FUNDAMENTAL
WRITTEN CHINESE

SECOND EDITION

FUNDAMENTAL WRITTEN CHINESE

MARGARET LEE, JIAYAN LIN, AND ROBERT SANDERS

UNIVERSITY OF HAWAI'I PRESS

HONOLULU

Library of Congress Cataloging-in-Publication Data

Names: Lee, Margaret Soo Kiak, author. | Lin, Jiayin, author. |
  Sanders, Robert, author.
Title: Fundamental written Chinese / Margaret Lee, Jiayin Lin, Robert
  Sanders.
Description: Second edition. | Honolulu : University of Hawai'i Press,
  [2024] | In English and Mandarin Chinese.
Identifiers: LCCN 2023032844 (print) | LCCN 2023032845 (ebook) | ISBN
  9780824894146 (trade paperback) | ISBN 9780824897086 (pdf)
Subjects: LCSH: Chinese language—Writing—Textbooks for foreign
  speakers—English.
Classification: LCC PL1171 .L336 2024 (print) | LCC PL1171 (ebook) | DDC
  495.11/1—dc23/eng/20231204
LC record available at https://lccn.loc.gov/2023032844
LC ebook record available at https://lccn.loc.gov/2023032845

University of Hawai'i Press books are printed on acid-free paper and meet the guidelines for permanence and durability of the Council on Library Resources.

Cover art by Libellule/Shutterstock.com. Cover design by Mardee Melton.

Brief Contents

Contents

Preface

APPROACH

Three core assumptions underlie the design of *Fundamental Written Chinese* and its relationship with *Fundamental Spoken Chinese*. The first assumption is that oral and written language represent two different but related systems that are most effectively taught by delinking the sequence in which the particulars of each system are taught, while at the same time ensuring that the instruction of reading and writing skills is done so while firmly grounded in the spoken vocabulary and grammar that the learner has already acquired. A consequence of this belief is that all instruction of vocabulary and grammar takes place exclusively in *Fundamental Spoken Chinese*, with the role of *Fundamental Written Chinese* clearly defined as providing instruction in reading and writing what users have already learned how to say elsewhere.

The second core underlying belief is that individual written characters should not be confused with the concept of a word, as many words in modern Chinese are composed of more than one syllable and as such are written as a combination of two or more different characters. A consequence of this is that quite a number of characters in modern Chinese can never stand alone as independent words. Instead they must always combine with another character before they can be considered linguistically whole. For example, the underlying meaning of the character 汉 is "China; Chinese", but in fact, it can never stand alone as an independent word. Instead, it must always combine with another character before it can be considered linguistically whole, e.g. 汉语 "Chinese language", 汉字 "Chinese character(s)", and 汉人 "person of Chinese Han ethnicity".

The third core assumption is that the optimum way to teach the mastery of the written system is by systematically focusing on structural regularities such as radicals, phonetic components, shared graphic components, stroke order, and principles of proportion, and to sequence the introduction of these characters according to a principle of graduated structural complexity from simple independent characters to the more complex compound characters. This is best carried out without distraction from the teaching of too many different radicals or too many structurally unrelated characters in any one chapter, or by failing to include a sufficient number of examples of characters containing the newly introduced radical to reinforce the saliency of that radical. From a practical standpoint this can be accomplished only after a sufficient number of spoken words has already appeared in *Fundamental Spoken Chinese* that, when written, happen to use at least one character constructed with the targeted radical. However, before a sufficient number of spoken vocabulary of this type has been learned, it is often more appropriate to simply use *Hànyǔ Pīnyīn* romanization rather than a Chinese character to represent a particular syllable in a *Fundamental Written Chinese* text.

For example, the word *shuō* "to speak" first appears in Chapter 4 of *Fundamental Spoken Chinese*, but in Chapter 4 of *Fundamental Written Chinese* it appears in the written text as *Hànyǔ Pīnyīn* romanization only. In Chapter 5 of *Fundamental Spoken Chinese*, three different syllables—*cí* "word", *huà* "speech", and *yǔ* "language"—all of which share that same speech radical in their character composition, appear in words for the first time, so the speech radical is then introduced in Chapter 5 of *Fundamental Written Chinese*, together with all four characters that illustrate the speech radical's use. Because the speech radical has been systematically taught in Chapter 5, it was then possible over the course of the remainder of *Fundamental Written Chinese* to immediately introduce, without need for further explanation, another thirteen additional examples of speech radical characters as soon as each character first appeared in a spoken word in the corresponding chapter of *Fundamental Spoken Chinese*.

Beyond our core assumptions, we wish to make two other points about Chinese characters, one having to do with the importance of practicing them in linguistic context, and the other being our decision to include a limited number of extended character combinations in our supplementary reading exercises.

It is our firm belief that one should avoid, as much as possible, practicing writing Chinese characters only as isolated symbols. Rather, as noted above, individual characters should always be treated as functioning as parts of larger words and phrases. Therefore, when practicing how to master 汉, in addition to practicing how to write it as an isolated character, one should also practice writing it as a part of real words they can already say, such as 汉语, 汉字, and 汉人, and not merely as 汉. And a word such as 汉字 or 汉语 can be further inserted into larger, already learned spoken phrases for further writing practice, regardless of whether or not every character in that known spoken phrase has already been learned, e.g. *xiě* 汉字 "write Chinese characters", 他 *huì* 说汉语 "He is able to speak Chinese", etc.

Finally, we wish to note that an individual Chinese character often exhibits a range of meanings that can vary from its core meaning, depending on the specific word in which the character is embedded. On such example is 商人, a new combination not included in the vocabulary list of either textbook, but composed of two known characters with known meanings: 商 "commerce" and 人 "person". It doesn't take too much head scratching to realize that 商人 means "business person". This phenomenon of known characters seeing their core meanings extended as they combine with other characters to form new words is quite common in written Chinese. A very limited amount of this vocabulary extension is included in the supplementary readings, although the main purpose of these readings is primarily to reinforce previously taught vocabulary and grammar in natural written contexts.

CHAPTER FORMAT

The first three chapters of *Fundamental Written Chinese* are designed to educate users about the writing system, preparing them to formally embark upon their study of this aspect of the language starting in Chapter 4, well equipped with the essential knowledge and understanding of the intrinsic nature of Chinese characters: what they are and what they are not, how they are constructed, and how native speakers and advanced non-native learners go about looking up written characters and words in a dictionary. As such, each of these three chapters first presents selected information about Chinese characters, including illustrative examples, which is then reinforced by hands-on exercises at the end of the chapter. It is not our expectation that users genuinely master the skills and knowledge introduced in these first three chapters before they begin their actual study of Chinese characters in Chapter 4. Rather, we believe that the very experience of getting one's hands "dirty" while going through the chapter exercises helps users to better familiarize themselves with the general nature of the task that they are about to embark upon, thus allowing them to be more knowledgeable and at ease with what lies ahead for them.

Starting with Chapter 4, then, every chapter of *Fundamental Written Chinese* is organized as follows:

1. Long written text
2. A list of vocabulary items being used for the first time in the textbook with:

   - Romanized pronunciation
   - English meaning
   - Part of speech label

3. Exercises related to the reading passage
4. A chart introducing the chapter's independent characters (graphically minimal autonomous characters) showing:

   - Romanized pronunciation
   - Traditional form in brackets[1]

---

1. This information is provided for reference purposes only and is only done so when the traditional and simplified forms of the character differ from one another.

- An asterisk when the character is not an independent word in modern Chinese[2]
- Basic underlying meaning
- Total number of strokes and stroke order
- Classificatory radical
- The character's inventory of identifiable graphic components
- Box schema indicating the character's proper balance and proportion

5. A chart introducing the chapter's new compound characters constructed using already taught radicals showing:

- Romanized pronunciation
- An asterisk when the character is not an independent word in modern Chinese
- Basic underlying meaning
- Classificatory radical
- Composite meaning clue (if present)
- Composite phonetic clue (if present)
- Total number of strokes and stroke order
- All identifiable graphic components used to construct the character
- Box schema indicating the character's proper balance and proportion

6. The chapter's new radicals and example characters, presented in an informational chart similar to what has been described above
7. Suggested mnemonics and other clues for remembering how certain characters are put together[3]
8. Character exercises, vocabulary exercises, and structure exercises
9. One or two short supplementary texts and comprehension questions[4]
10. Eight empty squares next to each character for writing practice[5]

---

2. According to the *ABC Comprehensive Chinese-English Dictionary*.
3. These clues are not always historically or linguistically correct, but they do offer a possibly useful strategy for effectively remembering how the character in question is constructed.
4. The purpose of these supplementary texts is both to reinforce previously learned vocabulary, grammatical structures, and characters through additional readings and to provide the occasional opportunity for students to expand their knowledge of vocabulary through new combinations of known characters embedded in linguistically natural sentences and longer passages. Some in the later chapters also give students brief introductions to certain aspects of Chinese culture.
5. Beyond the point noted above that writing practice of individual characters should largely take place while using them in actual words and phrases, users should also keep in mind that learning how to write a new character is a lot like learning how to play a musical instrument or mastering a new sport. All require considerable, repetitive practice in order to develop the unconscious muscle memory necessary to perform all of the required movements smoothly and effortlessly. For beginning students of Chinese, writing a new character just eight times will not provide the muscle memory necessary to produce it smoothly from memory. Therefore, these eight squares should be taken as a starting point for writing practice and not as the complete course.

DISTINCTIVE FEATURES[6]

SYSTEMATIC INTRODUCTION OF CHARACTERS

Fundamental Written Chinese has many of the same features as its companion volume, *Fundamental Spoken Chinese*. It is designed not only to teach the content of the lesson but also to inculcate habits that are essential for further learning in later years. The emphasis on explaining characters explicitly in terms of radicals and phonetics is one such example. It explains every character in terms of the regularities that will make it easier to remember and raises awareness of the organizational principles of the written lexicon as a whole. The same is true for the emphasis that is placed on proper stroke order. Here it is shown why it is necessary from the start by teaching how to look up characters in the dictionary, and specific tests are devised to be sure that the students are learning it (e.g. "write the fourth stroke of this character"). Also, because many characters cannot stand alone as independent words in modern Chinese, those that cannot are marked with an asterisk when they are initially introduced.

Altogether, 505 basic, high-frequency characters are introduced over seventeen chapters, averaging 29 new characters per chapter. No chapter introduces fewer than 21 or more than 38 new characters. To put this total in perspective, depending on the study, the 500 most frequently used characters in Chinese constitute anywhere between 72% and 79% of the total number of characters that appear in a Chinese newspaper article.

PINYIN-PLUS-CHARACTER WRITING

In order to adhere to our vision that written language as being composed of words, not characters, that often encompass a natural linguistic scope greater than that of isolated sentences, while at the same time carefully controlling the sequence and manner in which individual characters are introduced, it has been necessary for written texts to make limited use of a Pinyin-plus-character system of writing. It should be noted, however, that this hybrid method of representing written language is more prevalent in the earlier chapters of *Fundamental Written Chinese* than it is in the later chapters.

SEPARATE DIALOGUES

A deliberate decision was made that the dialogues in the two volumes not be identical, thus requiring students to actually read and understand the dialogues and

---

6. Portions of this section are based heavily on written comments of one of the anonymous reviewers of the original manuscript proposal.

texts in *Fundamental Written Chinese*, not just read everything in *Hànyǔ Pīnyīn* in *Fundamental Spoken Chinese* to know what is being said.

MEETS THE NEEDS OF HERITAGE LEARNERS

Fundamental Written Chinese can be used independently of *Fundamental Spoken Chinese* by heritage learners and other semi-fluent speakers of Mandarin who do not require much attention to their spoken skills but who are in earnest need of support in acquiring a solid foundation in reading and writing.

FLEXIBLE COORDINATION OF THE TWO TEXTBOOKS

There is a sizable controversy in Chinese-teaching circles about whether one should introduce characters from the beginning or wait until the spoken language has progressed to a certain level and then introduce them, as happens with normal literacy acquisition in children—first they learn to speak, and then they learn to write. We have designed *Fundamental Written Chinese* in such a way that it can be used either way; since the lessons in the two books are keyed to each other in terms of vocabulary and grammar, they can be used simultaneously or the written material can be introduced at a later time, depending on how much of a gap between the two the user wishes to maintain. Regardless of which method of coordination one ultimately chooses to follow, however, it must be remembered that the first three chapters of *Fundamental Written Chinese* teach about the writing system rather than how to write any of the specific vocabulary that is introduced in Chapter 2 and Chapter 3 of *Fundamental Spoken Chinese*. By Chapter 4, however, it is possible to maintain no gap between the introduction of oral skills in *Fundamental Spoken Chinese* and the introduction of related written content in the parallel chapter of *Fundamental Written Chinese*.

前言

教学宗旨

　　《基石读写》是《基石口语》的姐妹教材。在编写这两部教材的过程中，我们有三点基本的构想。首先，口头和书面语言所代表的是两种不同但又相互关联的体系。它们各自的要点和特点都需分别教授，同时要确保阅读和书写技巧的教授必须基于学生已掌握的口语词汇和语法之上，这样才能取得最佳的教学效果。基于这一想法，词汇和语法集中在《基石口语》中教授，而《基石读写》则旨在教学生去阅读和写作他们已经学会说的东西。第二点，我们认为汉字不应与单词的概念混淆。因为现代汉语中有很多单词都包含一个以上的音节，因而由两个或多个汉字构成，所以现代汉语中有不少汉字并不能作为独立的单词使用，而必须与其他汉字结合才具有完整语义。譬如，"汉"的含义是"中国; 中国人"，但事实上，它并不能作为一个独立的词来单独使用，而必须与其它汉字连用才具有完整语义，例如："汉语"即"中文"，"汉字"即"中国文字"，"汉人"即"汉民族的人"。第三点，我们相信教会学生掌握读写体系的最佳方法是系统地教授汉字构成规律，如偏旁部首、语音组件、共有字形、笔划顺序及汉字书写比例分配原则；并按结构的复杂程度由简单的独体字到复杂的合体字依次讲解。讲解时最好不要在一个章节中介绍太多不同的偏旁部首及结构上互不相连的汉字来分散学生的注意力，同时又要注意给出足够的例子来强化学生对新学偏旁部首的记忆。要做到这一点，从现实角度来说，只有在学习《基石口语》后积累了足够数量的口语词汇，并且这些词汇在读写时又恰巧包含至少一个由所学偏旁部首构成的汉字时方能实现。不过，在没有学习足够数量的这类口语词汇之前，更恰当的做法是在《基石读写》的课文中用汉语拼音而不是汉字形式代表音节。

　　例如，"*shuō*"（说）首先出现于《基石口语》第 4 章，但在《基石读写》第4章中它只是以汉语拼音注释形式出现。在《基石口语》第 5 章中第一次出现三个不同的音节: *cí* (词), *huà* (话) 以及 *yǔ* (语)，它们的汉字字型结构中都有言字旁，因此《基石读写》第 5 章用这四个字一起对言字旁的用法加以说明。因为第 5 章中系统讲解了言字旁的用法，所以在其余章节口语词汇中出现的言字旁的字就无须另作解释了。

　　除了上述几点中心思想外，对于汉字学习还有两点需要补充。一是我们强调在自然语境中练习汉字的重要性；二是教材在补充阅读练习中加入了一定数量的有关汉字组合的延伸练习。

我们始终认为，进行书写练习时要尽量避免把汉字当作孤立的符号，而应如上文所说的，将个体汉字视为构成词语和短语的组件。因此，当练习写"汉"字时，除了把它当作一个孤立的字来练习书写外，学生更要把它作为已经学会说的真正的词语来练习书写，如"汉语""汉字"，或"汉人"。而作为词语，我们又可以将其放入更多的已学过的口语短语中作进一步读写练习——无论该短语中的字是否都已学过，例如，"xiě 汉字"(写汉字)，"他 huì 说汉语"(他会说汉语)，等等。

最后我们需要指出的是，个体汉字根据语境的不同，常常会有一系列与其核心字义不同的含义。例如，"商人"一词，由两个含义已知的汉字组成："商"即"商业"，"人"即"人们"，所以不太难猜测商人即"从事商业的人"。这种已知汉字因与其它汉字结合而使含义延伸从而组成新词的现象在汉语书面语中非常普遍。在补充的阅读材料中出现了部分这样的延伸词汇，当然阅读的主要目的首先在于巩固之前学过的语法和词汇，并加强对它们在自然书面语境中使用情况的理解。

章节结构

《基石读写》的前三章主要培养学生对读写体系的初步认识，为第 4 章开始的学习做好准备，了解汉字的基础知识——什么是汉字以及什么不是汉字，汉字如何构成，如何使用字典等。因此，前三章中，各章首先列出精选的汉字知识，并用例子说明。每章最后都要求学生动手练习加以巩固。我们并不期望学生在从第 4 章开始真正着手学习汉字之前就能完全掌握前三章中介绍的知识和技能，而是把它们作为学习汉语读写的一个基础。

从第 4 章开始，各章的结构如下:
1. 课文
2. 生词表，列出了课文中首次出现的词汇，并配有:

   - 用汉语拼音标注的发音
   - 英语含义
   - 词性标识

3. 与课文配套的阅读理解练习
4. 介绍本章独体字的图表，每个字包括:

   - 用汉语拼音标注的发音
   - 在括号中给出繁体字形式[1]
   - 以星号表示该汉字在现代汉语中不能独立使用[2]
   - 基本含义
   - 总笔划数及笔划顺序
   - 偏旁部首
   - 所有可识别的汉字组字要件
   - 用方框解构汉字书写的恰当比例

---

1. 繁体字形仅供参考，且仅在繁体和简体字形相异时给出繁体字形式。
2. 根据《ABC 综合汉英字典》编写。

5. 以图表形式列出本章由已学的偏旁部首组成的新的合体字, 每个字包括:

   - 用汉语拼音标注的发音
   - 以星号表示该汉字在现代汉语中不能独立使用
   - 基本含义
   - 偏旁部首
   - 综合语意线索(若存在)
   - 综合语音线索(若存在)
   - 总笔划数和笔划顺序
   - 所有可识别的汉字组字要件
   - 用方框解构汉字书写的恰当比例

6. 以图表形式列出本章新的偏旁部首及其组成的汉字, 形式同上
7. 顺口溜或其它线索, 以帮助记忆汉字组成[3]
8. 汉字书写练习、词汇练习和结构练习
9. 一至两篇补充材料[4]
10. 书写练习空格(每个汉字旁有八个空方框供书写练习)[5]

特点[6]

系统介绍汉字

　　《基石读写》与其姐妹篇《基石口语》有很多相似的特点。该教材的编写不仅着眼于授课内容, 更着重于为学生今后的学习培养良好的习惯, 教材在讲解汉字时对偏旁部首及语音的强调就是很好的例子。本教材对每个汉字的构成规律都加以解释使其便于记忆, 引导学生关注汉语书面语汇的组织原则。同样的, 本教材对于笔划顺序的强调也是出于上述目的。如, 从最初就强调查字典学汉字的重要性。教材还设计了一些小测试来检测学生的学习情况。比如, 让学生"写出该字的第四笔划"。另外, 由于很多汉字在现代汉语中不能独立使用, 教材对这一类字用星号加以标注。

---

3. 从历史学和语言学角度来说这些线索并不总是正确, 但却不失为有效记忆汉字结构的好方法。
4. 给出这些补充材料的目的一方面是通过额外阅读来巩固学生已学过的词汇、语法结构及汉字, 同时让学生通过阅读生动的语句及较长文章中出现的新的合成词来增加词汇知识。
5. 除上文所说汉字的书写练习应尽量放在词语和短语的背景下进行以外, 学习者还应记住学写新汉字就像学习弹奏乐器或掌握新的体育项目一样, 需用大量的重复练习来开发身体自主记忆能力, 从而流畅、自然地完成各种指定动作。对于汉语初学者而言, 把一个新汉字练习写八遍并不能实现身体自主记忆而流畅书写, 因此留出的八个方框只是书写练习的开始而非终了。
6. 该部分很大程度上采纳了一位匿名校阅者对初稿的意见。

　　本书在 17 章内总共教授 505 个基础的高频汉字，平均每章教 29 个汉字。每一章新教的汉字数量在 21–38 个之间。为了更好地理解这个汉字量的意义，有研究表明，汉语中使用频率最高的 500 个汉字占新闻报道文章总汉字量的72%–79%。

拼音加汉字的书写方式

　　如我们所认为的，语言是由词语而不是单个汉字组成，而且往往涵盖比单个句子更大的语言范畴，同时语言的使用又关联着每个汉字的使用顺序和方式。因此，课文中必须限制性地使用拼音加汉字的书写方式。不过，这种混合的书写表达方式只在本教材的前几章中较为常见。

独立的课文编写

　　两本教材中的课文内容互相独立，这样就需要学生切实读懂《基础汉语读写》中的课文内容，才能搞清课文含义，而不能仅仅依靠《基石口语》的拼音版本来理解课文。

满足华裔学生的汉语学习需求

　　《基石读写》可以独立于《基石口语》而单独使用，从而满足那些父辈为华人的学生或口语较流利而不需要过多关注口语能力的学生学习汉语的需求。

两本教材的互动

　　在汉语教学界，存在着一个颇有争议的课题，即究竟应该是从一开始就教授汉字读写，还是如儿童的正常学习顺序那样，在口语已经达到一定程度之后再教学汉字。我们在编写《基石读写》时兼顾这两种意见。由于两本教材中的词汇和语法彼此对应，因此它们既可以同时使用，也可以先学口语稍后再学汉字读写，这取决于使用者想在这两者之间保持多大的学习间距。无论最终选择哪种教学方式，都要记住一点，即《基石读写》的前三章讲授的是关于书写体系的知识，而不是真正教写《基石口语》第 2 和第 3 章中出现的具体词汇。从第 4 章开始，口语和书写技能的教授则可齐头并进，一边教授《基石口语》中的口语技能，一边教授《基石读写》中相对应章节的相关书写内容。

Acknowledgments

It is said that it takes a village to raise a child. The same can also be said for producing a textbook, even as a second edition. While the names of three authors appear on the cover, none of this would have been possible without the additional generous contributions and support of numerous other people. Heartfelt thanks are particularly extended to our colleague Nora Yao, who wrote many of the dialogues, reading texts, and exercises that appear in the first edition of each book and have been retained here either in their original or modified forms. We wish to additionally express our profound appreciation to Xiaozao Huang (黄小枣) and her team at Nanjing Normal University for recording all of the dial ogues, reading texts, and vocabulary lists found in both textbooks, as well as to Ying Liao (廖莹), Liang Liu (刘亮), and Ying Xie (谢颖), who produced all of the color illustrations used here, some of which were designed using resources from Freepik.com. Finally, we wish to express our undying gratitude to Stephanie Chun, Gianna Marsella, and Trond Knutsen of the University of Hawai'i Press, along with Lori Paximadis, Wendy Bolton, and Wanda China, for their unflinching patience, encouragement, and support over a very long road filled with inevitable surprises and challenges. Any shortcomings, oversights, or errors are exclusively the fault of the authors.

Robert Sanders
Margaret Lee
Jiayan Lin

Note on Online Content

Audio, exercise model answers, and other resources for *Fundamental Written Chinese* may be accessed at www.fundamentalchinese.com or by using the QR code below.

1 Demystifying Chinese Writing

Welcome to the exciting world of Chinese characters, where you have the chance to learn a system of writing with a history of over 3,500 years and that today is used by hundreds of millions of people. For many people embarking upon the study of Chinese, however, this writing system represents an intimidating object of fear. While it is certainly true that you will first need to put in a significant number of "hard yards" before you are able to read a Chinese newspaper or write a Chinese letter to a friend, nevertheless, many misconceptions and exaggerations about the writing system exist, not only within the minds of the general public outside of China but even within the minds of many native speakers. These misconceptions and exaggerations include:

1. Chinese characters are mostly pictures and ideographs (pictures of abstract concepts).

"日" 字的演化

2. Chinese characters don't indicate anything about their pronunciation.
3. There is no systematic rhyme or reason as to how Chinese characters are constructed. Because of this they are extremely difficult to memorize.

4. One needs to memorize thousands upon thousands of Chinese characters in order to become literate.

5. If you are not extremely careful while writing down a particular character, you can easily and erroneously transform the intended character into a completely different one instead.

6. People on the Chinese mainland and in Taiwan use two completely different systems of writing. Knowing only one of these systems means that it is next to impossible to understand the other system.

Let us now examine each of these statements in more detail:

1. Chinese characters are mostly pictures and ideographs.

Pictographs (simplification of shapes of real objects) and ideographs comprise just 3% of all Chinese characters.

From a logical perspective alone, such a situation makes little practical sense. While it is easy to draw a picture of a mountain or a horse and project the concept of "top, upper" or "brightness" by means of a diagram, it becomes much more difficult to imagine how to do this for absolutely everything we would ever want to write down on paper. What unambiguous picture or diagram could be easily drawn to express "democracy", "ideal", or completed action? What about the difference among "ideal", "ideals", and "idealism"? And how easy would it be to write a short paragraph like this one if we were limited only to using pictures and diagrams?

Thus it is not at all surprising that pictographs and ideographs are not the only types of Chinese characters in existence. Traditionally, Chinese have recognized six kinds of characters according to their construction strategy: pictographs, simple indicatives (graphic expressions of concepts), compound indicatives, phonetic loans, semantic-phonetic compounds, and mutual explanatories, with indicatives corresponding to ideographs. In modern times, however, this system has been reanalyzed and reduced to a total of four: pictographics, which are simplified drawings of an object's shape (e.g. 月 ⏾ "moon"; 日 ☼ "sun"); simple indicatives, signs used to suggest a certain meaning (e.g. the simple characters 一 "one", 二 "two", and 三 "three"); compound indicatives, formed by combining simple elements or characters to provide new meanings (e.g. 休, "to rest", showing a person 人 leaning against a tree 木; 明 "bright" showing the combination of the sun and moon ☼⏾); and semantic-phonetic compounds, which are characters that consist of one component providing a pronunciation clue (called the phonetic) and another component providing a meaning clue, e.g. 妈 *mā* "mother", which is composed of the meaning clue "female" 女 plus the pronunciation clue 马 (*mǎ*). While pictographs and ideographs (i.e. indicatives) comprise 75% of the existent categories, in point of fact those three categories only account in total for 3% of all the characters found in a dictionary. In other words, 97% of all Chinese characters actually belong to the semantic-phonetic compound category, whose name indicates that sound plays a role in their construction. Semantic-phonetic compounds are discussed under point 2 below.

Why, then, have Chinese characters been almost universally categorized as pictures and ideographs, completely devoid of pronunciation information? This is a direct result of their history.

The earliest examples of Chinese writing we have were carved on cattle bones and tortoise shells more than 3,000 years ago. The purpose of these inscriptions was to record events, with a very large percentage being concerned with the prophecies of fortune-tellers. Later, inscriptions of worship were found on ceremonial bronze vessels. Due to the content and limited nature of what was written there, a very large proportion of those characters were indeed pictographs and ideographs, and the system worked. However, as we have already seen, if writing is actually intended to record anything and everything one might say, then these pictures and ideographs would not be sufficient to fully meet the needs of its users. The way that this problem was overcome was to ignore the meaning of a picture altogether and focus instead on its pronunciation.

Imagine the picture of an eye: ◁◉▷. If we focused only on its meaning, then it could only be used to write the meaning "eye". However, if we were to focus instead on its pronunciation in English, then not only could it be used to represent the words "eye" and "I", but it could also be used to indicate the *ai* sound in "ideal", "island", "ivy", and so on. In this manner, the power of a picture to record spoken language has now been expanded hugely. What has just been illustrated is called the rebus principle, and it is a key operating principle in the construction of semantic-phonetic compounds in Chinese. This principle is not unique to the history of Chinese, and in fact is observed in many other so-called pictographic orthographies, including Egyptian hieroglyphics and Mayan writing.

2. Chinese characters don't indicate anything about their pronunciation.

Approximately 97% of all Chinese characters contain a sound clue, although these clues are rarely as predictive of pronunciation as an alphabetic spelling.

As its name implies, the idealized semantic-phonetic compound contains two pieces of information about itself—a meaning clue and a pronunciation clue. The meaning clue is called the **radical**, and the pronunciation clue is called the **phonetic**. As with all clues, some are clearer and more helpful than others. Let us look at a few commonly used radicals (meaning clues) in Chinese:

王 "jade"
石 "stone"
虫 "insect"
女 "female"
木 "tree"
口 "mouth"

Combining each of these radicals with the phonetic clue 马, which by itself is pronounced *mǎ* and means "horse", we end up with the following results:

Radical	Phonetic	Semantic-phonetic compound
王 "jade"		玛 *mǎ* "agate"
石 "stone"		码 *mǎ* "weights"
虫 "insect"		蚂 *mǎ* "ant"
女 "female"	(马 *mǎ* "horse")	妈 *mā* "mother"
木 "tree"		杩 *mà* "clamp"
口 "mouth"		骂 *mà* "scold"
口 "mouth"		吗 *ma* "question particle"

Though not always able to indicate the correct tone, the phonetic clue in the above set is nevertheless highly predictive of the overall correct pronunciation for each of the compound characters in which it is used.

Many similar phonetics also exist in Chinese, though a fairer example of the degree of reliability of a sound clue in Chinese might be something like:

Radical	Phonetic	Semantic-phonetic compound
亻 "person"		侥 *jiǎo* "lucky"
氵 "water"		浇 *jiāo* "sprinkle"
日 "sun"		晓 *xiǎo* "dawn"
马 "horse"		骁 *xiāo* "fine horse"
扌 "hand"		挠 *náo* "scratch"
女 "female"	尧 (*yáo* "legendary emperor")	娆 *ráo* "graceful"
纟 "silk"		绕 *rào* "wind around"
艹 "grass"		荛 *ráo* "rushes"
饣 "food"		饶 *ráo* "abundant"
火 "fire"		烧 *shāo* "burn"

And there are many more even less helpful sound clues than what we see illustrated immediately above. There are three important reasons why sound clues in Chinese characters are usually less helpful than an alphabetic spelling. First, most of these characters were put together well over 2,000 years ago. Language, including pronunciation, changed radically over that period of time, so it is understandable that irregularities will arise as a result. Second, pronunciation varies over time and space, and not all characters were created at one time or in one place. Third, we cannot say for sure how meticulous the people who created a particular semantic-phonetic compound were in choosing a phonetic clue that would exactly match the intended pronunciation of the new character.

3. There is no systematic rhyme or reason as to how Chinese characters are constructed. Because of this they are extremely difficult to memorize.

Writing by itself is not an independent language. Rather, it is based very heavily on speech, and in fact cannot exist without it. Therefore, a Chinese character, especially a semantic-phonetic compound, is much easier to memorize if you already have its meaning and pronunciation in your spoken language. For that reason, for a longer while than you probably care to contemplate, it will probably not be very easy for you to quickly memorize new characters. However, you will eventually reach a point when your spoken vocabulary is great enough and your familiarity with a range of radicals, phonetics, and repeating combinations of individual character strokes (see Chapter 2) is also great enough to allow you to see a new character and immediately be able to identify its sound, meaning, and structural properties and lodge that information away for later use. Once you reach that stage, new characters will not usually present themselves as a particularly formidable challenge. In the meantime, this textbook introduces the structure, meaning, and pronunciation of each character in a systematic, coherent fashion that will assist you in gaining an overall sense of the writing system as smoothly as possible.

4. One needs to memorize thousands upon thousands of Chinese characters in order to become literate.

Although authoritative Chinese dictionaries can list up to more than 48,000 different characters, achieving basic, native literacy in Chinese requires a knowledge of around 3,000 characters. Of those 3,000 characters, the first 500 most frequently used ones normally constitute anywhere between 72% and 79% of the total character content of any given Chinese newspaper article. Having said that, however, you will discover that many words in Chinese are made up of two characters and not just one, and it is very common in Chinese to take one character from one word and join it to a single character from a second word in order to form yet a third word, e.g. taking the 中 Zhōng of Zhōngguó "China" and the 美 Měi of Měiguó "America" to form 中美 Zhōng-Měi "Sino-American". And adding to that problem is the fact that the basic meaning of 中 is "middle", while the basic meaning of 美 is "beautiful". For these reasons, although basic literacy requires a knowledge of roughly 3,000 characters, it actually requires command of a much larger quantity of vocabulary items.

5. If you are not extremely careful while writing down a particular character, you can easily and erroneously transform the intended character into a completely different one instead.

Very few Chinese characters differ from one another by just the variation of a single stroke. Failure to write your strokes in the proper way is rather a sign of sloppy penmanship. Many native speakers consider penmanship to be a window into the personality, level of education, and makeup of the writer. Also, a lack of certainty about the proper formation of strokes and the correct sequencing of these strokes in the formation of individual characters will disadvantage you later on when you encounter and try to decode the mature handwriting of native speakers.

It is true that there are one or two examples where the graphic difference between one character and another can be boiled down to just a slight variation in one stroke. However, this is very rare. In fact, even when we examine the classic set to illustrate this supposedly dangerous situation, comprised of the following set of four characters, we can see just how limited the danger really is:

田	"cultivated field"
由	"from"
甲	"first of the ten Heavenly Stems"
申	"ninth of the twelve Earthly Branches"

Fearmongers will point out that depending on whether the central vertical stroke (line) stays completely within the borders of the box, extends upward above the box, extends downward below the box, or extends both upward above the box *and* downward below the box determines what the final written result will mean. But keep in mind the following point: this relates only to that one particular stroke in that one particular character set. Should any one of the other strokes for any one of those four characters vary in any way (e.g. if the box shape of the third or fourth character was completely square, as is observed with the box shape for characters one and two), then the end result would merely be a somewhat odd-looking character whose intended meaning could still be understood. Rather than erroneously writing the wrong character, the variation in a single stroke or two is much more likely going to broadcast the message that you possess sloppy penmanship and don't know, or don't care about, the proper way to write the strokes.

Although bad penmanship will not likely cause confusion to others, there are two compelling reasons why you should know the proper way to write each stroke and why you should know the proper sequencing of those strokes ("stroke order") to form each character. First, for many Chinese, the visual qualities of your written characters say a lot about the quality of your personal character. The positive reaction that can be generated by good penmanship can never be underestimated. Second, in the real world, most native speakers don't actually take the time to write out every stroke in painstaking detail once they have become adept at the basics of writing. Instead, they speed through the process, following customary shortcuts based on conventions established over the centuries (much the same way that older native English speakers rarely print out their words, but write them in script instead). These conventions set out the pen in a fixed sequence of movements in a fixed pattern that can be traced from start to finish only if you (as the writer or as the reader) are well grounded in both the basic stroke directions and the particular stroke order of each character involved. Some examples of "print forms" (the way they are first learned by native-speaking children and the way they are taught in this book) and their script alternatives (the way they are often written by mature native writers) are shown below:

English	Romanization	Print form	Script form
Beer	*píjiǔ*	啤酒	啤酒
Bustling	*rènào*	热闹	热闹
Car	*qìchē*	汽车	汽车
Chinese language	*Hànyǔ*	汉语	汉语
Pencil	*qiānbǐ*	铅笔	铅笔
Trousers	*kùzi*	裤子	裤子

6. **People on the Chinese mainland and in Taiwan use two completely different systems of writing. Knowing only one of these systems means that it is next to impossible to understand the other system.**

The problems involved in being able to read the other system are not insurmountable. First, quite a large number of characters are written exactly the same way in both systems. Second, there are a lot of regularized differences between the two systems that, once learned, allow the users of one system to mechanically convert a character into the form used in the other system. This being the case, however, it does require less effort for those who only know traditional forms to be able to recognize simplified forms than it is for those who only recognize simplified forms to be able to recognize traditional forms.

As mentioned immediately above, for centuries a gap has existed between the meticulous appearance of the official print forms of Chinese characters and that of the unofficial, flowing script employed by many Chinese on an everyday basis. These script forms have always embodied conventions for systematically simplifying graphic complexity, thus saving time. The government on the Chinese mainland in 1956 introduced new official versions of the characters that, with some glaring exceptions, better matched the everyday writing habits followed for centuries in China and are still employed unofficially in Taiwan today. This can be illustrated below:

English	Romanization	Traditional print form*	Traditional script form	"Simplified" print form
Beer	*píjiǔ*	啤酒	啤酒	啤酒
Bustling	*rènào*	熱鬧	热闹	热闹
Car	*qìchē*	汽車	汽车	汽车
Chinese language	*Hànyǔ*	漢語	汉语	汉语
Pencil	*qiānbǐ*	鉛筆	铅笔	铅笔
Trousers	*kùzi*	褲子	裤子	裤子

*And still officially recognized in Taiwan

For these reasons most people in Taiwan do have the ability to read simplified characters without too much prior training, and vehement claims to the contrary likely have more to do with subjective factors than with objective ones. As for language students who only know traditional print forms but not the unofficial script ones, their ability to recognize simplified characters is dependent on the same sort of training, only in the opposite direction, required of simplified characters users discussed immediately below.

For people on the Chinese mainland who may never have been formally taught the traditional forms of characters at school, it might seem difficult to imagine how they could possibly learn to read these older forms without considerable training. However, many characters often differ from one another only in terms of the way a radical or phonetic (both discussed in point 2 above) is written, as the remaining part of the character beyond the radical is still written exactly the same in both systems. By learning the correspondences between the simplified and traditional forms of a relatively small number of radicals, together with some other mechanical correspondences involving other graphic elements in the character, it is possible to account for a relatively high percentage of the characters that are written differently in each system. Examples of a few common radical correspondences are shown below:

Traditional radical	Simplified radical	Examples	
		Traditional	Simplified
金	钅	銀 鏡 鉛 釘	银 镜 铅 钉
門	门	問 聞 間 閣	问 闻 间 阔
食	饣	飯 餃 館 餓	饭 饺 馆 饿
言	讠	話 語 課 謝	话 语 课 谢
車	车	軋 較 輩 轍	轧 较 辈 辙
鳥	鸟	島 鴨 鶩 鵡	岛 鸭 鹜 鹉

To be fair, it should be noted that many more character pairs differ from one another not only in terms of the respective ways their shared radical is written, but also in terms of the phonetic element each character uses, or in terms of some other systematic graphic differences between the two characters. Occasionally, however, the simplified system uses just one graphic element to take the place of more than one graphic element in the traditional system. This can be illustrated by what is unquestionably the single most extreme example of collapsing multiple traditional graphic elements into a single simplified element:

Traditional element	Traditional character	Simplified element	Simplified character
又	反, 友, 取, 受	又	反, 友, 取, 受
茣	漢, 艱, 灘		汉, 艰, 滩
雚	歡, 觀		欢, 观
丵	對		对
奚	鷄		鸡
	聖		圣
	雙		双
	發		发

Because of examples like this, it does require more training for someone who only knows the simplified system to be able to recognize the traditional system than it does for someone who only knows the traditional system to be able to recognize the simplified system. Nevertheless, even for those who are learning to recognize traditional characters from the perspective of the simplified system, so many similarities and systematic correspondences exist that the process of learning how to recognize the other system is not as difficult as is often claimed.

EXERCISES

1. **Try to match each pictograph or ideograph in column A with an English meaning in column B.**

A	B
二	"mountain"
上	"sun"
月	"one"
雨	"top"
三	"sheep"
下	"rain"
日	"three"
一	"moon"
羊	"two"
山	"bottom"

2. Give the meanings of each of the following nine radicals and the pronunciation of each of the following two sound clues.

Radicals: **Sound clues:**
亻 "person"   巴 *bā*
口 "mouth"   主 *zhǔ*
氵 "water"
火 "fire"
疒 "illness"
虫 "insect"
木 "tree"
米 "rice"
扌 "hand"

Match the character in column A with the Chinese pronunciation and English meaning in column B.

A	B
注	*zhù* "reside"
粑	*bǎ* "grasp"
炷	*zhù* "moth"
住	*bā* "scar"
疤	*ba* "interjection particle"
吧	*zhù* "pour"
柱	*zhù* "burn"
疰	*bā* "cake"
把	*zhù* "post, pillar"
蛀	*zhù* "a type of summer disease"

3. Using the tables presented under point 6 on page 10, try to match the character in column A with the character in column B.

A	B
鵶	轮
餞	辆
飾	钓
釣	钱
閣	饯
鵑	鸦
輸	饰
錢	鹃
悶	阁
輌	闷

2   The Design and Construction of Chinese Characters

BACKGROUND

Architecture and the process of erecting buildings are two very useful metaphors for understanding how Chinese characters are put together. They explain much about the process by which one starts with a handful of basic building materials that are then assembled to form larger structural units. Then, depending on the particular design pattern shown on the blueprint, some of those larger units are given additional customized add-on pieces, until the building itself is finally completed. At the same time, as these structures are being assembled, one must continually pay attention to questions of structural integrity, design aesthetics, and fitting in with the immediately surrounding environment. All but the aesthetic points will be touched upon in this chapter.

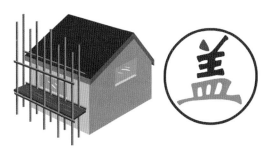

THE BASIC STROKES

The structure of any and all Chinese characters, regardless of how complex they are, share a common process of formation. This process begins with a closed set of 11 basic strokes that combine together to form increasingly larger and larger clusters. The direction of movement of each stroke and the type of ending it should take are very crucial, and will be discussed in slightly more detail later in this chapter.

Stroke	Direction	Name	Example
丶	↘	diǎn 点	小 家 觉
一	→	héng 横	木 兰 同
｜	↓	shù 竖	半 下 做
ノ	↙	piě 撇	公 话 具
㇏	↘	nà 捺	八 全 两
╱	↗	tí 提	冰 打 我
㇇	↘	hénggōu 横钩	写 学 安
｜	↓	shùgōu 竖钩	水 拉 事
㇁	↘	xiégōu 斜钩	找 成 试
㇕	↘	héngzhé 横折	因 星 漂
㇄	↘	shùzhé 竖折	东 他 每

At each step along the way, a certain unit or combination of units may be able to stand alone as an **independent character**. An independent character possesses both a known meaning and a known pronunciation, but *it cannot be further subdivided into one or more smaller units capable of standing alone in a written text.* Of the basic 11 strokes shown above, only one of them, 一, referred to as *héng* when it functions as a stroke, can function as an independent character. As an independent character it has the meaning of "one" and is pronounced *yī*.

THE CONSTRUCTION PROCESS

It doesn't take very much effort, however, to combine two or more of these basic strokes to form other full-fledged characters. For example, we can combine two *héng* strokes to form 二, *èr* "two". We can also combine a *piě* stroke, ノ, and a *nà* stroke, ㇏, to form 人, *rén* "person". Or, we can combine a *héng* stroke, 一, a *piě* stroke, ノ, and a *nà* stroke, ㇏, to form 大, *dà* "big".

Most full-fledged characters, however, are not composed of just two or three basic strokes in total, but are rather the end product of the joining together of two or more graphically complex subparts, e.g. the character 到 *dào*, meaning "to arrive", which can be broken down into the two different subparts 至 and 刂, as illustrated in the following schema: 到.

How this plays out is that one starts with one piece/sector of the full character (in this case 至) and assembles that piece stroke by stroke until it is finished before moving on to the next piece (in this case 刂) and if necessary the next piece (not applicable for 到), until the final mosaic, in this case 到, is complete, i.e.

Which piece of a character one should start with, which piece one should move on to next, and the stroke order one should follow when constructing each piece are all subject to very strict rules, which will be discussed later in this chapter.

As your experience reading and writing Chinese increases, you will begin to recognize more and more familiar sub-character building blocks shared across characters. Some common examples will possess very little significance beyond their visual similarity.

However, other common clusters of strokes will have great relevance, owing to centuries-old conventions used to arrange characters in Chinese dictionaries based on a list of over 180 (214 in the case of traditional characters) different key graphic elements that in most cases only constitute one part of the character in which it is embedded. That is, for every Chinese dictionary, each entry is arranged either in the index or in the main body itself according to which particular key graphic cluster from that list of 180+ items happens to be embedded in it. These 180+ graphic classifying labels are called **radicals**. In terms of the semantic-phonetic compounds discussed in the previous chapter, what we have called meaning clues there correspond to what we are calling radicals here. Having said this, not every radical is a meaning clue, and even if it were, not every meaning clue is useful in revealing the meaning of the character in which it is contained. Nevertheless, for dictionary bookkeeping purposes, every character does have a radical.

As a group, radicals fall into two major types: those that are able to stand alone as full-fledged characters and those that cannot. Of those radicals that are unable to stand alone as full-fledged characters, most have meaning but lack a pronunciation. Of these, some are graphic abbreviations of full-fledged characters and continue to convey the same meaning contained in their original, fuller forms. Some common examples of these include:

Radical form	Character form	Meaning	Examples
讠	言	"language"	话 "words", 说 "say", 语 "language", 谚 "proverb"
氵	水	"water"	汗 "sweat", 江 "river", 沙 "sand", 泳 "swim"
扌	手	"hand"	打 "hit", 扔 "throw", 扯 "pull", 摸 "stroke"
钅	金	"metal"	钉 "nail", 铅 "lead (Pb)", 铜 "copper", 锁 "lock"

On the other hand, there exist other meaning-containing radicals that cannot stand alone as full-fledged characters and are not themselves derived from full-fledged characters. Some common examples of these include:

	Meaning	Examples
宀	"roof"	安 "peace", 室 "room", 家 "family", 宿 "lodge for the night"
辶	"road, walking"	达 "arrive", 过 "pass over", 返 "return", 退 "retreat"
艹	"grass, plant"	花 "flower", 芽 "bud, sprout", 菜 "vegetable", 茶 "tea"
疒	"illness, disease"	疼 "ache", 病 "illness", 痴 "idiotic", 癌 "cancer"

Of the radicals that can also stand alone as full-fledged characters without any change to their appearance, some common examples include:

Radical	Meaning	Example
女	"female"	妈 "mother", 妹 "younger sister", 姑 "father's sister", 妻 "wife"
马	"horse"	驴 "donkey", 驾 "harness", 骑 "ride", 骠 "fast (of horses)"
木	"tree"	杖 "cane, stick", 杏 "apricot", 板 "board", 松 "pine tree"
石	"stone"	岩 "cliff", 矿 "ore", 砚 "inkstone", 碗 "bowl"

CONSTRUCTION PRINCIPLES

As briefly noted above, the assembling of a Chinese character is not a random or arbitrary process, but is in fact subject to very strict rules. Of these rules, the type you should be most concerned about is proper stroke order, because as is noted in the previous chapter, one must pos-

sess command of the specific stroke order for a very large number of individual characters before being able to read the everyday handwriting of most native speakers and to look up a character in a dictionary. In this regard, there is a widely quoted pair of principles that can generally account for the proper stroke order of most characters in a very simple way: top to bottom and left to right. That is, when writing a character, you should start from the top and work your way down, step by step. And likewise, when writing a character, you should take care of the left part before taking care of the right part.

Besides the obvious potential for contradiction between these two principles, another problem with the simple way that these two ideas are ordinarily conveyed is that they assume, without ever explicitly saying so, that top to bottom and left to right does not usually apply to the character as an integral whole (unless that character is an independent character), but rather to its subcomponents. That is, because most Chinese characters are **compound characters**, i.e. characters that are made up of an independent character plus at least one extra stroke and not independent characters, top to bottom and left to right actually work first to prioritize the sequence in which each individual building block within the character undergoes construction, and then determines the order in which each of the strokes are written within each of the individual building blocks.

Let us examine a few representative examples to see how this plays out in practice:

Type	Block sequencing	Example	Stroke cluster distribution	Block-internal stroke order
日 (stacked)	1 / 2	怎	乍 / 心	ノ 广 乍 乍 乍 丶 心 心 心
		条	夂 / 木	ノ 夕 夂 一 十 才 木
川 (side-by-side)	1 2	到	至 刂	一 工 互 至 至 至 ／ 刂
		休	亻 木	ノ 亻 ／ 一 十 才 木

Type	Block sequencing	Example	Stroke cluster distribution	Block-internal stroke order
▤ (stacked 1/2/3)	1 / 2 / 3	常	常 (宀 / 吕 / 巾 stacked)	⺌ ⺌ ⺌ 芯 芯 芯 ｜ 冂 巾 (stroke order for 常)
		桌	桌 (⺊ / 日 / 木 stacked)	⺊ ⺊ 冂 日 日 一 十 才 木 (stroke order for 桌)
▥ (three columns)	1 2 3	搬	扌 舟 殳 / 搬	一 十 扌 ⺉ 夃 舟 舟 ⺉ 几 殳 殳
		谢	讠 身 寸	讠 讠 ⺅ 竹 白 白 身 一 十 寸
▤ (2 over 1)	1 2 / 3	坐	人 人 / 土	丿 人 丿 人 一 十 土
		然	夕 犬 / 灬	丿 夕 夕 一 ナ 大 犬 丶 ⺍ 灬 灬

Type	Block sequencing	Example	Stroke cluster distribution	Block-internal stroke order
		骑		
		楼		
		前		
		最		
		数		
		影		
		慢		
		镜		

Type	Block sequencing	Example	Stroke cluster distribution	Block-internal stroke order
⌐	1 / 2	还	不 / 辶	、、丶 ; 辶 ; 一 丆 オ 不
		建	聿 / 廴	了 ; 廴 ; 一 ㇕ 彐 彐 肀 聿 ; 丬 廴
⌐	1 / 2	有	ナ / 月	一 ナ ; 丨 几 月 月
		病	疒 / 丙	、一 广 疒 ; 疒 ; 一 厂 厇 丙 丙
□	1 2 *	因	囗 大	丨 冂 ; 一 ナ 大 ; 囗
		国	囗 玉	丨 冂 ; 一 二 干 ; 王 玉 ; 囗
⊓	1 / 2	间	门 间	、丷 门 ; 丨 冂 月 日
		问	门 问	、丷 门 ; 丨 冂 口

As one can see, the prioritization of the ordering of the subcomponents is determined by the internal structure of the character. As a rule, one usually starts with the component that occupies the upper-left corner, though there are exceptions to this (see the "walking person last" and "X" principles below for two such counterexamples). Generally speaking, there is a tendency to take care of every component on the left of the character before proceeding to the component(s) on the right. The only exception to this tendency involves cases where the very bottom component of a character serves as its base/foundation and extends fully across from the bottom left to the bottom right, e.g. ⊞ and ⊞ .

Beyond the very general top to bottom and left to right principles illustrated above, there are other stroke order principles specific to particular stroke order clusters. These include:

a. The Kebab Principle (open at bottom):

When skewering one or more horizontal strokes with a single vertical stroke that protrudes through the bottommost horizontal stroke, first write every horizontal stroke, including the very bottom one 三, then finish with the vertical stroke 丰, e.g. 十, 用, 丰, 干.

b. The Kebab Principle (closed at bottom):

When skewering two or more horizontal strokes with a single vertical stroke that finishes immediately upon reaching the bottommost horizontal stroke, first write every horizontal stroke *except* the very bottom one 二, followed by the vertical stroke that temporarily protrudes at the bottom 干, and then finish up with the bottommost horizontal stroke that seals the skewer 王, e.g. 土, 王, 难, 住.

c. The Box Principle:

When writing a box that contains additional writing inside of it, first write the left side of the box 丨, followed by a single stroke that takes care of both the top and then right sides 冂, then insert inside the box all of the contents that are fully contained within it 因, and finally seal the box at the bottom 因, e.g. 国, 因, 田.

d. The "X" Principle:

When forming an *X*-like shape using two diagonal strokes, first write the stroke that starts toward the upper right and finishes around the lower left before writing the stroke that starts toward the upper-left corner and finishes around the lower right, e.g. 义, 更, 人.

e. The Walking Person Last Principle:

Anytime that the radical 辶 is used, it should be written last 辶这, e.g. 边, 这, 道.

Returning once again to the 11 basic strokes:

Stroke	Direction	Name	Example
ヽ	↘	diǎn 点	小 家 觉
一	→	héng 横	木 兰 同
丨	↓	shù 竖	半 下 做
ノ	↙	piě 撇	公 话 具
丶	↘	nà 捺	八 全 两
ノ	↗	tí 提	冰 打 我
㇆	↘	hénggōu 横钩	写 学 安
亅	↓	shùgōu 竖钩	水 拉 事
乀	↘	xiégōu 斜钩	找 成 试
㇆	↘	héngzhé 横折	因 星 漂
ㄴ	↳	shùzhé 竖折	东 他 每

You will need to master these 11 strokes in order to write characters correctly, decode the mature handwriting of native speakers, and be able to look up characters in a Chinese dictionary. In order to master each stroke, you will need to pay special attention to several features, including:

1. In which direction does the stroke flow—horizontally, vertically, diagonally?
2. Is the movement to the left or right?
3. Does it move up or down?
4. Is the stroke a straight line, or is there some degree of curve?
5. Is there a single direction to the stroke, or is there an abrupt change of direction?
6. Does the stroke end without ceremony, or does it end with a hook?

Paying attention to each of these questions will help you to master the 11 basic strokes as quickly as possible. How to put everything together in as aesthetically appealing a manner as possible is discussed immediately below.

AESTHETICS: COHERENCE AND BALANCE

It is not enough simply to know how to write each individual stroke separately. Ultimately, one must know how to assemble these many individual strokes into a single, holistic, and well-proportioned structure. The frame of reference for what is meant by "well-proportioned" is a square box, usually imaginary, but often, especially at the beginning stages of learning how to write properly, laid out boldly on paper.

Generally speaking, a character, especially one with many strokes, should spread out equally in all directions within that real or imaginary square and should not look as if it has been squashed, squeezed, pinched, or tilted. Nor should it look as if it is too top-heavy or that one half of the character dwarfs the other half. Let us examine some concrete examples of common beginning student problems to illustrate this:

Problem	Ill-proportioned example	Well-proportioned example
Top-heavy	黑	黑
Tilted	多	多
Squashed	街	街

Problem	Ill-proportioned example	Well-proportioned example
Squeezed	学	学
Pulled apart	行	行
Deflated-inflated	越	越
Inflated-deflated	就	就

Let us now convert each of the poorly proportioned forms shown above into its corresponding well-proportioned form.

Key:

→	move in this direction
→←	reduce in size
| |	involving portion of character on this side of the square within these lines

Problem	Ill-proportioned example	Well-proportioned example
Top-heavy	黑	黑
Tilted	鸟	多
Squashed	街	街
Squeezed	学	学
Pulled apart	行	行
Deflated-inflated	越	越
Inflated-deflated	就	就

EXERCISES

1. Indicate the direction of the following strokes in gray using a line with an arrow at the end.

大　　　汉　　　形　　　语

解　　　书　　　升　　　里

口　　　家　　　笔　　　空

2. For each character below, try to identify as many different stroke types as you can that have been used to make the character.

a. 休　　＿＿＿＿

b. 小　　＿＿＿＿

c. 我　　＿＿＿＿

d. 他　　＿＿＿＿

e. 把　　＿＿＿＿

f. 买　　＿＿＿＿

3. Draw lines that match each character below with its correct corresponding structural box.

a. 

1. 床

b. 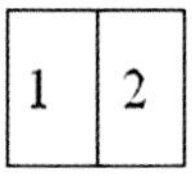

2. 意

c. 

3. 前

d. 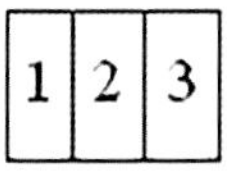

4. 伟

e. 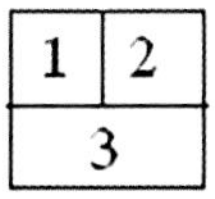

5. 道

f. 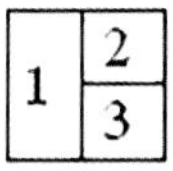

6. 想

g. 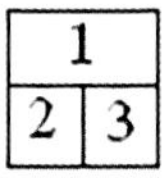

7. 颈

h. 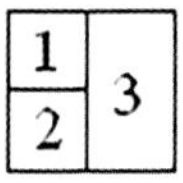

8. 谢

i. 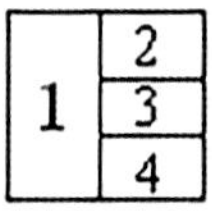

9. 临

j. 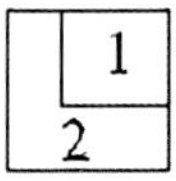

10. 阁

k. 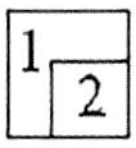

11. 漠

l. 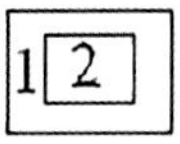

12. 囚

m. 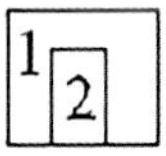

13. 尘

4. Draw a suitable box for each of the following characters, e.g. 好 ▯

a. 楼　　　　＿＿＿＿

b. 新　　　　＿＿＿＿

c. 热　　　　＿＿＿＿

d. 最　　　　＿＿＿＿

e. 茶　　　　＿＿＿＿

f. 边　　　　＿＿＿＿

g. 右　　　　＿＿＿＿

h. 做　　　　＿＿＿＿

i. 因　　　　＿＿＿＿

j. 人　　　　＿＿＿＿

k. 闸　　　　＿＿＿＿

l. 晚　　　　＿＿＿＿

3 How to Use Reference Books

TOWARD INDEPENDENCE

Eventually becoming a proficient reader and writer of Chinese requires a considerable investment of time and effort, most of which must take place outside of the classroom in your own time. To set the foundation for this you will need to know how to make full use of the content of the chapters that follow this one. And once you have acquired a sufficient number of written characters and words to embark upon new texts with less-controlled content, you will also need to know how to look up unknown characters, words, and phrases.

LOOKING UP AN UNKNOWN CHARACTER IN A DICTIONARY

What happens when someone encounters an unknown character or string of characters and wants to know the correct pronunciation and meaning? In the past, the only option for doing this was to look that material up in an old-fashioned printed dictionary, one character or word at a time. Many would argue that in this day and age of smartphones, with their many apps, and online dictionaries, where you only need to copy and paste from the digital document or website to get an instantaneous answer, that knowledge of how to decompose characters into their

radical and remaining strokes, in order to look up their pronunciation and meaning in a written dictionary is now a completely passé and unnecessary skill. This is not completely true for a multitude of practical reasons.

First, you will not always be dealing with digital documents. What you might be reading could be printed or even written by hand, often in a cursive form that requires a knowledge of stroke order in order to identify each individual character. Second, you may not always have online access to the apps or dictionaries you plan to rely on, especially if you are in China. Third, the quality of existing Chinese–English and English–Chinese translation apps to handle material beyond the scope of individual words or short phrases is still sometimes not accurate enough. Fourth, knowledge of character stroke order is a necessary prerequisite to facilitating popular Chinese learning apps such as Pleco. Fifth and most importantly as you embark on your Chinese language study, relying on apps to do the heavy lifting for you does not teach you any of the knowledge or skills you need in order to smoothly read and write connected Chinese texts of any length, especially outside of a digital environment. The sooner you master the knowledge of radicals, phonetic sound clues, stroke shapes, and fundamental stroke order principles, the sooner you will be able to confidently carry out reading and writing Chinese texts, be they digital, printed, or written by hand, completely on your own.

How to decompose a character into its organizational structure is best demonstrated through the process of looking up an unknown character the old-fashioned way. While in reality you may never actually need to look up the meaning or pronunciation of a character in this way, walking through the process of how this is done illustrates how to deconstruct a character into its useful parts and what information can be gleaned from each of these parts. How, then, does one do this?

First you need to identify that character's radical and then after that, count the total number of remaining strokes beyond—not including—that radical. With that information, you are then in a position to locate that character in a dictionary and, once you have done this, to learn both its pronunciation and meaning if you are looking it up in a *zìdiǎn* (character dictionary), or its pronunciation, meaning, and the meaning of compounds in which it serves as the first character if you are looking it up in a *cídiǎn* (word dictionary). Let us work this through using the following examples: 他, 做, 话, 说, 国, and 图. To be able to look each of these characters up in a dictionary one should follow the following steps:

Step 1. Identify the character's radical.

Step 2. Count the number of strokes within that radical.

Step 3. Locate the radical within the dictionary's radical index and use that index to identify the page number on which all characters with that shared radical are listed.

Step 4. Count the number of remaining strokes in the character outside of the radical.

Step 5. Go to the correct radical page number and then locate the desired character under its radical header according to the number of its remaining strokes.

Step 6. Go to the character's indicated page number to learn its pronunciation and meaning(s).

Step 1: Identify the character's radical.

Character	Radical
他	亻
做	亻
话	讠
说	讠
英	艹
草	艹
国	囗
图	囗

Step 2: Count the number of strokes within that radical.

Radical	Stroke order	Number of strokes
亻	丿 亻	2
讠	丶 讠	2
艹	一 十 艹	3
囗	丨 冂 囗	3

Step 3: Go to the dictionary's radical index, which lists every radical sequentially by stroke number, and locate the desired radical. Indicated next to each radical is the page number on which all characters sharing that same radical are listed.

One stroke		亠	18	彳	30	木	39
一	14	冫	19	忄	31	车	41
丨	15	讠	19	广	31	戈	41
丿	15	阝	20	门	31	日	42
丶	15	刀	21	氵	32	水	42
乙	15	厶	21	忄	34	见	43

Two strokes		又	21	宀	34	牛	43
二	15	**Three strokes**		辶	35	手	43
十	15	土	21	女	36	毛	43
厂	16	**艹**	**22**	子	37	气	43
亻	**16**	大	24	纟	37	攵	43
八	18	扌	25	马	38	父	44
人	18	小	26	幺	38	月	44
儿	18	口	27	**Four strokes**		文	45
几	18	**囗**	**29**	王	38	方	45

From the above radical index, we now know the following:

Character	Radical	Radical page number
他	亻	16
做	亻	16
话	讠	19
说	讠	19
英	艹	22
草	艹	22
国	囗	29
图	囗	29

Step 4: Count the number of remaining strokes in the character outside of the radical.

Character	Remainder	Remaining stroke breakdown	Remaining stroke count
他	也	㇇ 也 也	3
做	故	一 十 十 古 古 古 古 故 故	9
话	舌	一 二 干 千 舌 舌	6
说	兑	、 丷 丷 丷 台 户 兑	7
英	央	丶 冂 冂 央 央	5
草	早	丶 冂 冃 旦 旦 早	6
国	玉	一 二 千 王 玉	5
图	冬	丿 夕 夂 冬 冬	5

The necessary information about these unknown characters has now expanded to:

Character	Radical	Radical page number	Remaining stroke count
他	亻	16	3
做	亻	16	9
话	讠	19	6
说	讠	19	7
英	艹	22	5
草	艹	22	6
国	囗	29	5
图	囗	29	5

Step 5: Go to the appropriate radical page number and locate the desired character under its radical header according to the number of its remaining strokes.

Page 16 (for 他 and 做):

Radical 厂		仍	1068	使	1149
厂	6 143	化	536 534	供	439 442
2 to 6 strokes		**3 strokes**		7 to 8 strokes	
厅	1257	仗	1587	俪	780
历	776	代	240	修	1416
厕	126	仙	1360	保	44
7 to 8 strokes		**他**	**1215**	借	651
厚	528	4 to 6 strokes		候	529
原	1547	休	1415	**9 strokes**	
9 to 10 strokes		伤	1103	债	373
厢	1374	伙	576	**做**	**1688**
厨	188	伪	1311	偷	1269
Radical 亻		何	509	Radical 八	
1 stroke		但	247	2 to 4 strokes	
亿	1490	你	924	公	434
2 strokes		佳	604	半	35
仁	1065	侨	1020	共	441

From the information above we now know which pages to turn to in order to find the meaning and pronunciation of both 他 and 做.

Character	Character page number
他	1215
做	1688

Step 6: Go to the character's indicated page number to learn its pronunciation and meaning(s).

Page 1215 (for 他):

它	tā	it
他	**tā**	① he, ② s/he, ③ other, another, some other
她	tā	she
塔	tǎ	① (Buddhist) pagoda, ② tower, ③ surname

Page 1688 (for 做):

柞	zuò	oak tree (*quercus*)
胙	zuò	sacrificial meat (in ancient times)
座	zuò	① seat, place, ② stand, pedestal, base, ③ constellation āstr., ④ classifier for large buildings and mountains
做	**zuò**	① make, produce, manufacture, ② cook, prepare, ③ do, act, engage in, ④ be, become, ⑤ write, compose, ⑥ hold a family celebration, ⑦ be used as, ⑧ form or contract a relationship

LOOKING UP AN UNKNOWN WORD OR PHRASE IN A DICTIONARY

A word in Chinese is usually made up of more than one character. Looking up an unknown word or phrase in a dictionary merely involves focusing on the first character in the word and following the procedures outlined just above for how to look up that first character in a dictionary.

Returning to the character 做 directly above, then, we could now imagine needing to look up the following four words or phrases in a dictionary: 做伴, 做法, 做事, 做贼心虚.

Going through the procedures for finding 做, we now come to page 1688. On that page we find 做 and a list of words and phrases beginning with 做 placed immediately below it, arranged in semi-alphabetical order based on the romanized spelling of the character immediately following 做. Assuming that you do not know the pronunciation of that second character, you would then simply need to start from the beginning of the word/phrase entry list and go down until you find the desired entry.

Page 1688 (for 做):

做	zuò	① make, produce, manufacture, ② cook, prepare, ③ do, act, engage in, ④ be, become, ⑤ write, compose, ⑥ hold a family celebration, ⑦ be used as, ⑧ form or contract a relationship
[做伴]	**zuòbàn**	**keep sb. company**
[做东]	zuò dōng	play the host, host sb., act as host to sb.
[做法]	**zuò.fǎ**	**way of doing or making sth., method of work, practice**
[做客]	zuò kè	be a guest
[做媒]	zuò méi	be a matchmaker
[做梦]	zuò mèng	① have a dream, dream, ② have a pipedream, daydream
[做事]	**zuò shì**	**① handle affairs, do a deed, act, ② work, have a job**
[做寿]	zuò shòu	celebrate the birthday (usu. of elderly people), hold a birthday party
[做贼心虚]	**zuòzéi-xīnxū**	**have a guilty conscience**
[做作]	zuòzuo	affected, artificial

FINAL BITS OF INFORMATION ABOUT HOW TO USE THIS TEXTBOOK

So far you have learned some important information about the nature of the Chinese writing system, including the prominent role that sound and meaning clues play in knowing what a character means and how to pronounce it, as well as the use of radicals as a bookkeeping device to classify characters and the central role they play in the process of looking up characters in a dictionary.

You also learned about the 11 basic stroke types and the principles used to put them together to form larger and larger building blocks in a stable, well-balanced manner within an imaginary square. Additionally, you have seen how to reverse the construction process, i.e. how to go about decomposing independent and complex characters into smaller and smaller units, eventually boiling them down to individual, countable strokes of the pen or pencil.

In the following chapters each new character will be systematically introduced together with the specific factual details of how it is constructed and classified.

Keeping in mind that not every character can stand alone as a full-fledged word in modern Chinese, each character that is unable to do this will be marked with a (*).

Also, from time to time, a brief mnemonic clue will also be offered. Recognizing that these mnemonic clues are not always etymologically correct, the point to remember is that their utility lies primarily in helping you to quickly remember how to write a character and not in providing you with an accurate picture of how a particular character actually came to be written the way it is.

Finally, next to each new character are eight blank squares for you to practice how to properly write each character. Please bear in mind that, like learning to play a musical instrument or mastering a sport, learning how to write Chinese characters requires constant repetition in order to develop muscle memory. In other words, you will need to practice writing each new character many, many more times than just eight.

You are about to embark on an exciting journey. Good luck!

EXERCISES

1. **Identify the radicals of each of the following characters, then count the number of the strokes of the radical for each.**

   a. 作 _____   c. 汤 _____   e. 国 _____

   b. 楼 _____   d. 谢 _____   f. 花 _____

2. **Write down the number of remaining strokes beyond its radical for the following characters.**

   a. 吵 _____   c. 妈 _____   e. 双 _____

   b. 除 _____   d. 位 _____   f. 忙 _____

3. **Using the radical table shown under step 3 above, identify the radical of each of the following characters. You may like to find each radical in the radical index of your own dictionary as well.**

   a. 快 _____   c. 昨 _____   e. 架 _____

   b. 肚 _____   d. 奶 _____   f. 咱 _____

4. **Look up the following characters in any dictionary of your choice. Then write down the pronunciation of the character you find.**

   a. 超 _____   c. 志 _____   e. 笔 _____

   b. 和 _____   d. 所 _____   f. 钟 _____

5. **Try to find the following words in a printed or online/digital dictionary, then write down their English definitions.**

a. 词典 _____   c. 小说 _____   e. 办公楼 _____

b. 杂志 _____   d. 外衣 _____

4

第四课

TEXT 1

我 kàn 书, 我也 mǎi 书。[1] 我 yǒu 中文书, 也 yǒu 日文书, 一、[2] 二、三、sì、五、liù、七、八、九、十。我 de 书不大, 也不小。Nǐ ne? Nǐ yǒu 中文书 háishi 日文书?

生词 NEW WORDS

我	wǒ	(Pr) I, me
书	shū	(N) book
也	yě	(Adv) also

---

1. The Chinese period/full stop is written as a small circle rather than as a dot.
2. Chinese has two kinds of commas. One looks like the English comma, while the other, "、", is used exclusively between parallel items (things, actions, etc.) in a list. The English comma is used everywhere else that a comma would be used in English.

中文	Zhōngwén	(N) Chinese (language)
一	yī, yì, yí	(Nu) one
二	èr	(Nu) two
三	sān	(Nu) three
五	wǔ	(Nu) five
日文	Rìwén	(N) Japanese (language)
七	qī	(Nu) seven
八	bā	(Nu) eight
九	jiǔ	(Nu) nine
十	shí	(Nu) ten
不	bù-, bú-, -bu-	(Adv) not
大	dà	(SV) be big, be large
小	xiǎo	(SV) be small, be minor

TEXT 2

Tā shì 中 guó[3] 人, míngzi jiào 王中书。Tā shuō 中文, 也 huì shuō Yīng 文。我 shì 日本人, 我 xìng 中本, jiào 一也, 我 shuō 日文。我 de péngyou shì Xīn 西 lán 人, tā shuō Yīng 文。我 men dōu xué 中文, 王中书 jiāo 我 men 中文。

生词 NEW WORDS

| 中 guó | Zhōngguó | (PW) China |
| 人 | rén | (N) person, human being |

---

3. Proper nouns that cannot be further decomposed into smaller words are underlined in Chinese.

王	Wáng	(N) a Chinese surname
王中书	Wáng Zhōngshū	(N) a personal name
Xīn西lán	Xīnxīlán	(PW) New Zealand
日本	Rìběn	(PW) Japan
中本 一也	Zhōngběn Yīyě	(N) a Japanese personal name
Yīng 文	Yīngwén	(N) English (language)

COMPREHENSION QUESTIONS

1. Read the text at the beginning of the chapter and answer the following questions, using Chinese characters wherever possible.

TEXT 1:

a. Nǐ kàn 书 ma?

_____

b. Nǐ mǎi shénme?

_____

c. Nǐ yǒu 中文书 háishi 日文书?

_____

d. Nǐ de 书大不大?

_____

TEXT 2:

a. 王中书 shì 中 guó 人 háishi 日本人?

_____

b. Nàge 日本人 jiào shénme míngzi?

_____

c. Shéi xué 中文?

_____

d. Shéi shuō 中文?

_____

WRITING HELP

As noted in the previous chapter, every Chinese character can be divided into a radical plus a remainder, unless the character itself is a radical. Structure-wise, most characters embody more complexity than just a radical, and contain one or more substructures beyond the radical itself. Characters that Chinese have historically considered to be of a single structure are called **independent characters** and are written mentally in a simple, undivided square, though they are presented in this textbook with an actual empty square for you to work with. Characters that contain substructures beyond the radical are called **compound characters** and fill out that same mental square, which can be divided according to the compound structure. In this book, all characters are introduced according to these two categories.

INDEPENDENT CHARACTERS

Character	Basic meaning	No. of strokes	Stroke order	Radical	Components	Structure
一 yī, yì, yí	one	1	一	一	一	□
七 qī	seven	2	一七	一	七	□
八 bā	eight	2	一八	八	八	□
九 jiǔ	nine	2	丿九	丿	九	□
十 shí	ten	2	一十	十	十	□
人 rén	person	2	丿人	人	人	□
大 dà	big	3	一ナ大	大	大	□
小 xiǎo	small, little	3	丿亅小	小	小	□
也 yě	also	3	乛也也	乛	也	□
五 wǔ	five	4	一丁丆五	一	五	□
*1 中 zhōng	middle	4	丶冂口中	丨	口丨	□

Character	Basic meaning	No. of strokes	Stroke order	Radical	Components	Structure
*文 wén	language	4	丶 亠 ナ 文	文	文	☐
不 bù-, bú-, -bu-	not	4	一 ア 不 不	一	不	☐
*日 rì	sun	4	丨 冂 月 日	日	日	☐
王 wáng	king, surname	4	一 二 干 王	王	王	☐
书 (書)² shū	book	4	⼬ 乛 书 书	乛³	书	☐
*本 běn	origin	5	一 十 オ 木 本	木	木 一	☐
西 xī	west	6	一 丆 兀 丙 西 西	西	西	☐
我 wǒ	I, me	7	丿 二 于 手 扸 我 我	戈	我	☐

1. An asterisk next to a character indicates that the character can never stand alone as an independent word in modern standard Chinese.
2. When the traditional form of the Chinese character differs from its simplified form, that traditional form of the character is placed in brackets for reference purposes.
3. Sometimes there are variant ways in which a particular component, including a radical, is written. As we can see from the radicals of 也 and 书, they look slightly different, but they are just variants of the same radical. This radical can be written in five ways altogether: 乛, 乛, 乙, ㄴ, 乁.

Compound characters are formed by combining a radical with one or more independent characters and/or symbols. The radical usually indicates something of the meaning in the compound character.

RADICAL

The radical of focus in this chapter is: 一. The characters in this chapter that contain this radical are 二 and 三.

Character	Basic meaning	No. of strokes	Stroke order	Radical	Components	Structure
二 èr	two	2	一 二	一	一 一	⊟
三 sān	three	3	一 二 三	一	一 一 一	☰

EXERCISES

CHARACTER EXERCISES

1. Add one or two strokes to each of the following characters to form a new character.

   一 _____   十 _____   口 _____   人 _____

2. Delete one or two strokes from each of the following characters to form a new character.

   七 _____   三 _____   大 _____   王 _____

3. Write the third stroke for each of the following characters.

   书 _____   西 _____   文 _____   我 _____

4. Write the characters for the following Pinyin.

   Zhōngwén yī, qī, shí, sān, wǔ, jiǔ, èr, bā, sì

   Shū bú dà, yě bù xiǎo. Rìběn

---

5. Circle the wrong character in each sentence and correct it in the brackets.

a. 我 yǒu 中 文 书, 一, 二, 三, 四, 互, liù, 七, 八, 九, 十。(　　)

b. 王 中 书 shuō 中 文, 我 乜 shuō 中 文, 我 men dōu shuō 中 文。(　　)

c. 我 péngyou shì 日 本 入, tā shuō 日 文, xǐhuan kàn 日 文 书。(　　)

6. Choose the appropriate character from the four characters given below and fill in the brackets. Each character can only be used once.

西　大　王　日

a. 我 xìng (　　), jiào Guìyí。我 shì 中 guó 人, 我 shì lǎoshī。

b. 我 de 书不 (　　), kěshì hěn guì。

c. Nǐ xǐhuan kàn 中文书 háishi (　　) 文书?

d. Tā shì Xīn (　　) lán 人, tā shuō Yīng 文。

STRUCTURE EXERCISES

1. Complete the following phrases/sentences in Chinese characters.

a. 我 kàn 书, 我 ＿＿＿＿ mǎi 书。

b. 我 de 书＿＿＿ 大, 我 de ＿＿＿ 也 不 ＿＿＿。

c. 我 shì 日本 ＿＿＿, 我 shuō ＿＿＿＿＿。

2. 中本一也 is a Japanese boy. He speaks Japanese and is learning Chinese. His telephone number is 439-1872. Fill in the following form for him in Chinese characters.

Surname	
First name	
Native language	
Learning language	
Phone number	

3. **Translate the following sentences into Chinese, using Chinese characters for learned words.**

a. Can you write 1, 2, 3, 4, 5, 6, 7, 8, 9, 10 (numbers in Chinese)?

_____

_____

b. He is Japanese. He can speak Japanese.

_____

_____

c. Hello, my name is *Wáng Dàlán*. I am Chinese. My friend is also Chinese.

_____

_____

d. My book is big, but *Xiǎoxī's* book is small.

_____

_____

COMPOSITION

Write a short passage about *Meimei* based on the information given below. You only need to use the vocabulary and grammar that you have learned up to Chapter 4, which includes the vocabulary and grammar points from *Fundamental Spoken Chinese*. The passage has to be in your own words; do not translate the information given word by word. For characters you have not yet been taught, please use *Hànyǔ Pīnyīn* together with the original tone marks.

Information about *Meimei*:

Meimei is an American. She has a lot of friends. She has Japanese, Korean, English, Chinese, and New Zealander friends. *Meimei* not only is pretty, she is also very rich. She is of medium height. She can speak Japanese and English. She can't speak Chinese and Korean. Her Chinese friend *Wang Dazhong* teaches her to speak Chinese. He taught her how to say "May I ask what is your name?" "Thank you", "goodbye", "it does not matter", and "no problem" in Chinese. *Dazhong* taught *Meimei* Chinese. *Meimei* gave him a writing brush.

Write a passage of 120 characters about *Meimei*.

_____

_____

_____

_____

_____

_____

_____

_____

SUPPLEMENTARY READING

王小文:　　Zǎo!

中本一也:　Zǎo!

王小文:　　Nǐ shì 中 guó 人 háishi 日本人?

中本一也:　我 shì 日本人。Nǐ shì 中 guó 人 ma?

王小文:　　我 shì 中 guó 人。我 jiào 王小文。Nǐ jiào shénme míngzi?

中本一也:　我 jiào 中本一也。

COMPREHENSION QUESTIONS

1. 王小文 shì 中 guó 人 ma?

_____

2. 中本一也 shì 中 guó 人 háishi 日本人?

_____

CHARACTER PRACTICE

一	一								
七	七								
八	八								
九	九								
十	十								
人	人								
大	大								
小	小								
也	也								
五	五								
中	中								
文	文								
不	不								

日	日								
王	王								
书	书								
四	四								
本	本								
西	西								
我	我								
二	二								
三	三								

TEXT 1

王先生 yǒu 一千二百五十 sì 本书, 他 yǒu 中文书、[1] Yīng 文书, hái yǒu 日文书。他问 文文 yǒu 什么书, yǒu 几本书。文文只 yǒu 几本 Yīng 文小说。王先生说文文可以 kàn 他 de 中文书, 可 shì 文文不 dǒng 中文, 不会说中 guó 话, 也不会 kàn 中文书。文文只会说 "你 hǎo! 再见", 文文 yào xué 中文。王先生说他可以 jiāo 文文中文, 他 hái sòng 文文一本中 Yīng 词 diǎn。

---

1. In lists of items, objects or things, Chinese uses a special comma, which is written as "、". In all other instances where a comma is used, the ordinary "," is employed.

生词 NEW WORDS

先生	xiānsheng	(N) teacher, sir, Mr., husband
王先生	Wáng xiānsheng	(N) Mr. Wang
千	qiān	(Nu) thousand
百	bǎi	(Nu) hundred
-本	-běn	(Cl) volume (for books)
他	tā	(Pr) he, him
问	wèn	(V) ask (a question)
文文	Wénwen	(N) a personal name
什么	shénme	(QW) what
几?	jǐ?	(Q) How many? (classifier required)
只	zhǐ	(Adv) only, just
几-	jǐ-	(Q) a few, several (classifier required)
小说	xiǎoshūo	(N) fictional work (Cl -本)
说	shuō	(V) say, speak
可以	kěyǐ	(Aux) allowed to, can
可shì	kěshì	(Conj) but, however
会	huì	(Aux) may, can
话	huà	(N) spoken language
你	nǐ	(Pr) you (singular)
词 diǎn	cídiǎn	(N) dictionary (Cl -本)
再见	Zàijiàn!	(Ex) Goodbye, au revoir!

TEXT 2

我 shì <u>Xīn 西 lán</u> 人。我会说 Yīng 语、日语, 我也会 xiě 几个中文 zì。<u>王太太</u> de 儿子、女儿 shì 中 xué 生, 我 jiāo 他们说日语。王太太 sòng 我三支毛 bǐ。我问 tā: "你可以 jiāo 我 xiě 毛 bǐzì 吗?" Tā 说: "可以。" Tā 真 hǎo! 你们呢? 你们 yào xué xiě 毛 bǐzì 吗? 我可以 sòng 你们两支毛 bǐ。

我可以 sòng 你们两支毛 bǐ。

生词 NEW WORDS

Yīng 语	Yīngyǔ	(N) English (language)
日语	Rìyǔ	(N) Japanese (language)
一个	-gè	(Cl) (general classifier)
太太	tàitai	(N) Mrs., wife
王太太	Wáng tàitai	(N) Mrs. Wang
儿子	érzi	(N) son
女儿	nǚ'ér	(N) daughter
中 xué 生	zhōngxuéshēng	(N) secondary school students
他们	tāmen	(Pr) they, them
一支	-zhī	(Cl) (for pens, pencils)
毛 bǐ	máobǐ	(N) writing brush (Cl -支)
吗	ma	(P) (indicates a question)
真	zhēn	(Adv) really, truly
你们	nǐmen	(Pr) you (plural)
呢	ne	(P) (forms a reverse question)
两	liǎng	(Q) two (classifier required)

COMPREHENSION QUESTIONS

TEXT 1:

1. Read the texts of this chapter and answer the following questions.

a. 王先生 yǒu duōshao 本书?

_____

b. 王先生 yǒu 什么书?

_____

c. 文文 yǒu 几本书?

_____

d. 文文 yǒu 什么书?

_____

e. 文文会说中 guó 话 ma?

_____

f. 王先生 sòng 文文什么?

_____

g. Shéi 可以 jiāo 文文中文?

_____

h. 文文 yào 不 yào xué 中文?

_____

TEXT 2:

1. Complete each of the following sentences according to the passage.

a. 我 shì _____

b. 我会 _____

c. 我 jiāo _____

d. 王太太 sòng 我 _____

WRITING HELP

INDEPENDENT CHARACTERS

Character	Basic meaning	No. of strokes	Stroke order	Radical	Components	Structure
儿 (兒) ér	son	2	丿 儿	儿	儿	☐
*几 (幾) jǐ	several	2	丿 几	几	几	☐
千 qiān	thousand	3	ノ 二 千	十	丿 十	☐
*么 (麼) me		3	丿 厶 么	丿	丿 厶	☐
*子 zǐ	son, little boy, child	3	乛 了 子	子	子	☐
*女 nǚ	female, daughter	3	乀 夊 女	女	女	☐
毛 máo	hair, surname	4	ノ 二 三 毛	毛	毛	☐
太 tài	overly	4	大 太	大	大 丶	☐
*可 kě	can	5	一 口 可	口	口 丁	☐☐
生 shēng	student	5	ノ 一 七 牛 生	生	生	☐
*两 (兩) liǎng	two	7	一 厂 丙 丙 两	一	一 冂 人 人	☐
见 (見) jiàn	see	4	丨 冂 见 见	见	冂 儿	☐

COMPOUND CHARACTERS

The new compound character with learned radical 一 in this chapter is 百.

Char-acter	Basic meaning	No. of stokes	Stroke order	Radical	Meaning clue	Phonetic clue	Compo-nents	Struc-ture
百 bǎi	hundred	6	一 ｢ 丆 丏 百 百	一	一	白	一, 白	⊟
再 zài	again	6	｜ 冂 贝 见	一	一		一 冉	⊟

RADICALS

The radicals of focus in this chapter are 儿, 亻, 讠, 人, 十, and 口.

1. 儿

This can be a character as well as a radical.

Character	Basic meaning	No. of strokes	Stroke order	Meaning clue	Phonetic clue	Compo-nents	Structure
先 xiān	first	6	ノ 一 牛 生 先			生 儿	⊟

2. 亻

As a character, this means "human" and is written as 人. As a radical it is often used as the left part in a compound character to form characters related to humans or to things related to human activities, and is written as 亻. The compound characters in this chapter that contain this radical are 什, 们, 他, and 你.

Character	Basic meaning	No. of strokes	Stroke order	Meaning clue	Phonetic clue	Components	Structure
*什 (甚) shén	what (什么)	4	ノ 亻 仁 什		十	亻 十	
*们 (們) men	(plural for personal pronouns)	4	亻 亻 价 们	亻	门 mén	亻 门	
他 tā	he/him	5	亻 他	亻		亻 也	
你 nǐ	you	7	亻 亻 价 你	亻 尔 (ěr, you)		亻 尔 (勹小)	

他: 他 is also (也) "human"!

3. 讠

As a character, this means "spoken words or speech" and is written as 言 *yán*. As a radical it is used as the left part in a compound character, and is written as 讠 to form characters related to words, speech, and the action of speaking. The compound characters in this chapter that contain this radical are 词, 说, 话, and 语.

Character	Basic meaning	No. of strokes	Stroke order	Meaning clue	Phonetic clue	Components	Structure
词 (詞) cí	word	7	` 讠 订 订 词	讠	司 sī	讠 司 (刁 一口)	
话 (話) huà	talk	8	讠 讦 话	讠 舌 (shé, tongue)		讠 舌 (千 口)	
说 (說) shuō	speak	9	讠 讠 讠 说 说	讠		讠 兑 (丷 口儿)	
*语 (語) yǔ	language	9	讠 语 语	口 (kǒu, mouth)		讠 五口	

语: Think of it as being composed of speaking with five mouths—language 语.

4. 人

This form of 人 is used as a radical in compound characters mainly of the top-bottom structure, and sometimes in characters of the left-right structure. In this chapter, the characters that contain this radical are 以, 会, and 个.

Character	Basic meaning	No. of strokes	Stroke order	Meaning clue	Phonetic clue	Compo-nents	Structure
*个 (個) gè	(a classi-fier)	3	丿 人 个	人, 丨 (一个人)		人, 丨	⊟
以 yǐ	according to	4	丄 丄 以			以, 丷 、 人	⊞
会 (會) huì	may, can	6	人 仝 会 会	人		人 云 (二厶)	⊟

5. 十

This can be both a character and a radical. Usually, as a radical, it is put on the top part of a character. The compound characters in this chapter that contain this radical are 支 and 真.

Character	Basic meaning	No. of strokes	Stroke order	Meaning clue	Phonetic clue	Compo-nents	Structure
支 zhī	branch	4	十 圥 支		十	十 又	⊟
真 zhēn	true, truth	10	十 市 肻 直 真			直 八	⊟

6. 口

This can be both a character and a radical. 口 *kǒu* means "mouth" as an independent character (see Chapter 6). As a radical it is often used to form characters related to the mouth or the action of the mouth. The compound characters in this chapter that contain this radical are 只, 问, 吗, and 呢.

Character	Basic meaning	No. of strokes	Stroke order	Meaning clue	Phonetic clue	Components	Structure
只 zhǐ	only	5	口 只			口 八	
问 (問) wèn	ask	6	丶 亻 门 问	口	门 mén	门 口	
吗 (嗎) ma	(question word)	6	口 叮 吗 吗	口	马 mǎ	口 马	
呢 ne	(forms a reverse question)	8	口 叮 叮 吷 呢 呢	口	尼 ní	口 尼 (尸 匕)	

EXERCISES

CHARACTER EXERCISES

1. Find the independent characters you have learned hidden in the following characters.

语 _____   太 _____   说 _____   个 _____

你 _____   什 _____   以 _____   生 _____

2. Add more strokes to each of the following to form new characters.

司 _____   儿 _____   口 _____   尸 _____

门 _____   也 _____   千 _____   又 _____

3. Write the fourth stroke for each of the following characters.

真 _____   两 _____   会 _____   吗 _____

4. Fill in the blanks with a character that has the same radical as shown.

亻: _____   _____   _____

讠: _____   _____   _____

5. Write the characters for the following Pinyin.

xiǎoshuō, xiānsheng, Nǐmen shuō Rìyǔ.   Wǒ kéyǐ wèn.

6. Circle the wrong character in each sentence and correct it in the brackets.

a. 他 xǐhuan mǎi 书, 他 yǒu 两干两百本中文书。　　　　（　　）

b. 王大大 de 女儿会说 Yīng 语、日语。　　　　　　　（　　）

c. 儿子不 dǒng 中文, 他只会说: "你好! 冉见。"　　　（　　）

d. 他 xǐhuan kàn 小说, 我问他 xǐhuan kàn 什么小说。 （　　）

VOCABULARY EXERCISES

1. Fill in each of the following squares with one proper character so as to form a two-character word with the character already shown.

a.

	儿

b.

	们

c.

日	

STRUCTURE EXERCISES

1. Write the correct classifier character to complete each of the following phrases.

十_____词 diǎn　　　　　　五_____儿子

七_____小说　　　　　　　九_____毛 bǐ

2. Complete each of the sentences below with appropriate adverbs. Use characters for words you've already learned, and use Pinyin for characters you haven't learned yet.

a. 他 yǒu hěn duō 书, 我_____ yǒu 三本书。

b. 小王 hěn gāo, 小文_____ hěn gāo, 他们_____ hěn gāo。

c. Mànhuà 书_____ hǎokàn, 他 zuì xǐhuan kàn mànhuà 书。

3. Choose the appropriate character from the characters given immediately below and fill in the brackets. Some characters may be used more than once.

a. 话　词　问　说　语

　　i. 王先生(　　)小文 yào 不 yào xué 中文, 小文(　　) yào xué 中文。

　　ii. 王太太 sòng 女儿一本日文(　　) diǎn。、

　　iii. 我会(　　)中 guó (　　), 可 shì 不会 xiě 中文 zì。

　　iv. 我 jiāo 儿子日(　　), 儿子 hěn xǐhuan xué。

b. 么　吗　呢

　　i. 他 kàn 书, 我不 kàn。你(　　)?

　　ii. 你会 xiě 什(　　)中文 zì?

　　iii. Gěi 我 kànkan 你 de 小说, hǎo (　　)?

4. Rearrange the elements of each of the entries to make a grammatical sentence.

a. 会　　　　中文　　　　王太太　　　说

_____

b. shì　　　他们　　　　人　　　　日本

_____

c. 他　　　yǒu　　　　个　　　　儿子　　　两

_____

5. Write four sentences about 我 in Chinese using Chinese characters you have already learned. You may, however, include vocabulary you have already learned how to say but don't yet know how to write in characters. In such cases you may use Pinyin.

_____

_____

_____

_____

6. Translate the following sentences into Chinese, using Chinese characters for learned words.

a. What kind of books do you have?

_____

b. Zhōnglán has 10 Japanese dictionaries.

_____

c. That gentleman can speak Japanese.

_____

d. Mrs. Wang has three daughters and two sons.

_____

e. This lady has four children.

_____

f. These two dictionaries are really big.

_____

g. This school has 2,001 students.

_____

COMPOSITION

Wang Zhenzhen meets *Xiaowen* at a friend's house, and *Wang Zhenzhen* discovers that *Xiaowen* is her mother's student and starts a conversation. Write a dialogue recording their conversation. Your dialogue has to be based on the information given below. You only need to use the vocabulary and grammar that you have learned up to Chapter 5 from *Fundamental Spoken Chinese*. The passage has to be in your own words. Use the characters that you have learned up to Chapter 5 of *Fundamental Written Chinese*. For characters that you have not yet been taught, please use *Hànyǔ Pīnyīn* together with the original tone marks.

Wang Zhenzhen is a secondary school student. There are 3,102 students in her school, 2,000 of whom are male students and 1,202 of whom are female students. Her English teacher is surnamed Han. Teacher Han is not British. He is Korean. His wife is Chinese. Mrs. Han can write Chinese calligraphy. She teaches *Wang Zhenzhen* to write Chinese calligraphy. *Wang Zhenzhen's* father is a university teacher and her mother is a secondary school teacher.

Xiaowen is a university student. She is a student of *Wang Zhenzhen*'s mother. There are 9,229 students in her university, 5,000 of whom are male students and 4,229 of whom are female students. *Xiaowen* is learning Chinese. She has two Chinese teachers. She likes writing Chinese calligraphy. *Wang Zhenzhen*'s mother teaches her to write Chinese calligraphy. *Xiaowen* can speak English. She can also speak Chinese. Her father and mother are both teachers.

SUPPLEMENTARY READING

中本一也: 你 hǎo! Qǐng 问, 你会说日语吗?

王文:　　 我只会说一、二、三、sì、五、liù、七、八、九、十。你 shì 日本人吗?

中本一也: 我 shì 日本人, 可 shì 我太太 shì 中 guó 人。

王文:　　 你会说中文。你太太会说日语吗?

中本一也: 我太太会说日语。

王文:　　 他 shì 你 de 儿子吗?

中本一也: Shì。

王文:　　 你 de 儿子会说中文 háishi 日文?

中本一也: 他会说中文, 也会说日文。

COMPREHENSION QUESTIONS

1. <u>王文</u>会说日语吗?

   _____

2. <u>中本一也</u> de 太太 shì <u>中</u> guó 人 háishi <u>日本</u>人?

   _____

3. <u>中本一也</u> de 儿子会说中文吗?

   _____

CHARACTER PRACTICE

儿	儿							
几	几							
千	千							
么	么							
子	子							
女	女							
毛	毛							
太	太							
可	可							

生	生								
两	两								
百	百								
先	先								
什	什								
们	们								
他	他								
你	你								
词	词								
话	话								
说	说								
语	语								
个	个								
以	以								

会	会							
支	支							
真	真							
只	只							
问	问							
吗	吗							
呢	呢							
再	再							
见	见							

COMPLETE THE DIALOGUE

1. Complete the dialogue based on the information given.

A: 你 hǎo! Qǐngwèn 你 shì <u>中 guó</u> 人吗?

B: Duì, _____?

A: 我 shì <u>Měiguó</u> 人, 我 jiào Tom, _____?

B: 我 jiào <u>小 yí</u>。_____?

A: 我 shì xuésheng, 也 shì lǎoshī。

B: _____?

A: Zhè 不 shì 我 de 毛bǐ。

B: _____?

A: Zhè shì 我 péngyou de_____。

FILL IN THE BLANK

1. **Fill in each blank by choosing the most appropriate word from the alternatives provided in the box. You should not use any word more than once. There are more choices than blanks.**

只 本 qǐng xíng jiāo 会 háishi méi(.yǒu) jiào 支 个 不 gěi qián

<u>Gāo</u> 太太 de 儿子 jiào <u>大中</u>, 他 shì 我 de hǎo péngyou。他_____xiě

毛 bǐzi, 也 xǐhuan xiě 毛 bǐzi。他 yào jiāo 我 xiě 毛 bǐzi, 我说: "不 xíng,

我_____毛 bǐ。"他说: "Méi guānxi, 我可以 sòng 你一_____。"

他 sòng 我一支毛 bǐ, 我 gěi 他什么 dōngxi 呢? 我 yǒu 四支 qiānbǐ、

五_____词 diǎn。我问他 yào_____yào qiānbǐ, 他说不 yào。他问我可

以不可以_____他一本 Yīng 文词 diǎn, 我说我_____yǒu 日文词 diǎn,

他不 yào 日文词 diǎn, 我说: "Nà, 我_____你 kàn diànyǐng hǎo 吗? "他

说: "Nà 也_____。我_____你 xiě 毛 bǐzi, 你 qǐng 我 kàn 一个 <u>Měiguó</u>

diànyǐng。"

TRANSLATION

1. **Translate the following passage into Chinese. For characters you have not yet been taught, you may use *Hànyǔ Pīnyīn* romanization together with the tone marks.**

Tom is an American. He is my friend. He is a teacher. He is able to speak English and is also able to speak Japanese. I am Korean. I am able to speak Chinese and am also able to write Chinese characters. Tom wants to learn to write Chinese characters. He asked me "Can you teach me to write Chinese characters?" I said, "No problem." I taught him to write "one, two three, four, five, seven, eight, nine, ten." I asked him, "Do you like to write Chinese characters?" He said, "(I) like to." Tom doesn't understand Chinese, but he likes to watch Chinese movies. He also likes to buy writing implements. He buys pencils, (but) he doesn't buy brush pens.

_____

_____

_____

_____

_____

_____

_____

_____

_____

_____

_____

_____

READING COMPREHENSION

1. Read the following passage and answer the questions that follow it.

王太太 yǒu 三个 hái 子。Dì 一个 shì 儿子, 他叫<u>大中</u>。Zuì 小 de 也 shì 儿子, 他叫<u>小 míng</u>。只 yǒu dì 二个 shì 女儿, 她 jiào <u>Yīngying</u>。他们 dōu shì 大 xué 生。<u>大中</u> xǐhuan kàn Yīng 文小说, <u>Yīngying</u> xǐhuan kàn wàiguó zázhì, <u>小 míng</u> 不 xǐhuan kàn 书, 他 xǐhuan kàn <u>Měiguó</u> diànyǐng, 他说<u>Měiguó</u> diànyǐng zuì hǎo。

QUESTIONS:

a. <u>王太太</u> yǒu 几个儿子?

_____

b. <u>王太太</u> de dì 二个 hái 子 jiào 什么 míngzi?

_____

c. <u>王太太</u> de 女儿 shì 中 xué 生, duì 不 duì?

_____

d. <u>Yīngying</u> xǐhuan kàn 什么 zázhì?

_____

e. <u>小 míng</u> 说 něi guó diànyǐng zuì hǎo?

_____

6

TEXT 1

我 yǒu 个好 péngyou, 姓万, jiào <u>万文生</u>。他家一共 yǒu 八口人, bàba、妈妈、一个姐姐、两个妹妹、一个哥哥、一个弟弟 hé <u>文生</u>。兄弟姐妹一半 shì nánde, 一半 shì 女 de。他姐姐 yǒu sì 本日文词典, 两份中文 zázhì, 三本 <u>Xīn</u> 西兰小说。他 de 两个妹妹 dōu shì 小 xué 生、她们不 xǐhuan kàn 小说、她们要 kàn màn 画书。她们说 màn 画书很好 kàn, 字也很 shǎo。他弟弟 hé <u>文生</u> dōu 不要 kàn 书, 他们要 kàn 电 shì, 他们说电 shì 很好 kàn。

生词 NEW WORDS

好	hǎo	(SV) be well, be good
姓	xìng	(V) be surnamed
万	wàn	(N) a Chinese surname
		(Q) ten thousand
万文生	Wàn Wénshēng	(N) a personal name
家	jiā	(N) family, home

一共	yígòng	(Adv) altogether
-口	-kǒu	(Cl) (classifier for persons)
妈妈	māma	(N) mother
姐姐	jiějie	(N) older sister
妹妹	mèimei	(N) younger sister
哥哥	gēge	(N) older brother
弟弟	dìdi	(N) younger brother
兄弟姐妹	xiōngdì-jiěmèi	(N) brothers and sisters, siblings
一半	yíbàn	(Q) half
女 de	nǚde	(N) woman, female
词典	cídiǎn	(N) dictionary (Cl -本)
-份	-fèn	(Cl) (issues of newspapers, magazines, etc.)
小 xué 生	xiǎoxuésheng	(N) elementary school pupil
她们	tāmen	(Pr) they, them (all females)
要	yào	(V) want, want to
màn 画(书)	mànhuà(shū)	(N) comic book, manga (Cl -本)
很	hěn	(Adv) quite, very
好 kàn	hǎokàn	(SV) good-looking, have an interesting story
字	zì	(N) (Chinese) character(s) (Cl -个)
电 shì	diànshì	(N) television

TEXT 2

我 hé 姐姐 dōu méi(.yǒu) 自行车。我得买一 liàng 自行车。自行车七百 sì 十 kuài 九毛五分一 liàng, 不 guì 也不便宜。我姐姐也要买一 liàng。两 liàng 车一共 duōshao qián? 你告诉我, 好吗? 哎呀! 一共要一千 sì 百八十一 kuài 九毛。不行, 我们只 yǒu 一千 kuài qián, 只 néng 买一 liàng。我父母 yǒu 很 duō qián, 他们 yǒu 几万 kuài qián。他们说他们可以 sòng 我们两 liàng 自行车。我父母真好!

生词 NEW WORDS

自行车	zìxíngchē	(N) bicycle (Cl -liàng -辆)
得	děi	(Aux) must
买	mǎi	(V) buy
-毛	-máo	(Cl) dimes
-分	-fēn	(Cl) pennies
便宜	piányi	(SV) be cheap
告诉	gàosu	(V) tell, inform
哎呀	āiyā!	(Ex) Oh! Oh my!
不行	bùxíng	(Ex) Can't be done.
我们	wǒmen	(Pr) we, us
父母	fùmǔ	(N) parents

COMPREHENSION QUESTIONS

1. Read the texts of this chapter and answer the following questions.

TEXT 1:

a. 你 de péngyou jiào 什么 míngzi?

_____

b. 他家 yǒu 几口人?

_____

c. 他 yǒu 几个兄弟姐妹?

_____

d. 他姐姐 yǒu 什么书?

_____

e. 他妹妹 ài kàn 什么书?

_____

f. 他 hé 弟弟 ài kàn 什么?

_____

TEXT 2:

a. 我 hé 姐姐要买什么?

_____

b. 两 liàng 自行车一共 duōshao qián?

_____

c. 他们 néng 买几 liàng 自行车?

_____

d. Shéi 可以 sòng 他们自行车? Wèi 什么 ("Why")?

_____

WRITING HELP

INDEPENDENT CHARACTERS

Character	Basic meaning	No. of strokes	Stroke order	Radical	Components	Structure
万 (萬) wàn	ten thousand, surname	3	一 丁 万	一	万	☐
口 kǒu	mouth	3	口	口	口	☐
车 (車) chē	vehicle	4	一 𠂦 𫐄 车	车	车	☐
*父 fù	father	4	八 父	父	父	☐
*半 bàn	half	5	丷 半 半	八	半	☐
*母 mǔ	mother	5	乚 𠃌 母 母 母	母	母	☐
电 (電) diàn	electrical	5	日 电	日	日 乚	☐
*自 zì	self	6	丿 𠂊 自 自	自	自	☐
买 (買) mǎi	to buy	6	乛 乛 乛 买	乙[1]	乛 头	☐
画 (畫) huà	to draw	8	一 厂 冂 𠃌 両 画 画 画	凵	一 田 凵	☐

1. 乙 is a variant of the first stroke in this character.

COMPOUND CHARACTERS

The new compound characters with learned radicals in this chapter are 兄, 份, 告, 呀, 诉, 哎, 便, and 哥.

Char-acter	Basic meaning	No. of strokes	Stroke order	Radical	Meaning clue	Phonetic clue	Compo-nents	Struc-ture
*兄 xiōng	elder brother	5	口 兄	口	儿		口 儿	
*份 fèn	portion	6	亻 伀 份 份	亻		分 fēn	亻 八 刀	
告 gào	to in-form	6	生 告	口	口		生 口	
呀 ya	Oh!	7	口 叿 吁 呀	口	口	牙 yá	口 牙	
*诉 (訴) sù	to in-form	7	讠 讠 讠 诉 诉 诉	讠	讠 斥 (chì, *to scold*)		讠 斥 (斤 丶)	
哎 āi	Oh!	8	口 吖 吖 哎 哎	口	口	艾 ài	口 艹 又	
*便 pián	conve-nient	9	亻 伫 佰 便 便	亻			亻 一曰 又	
哥 gē	elder brother	10	可 哥	口		可+可	可 可	

RADICALS

The radicals of focus in this chapter are 八, 女, 宀, and 彳.

1. 八

The 八 radical is sometimes written as 丷, and is used as the top or bottom part of a character. The compound characters in this chapter that contain this radical are 分, 兰, 共, 弟, and 典.

Character	Basic meaning	No. of strokes	Stroke order	Meaning clue	Phonetic clue	Components	Structure
分 fēn	to divide	4	分	刀 (dāo, "knife")		八 刀	⊟
*兰 (蘭) lán	orchid	5	丶 丷 兰 兰 兰			丷 三	⊟
*共 gòng	altogether	6	一 十 卄 共 共			卄 八	⊟
弟 dì	younger brother	7	丷 丷 兰 总 弟 弟			丷 弔	⊟
*典 diǎn	standard word	7	丨 冂 曰 由 曲 曲 典			册 卄	⊟

2. 女

女 can be both a character and a radical. It means "female" as an independent character. As a radical, it can be put on the left or underneath a character to indicate what are considered to be female-like things. The compound characters in this chapter that contain this radical are 妈, 她, 好, 姓, 姐, 妹, and 要.

Character	Basic meaning	No. of strokes	Stroke order	Meaning clue	Phonetic clue	Components	Structure
她 tā	she/her	6	女 她	女		女 也	⊟
妈 (媽) mā	mother	6	女 妈	女	马 mǎ	女 马	⊟
好 hǎo	good	6	女 好	女, 子		女 子	⊟
姓 xìng	surname	8	女 姓	女, 生 "birth"	生 shēng	女 生	⊟
姐 jiě	elder sister	8	女 刦 如 姐 姐	女	且 qiě	女 且	⊟
*妹 mèi	younger sister	8	妇 妷 妷 妹	女	未 wèi	女 未	⊟
要 yào	to want	9	西 要			西 女	⊟

好: 女 "woman/mother/daughter" + 子 "son" = good.
姓: 女 "woman" + 生 "birth" = surname; 生 is also a phonetic clue.

3. 宀

The 宀 radical is used at the top position of a character to indicate a roof or something under cover. The compound characters in this chapter that contain this radical are 字, 宜, and 家.

Character	Basic meaning	No. of strokes	Stroke order	Meaning clue	Phonetic clue	Components	Structure
字 zì	character	6	丶 丷 宀 字		子	宀 子	▭
*宜 yí	suitable	8	宀 宜			宀 且	▭
家 jiā	family, home	10	宀 宇 宇 宇 字 宇 家 家	宀, 豕 (shǐ, "pig")		宀 豕	▭

家: A pig lives under a roof—family. A pig was a must in traditional Chinese households, as pork is a common meat for Chinese.

4. 彳

彳 is called the double human radical and is often found in characters associated with walking (e.g. "street") and movement in general (e.g. "behavior"). It is used as the left part in a compound character of a left-right structure. The compound characters in this chapter that contain this radical are 行, 很, and 得.

Character	Basic meaning	No. of strokes	Stroke order	Meaning clue	Phonetic clue	Components	Structure
行 xíng	all right	6	丿 彳 彳 行 行	彳		彳 丁	▯
很 hěn	very	9	彳 彳 彳 彳 很 很 很		艮 gěn	彳 艮	▯
得 děi	must	11	彳 彳 得 得 得			彳 旦 寸	▱

EXERCISES

CHARACTER EXERCISES

1. Add one or more strokes to the following characters to form a new character.

十 _____　　　女 _____　　　也 _____　　　人 _____

2. Write the fourth stroke for each of the following characters.

她 _____　　　要 _____　　　兄 _____　　　份 _____

姓 _____　　　字 _____　　　画 _____　　　哥 _____

3. Write the third stroke for each of the following characters.

电 _____　　半 _____　　弟 _____　　母 _____　　共 _____

4. Write the Pinyin for the following characters and put the phonetic element to that character in the brackets.

字: _____ ( )　　　什: _____ ( )

哥: _____ ( )　　　支: _____ ( )

5. Add a radical to each of the following to make different characters.

? + 马, 且, 未 → ( ), ( ), ( )

? + 子, 且, 豕 → ( ), ( ), ( )

? + 马, 牙, 尼, 艾 → ( ), ( ), ( ), ( )

? + 分, 更, 门, 尔 → ( ), ( ), ( ), ( )

6. Solve the character riddles.

a. Take half of "you" and half of "she." Who is it? _____

b. One plus one is not two, but _____

c. One minus one is not zero, but _____

7. Write the characters for the following Pinyin.

fùmǔ　　　zìxíngchē　　　jiěmèi　　　yígòng　　　āiyā

8. Circle the wrong character in each sentence and correct it in the brackets.

a. <u>文生</u> yǒu 很 duō màn 画书, 他说 màn 画书很好 kàn, 学也很 shǎo。   (   )

b. 姐姐说 zhè liàng 白行车要九百四十块, 我只 yǒu 八百块, 不 néng
买 zhè liàng。   (   )

c. 我妹妹 xǐhuan kàn 电 shì, 可 shì 父母告拆她 kàn 电 shì 不好。   (   )

d. <u>王中书</u>家只 yǒu 三口人, 他 de tóngxué 文生家 yǒu 很 duō 兄弟姐妹。(   )

VOCABULARY EXERCISES

1. **Link a character in the left column with a character in the right column to form a word and write down the word in the bracket. An example is already given.**

妈	呀	( )
词	弟	( )
她	诉	( )
父	们	( )
告	典	( )
兄	妈	(妈妈)
哎	母	( )

2. **Add one or more characters to the following to form a word or phrase, then make sentences with each of the new words or phrases.**

吗: _____

妈: _____

分: _____

份: _____

STRUCTURE EXERCISES

1. Rearrange the elements of each of the following entries to make a grammatical sentence.

a. 自行车　　得　　我们　　买

_____

b. de　　我　　真　　màn 画书　好 kàn　妹妹　　说

_____

c. 一共　　人　　家　　八　　yǒu　　他　　口

_____

2. Introduce your family briefly, then write one or two sentences in Chinese characters about each of your family members.

_____

_____

_____

_____

_____

3. Make a sentence with each of the following words.

告诉: _____

兄弟姐妹: _____

父母: _____

4. Complete the passage by using appropriate characters, one character per blank.

我_____王, jiào 兰兰。我家 yǒu 四_____ _____, Bàba、_____ _____、哥哥 hé 我。_____méi(.yǒu)_____ _____、_____ _____, _____méi(.yǒu) 弟弟。我哥哥 shì 大 xuésheng, 他_____gāo, zuì ài kàn 书, hái ài xiě_____。我 shì 中 xuésheng, 我_____ài kàn 书, kěshì 我 ài kàn_____shì。

5. **Translate the following sentences into Chinese, using Chinese characters for learned words.**

a. The magazine is $5.50 and the comic book is $12.00. Altogether it's $17.50.

_____

b. There are a lot of people, more than 260,000.

_____

c. My little brother has three and a half dollars.

_____

d. Chinese bicycles are quite good.

_____

e. How many are there in your family?

_____

f. He told me that he would buy that work of fiction.

_____

g. There are six people (who) want to buy that dictionary.

_____

h. I have all together four older sisters.

_____

COMPOSITION

1. Compose a passage of approximately 100 characters on a given topic. Your passage must include the given sentence patterns and vocabulary items. Please highlight or underline in your essay each of the given sentence patterns and vocabulary items. Use the characters that you have learned up to Chapter 6 of *Fundamental Written Chinese*. You only need to use the vocabulary and grammar that you have learned up to Chapter 6 from *Fundamental Spoken Chinese*. For characters that you have not yet been taught, please use *Hànyǔ Pīnyīn* together with the original tone marks.

Topic: 我的一家

a. Sentence patterns:

Noun 1 shì Noun 2; "there exists"(yǒu) 有 sentence; měi…dōu…

b. Vocabulary items: 父母　一共　zuì　nánde　高

_____

_____

_____

_____

_____

2. Compose a dialogue of approximately 100 characters on a given topic. Your dialogue must include the given sentence patterns and vocabulary items. Please highlight or underline in your essay each of the given sentence patterns and vocabulary items. Use the characters that you have learned up to Chapter 6 of *Fundamental Written Chinese*. You only need to use the vocabulary and grammar that you have learned up to Chapter 6 from *Fundamental Spoken Chinese*. For characters that you have not yet been taught, please use *Hànyǔ Pīnyīn* together with the original tone marks.

Topic: 买 dōng 西

a. Sentence patterns: duōshao qián? Choice question:…háishi…?
b. Vocabulary items: xiǎng   自行车   méi guānxi   便宜

_____

_____

_____

_____

_____

SUPPLEMENTARY READING

READING 1

大西: 文生, 你家 yǒu 什么人?

文生: Bàba、妈妈、一个姐姐、两个妹妹、一个哥哥、一个弟弟 hé 我。

大西: 你家人 dōu 会说中文吗?

文生: 他们 dōu 会说中文。你 yǒu 几个兄弟姐妹?

大西: 我只 yǒu 一个弟弟。

文生: 你弟弟会说中文吗?

大西: 他只说 Yīng 文。

Comprehension questions

1. 文生 yǒu 几个兄弟姐妹?

_____

2. 文生 de 兄弟姐妹会说中文吗?

_____

3. 大西 yǒu 几个兄弟姐妹?

_____

READING 2

中本一也买 de nèi liàng 日本车不便宜, 可shì 他说不 guì。他说好 de 日本车一 liàng 要三四万 kuài qián, 他 de 只要一万 kuài qián, 他买 de 车真不 guì。

Comprehension questions

1. <u>中本一也</u> de nèi liàng 车 duōshao qián?

_____

2. <u>中本一也</u>说他 de 车 guì 不 guì?

_____

CHARACTER PRACTICE

万	万								
口	口								
车	车								
父	父								
半	半								
母	母								
电	电								
自	自								
买	买								
画	画								

兄	兄								
份	份								
告	告								
呀	呀								
诉	诉								
便	便								
哥	哥								
分	分								
兰	兰								
共	共								
弟	弟								
典	典								
她	她								
妈	妈								

好	好								
姓	姓								
姐	姐								
妹	妹								
要	要								
字	字								
宜	宜								
家	家								
行	行								
很	很								
得	得								

第七课

TEXT

快要吃午饭了, 我真饿, 可shì 不想做饭。我想 qù <u>中 guó</u> 饭馆儿吃小吃, 再喝一 diǎn 儿酒。<u>中 guó</u> 小吃很好吃, 可shì 不好做。兰兰也没吃午饭, 她也要 qù 吃午饭。我知道她想吃什么, 她想吃<u>日本</u> cài, 喝冰水, 喝<u>可口可乐</u>。<u>兰兰</u> de 伯伯 hé 伯母 shì 一家<u>日本</u>饭馆儿 de lǎobǎn, 生意很忙, 客人也不 shǎo。他们饭馆儿 de cài 很好吃, 可shì 他们 de 咖啡不好喝。他们以前也卖酒, xiànzài 不卖了。<u>兰兰</u>还说她知道伯伯不会要我们 de qián, 他很 xǐhuan 请客, 我们不必客气, 也不必送他东西, 没关 xi, 他 shì <u>兰兰</u> de 伯伯。可shì 伯伯 xǐhuan 说汉语, 我们 qù 他 de 饭馆儿吃饭得说汉语。太好了! 我会说一 diǎn 儿汉语, 我也 xǐhuan 说汉语, 我还会 xiě 几个汉字。

生词 NEW WORDS

快(要)......了	kuài (yào)…le	(Pat) about to…
吃	chī	(V) eat, consume
午饭	wǔfàn	(N) lunch
饿	è	(SV) be hungry
想	xiǎng	(V) think, want to
做	zuò	(V) do, take the role of
饭馆儿	fànguǎnr	(PW) restaurant (Cl -家)
小吃	xiǎochī	(N) snack, refreshment, simple dish
再	zài	(Adv) again, additionally
喝	hē	(V) drink
一 diǎn 儿	yìdiǎnr	(Q) a bit, a little
酒	jiǔ	(N) liquor (Cl -bēi 杯, -píng 瓶)
好吃	hǎochī	(SV) be delicious
好做	hǎozuò	(SV) be easy to do
兰兰	Lánlan	(N) a personal name
没(.yǒu)	méi(.yǒu)	(V) not have, has not
她	tā	(Pr) she, her
要	yào	(Aux) going to, will, must, should
冰水	bīngshuǐ	(N) ice water
可乐	kělè	(N) cola, Coke (Cl -guàn 罐, -píng 瓶)
可口可乐	Kěkǒu Kělè	(N) Coca Cola (Cl -guàn 罐, -píng 瓶)
伯伯	bóbo	(N) uncle (father's elder brother)
伯母	bómǔ	(N) aunt (wife of father's elder brother)
-家	-jiā	(Cl) (for businesses)
生意	shēngyi	(N) (commercial) business
忙	máng	(SV) be busy
客人	kè.rén	(N) guest, shop/restaurant customer
卖	mài	(V) sell
咖啡	kāfēi	(N) coffee
好喝	hǎohē	(SV) be delicious to drink
以前	yǐqián	(TW) formerly, before
了	le	(P) (indicates a new situation)

还	hái	(Adv) also, additionally
知道	zhī.dào	(V) know, know of, know that
请客	qǐng kè	(VO) to treat someone to food or entertainment
不必	búbì	(Aux) need not, not have to
客气	kèqi	(SV) be polite
送	sòng	(V) escort, deliver, present, give
东西	dōngxi	(N) thing (physical)
没关 xi	méi guānxi	(Ex) Never mind. It doesn't matter.
汉语	Hànyǔ	(N) Chinese (language)
太	tài	(SV) overly, too
汉字	hànzì	(N) Chinese character(s)

COMPREHENSION QUESTIONS

1. Read the text of this chapter and answer the following questions.

a. 兰兰 de bàba shì 一家饭馆儿 de lǎobǎn, duì 吗?

_____

b. Zhèi 家饭馆儿卖什么?

_____

c. 兰兰 de 伯伯只说<u>日本</u>话, shì 吗?

_____

d. 饭馆儿 de 生意不忙, 客人也不 duō, duì 吗?

_____

WRITING HELP

INDEPENDENT CHARACTERS

Character	Basic meaning	No. of strokes	Stroke order	Radical	Components	Structure
了 le	(particle)	2	一 了	乙	了	☐
*午 wǔ	noon	4	丿 𠂉 午	丿	丿 干	☐
水 shuǐ	water	4	丿 才 水	水	水	☐
气 (氣) qì	air	4	丿 𠂉 气	气	气	☐
*必 bì	surely	5	丶 心 心 必 必	心	心 丿	☐
乐 (樂) lè	happy	5	丿 𠃋 乐	丿	一乙小	☐
东 (東) dōng	east	5	一 𠂇 东	一	一乙小	☐

COMPOUND CHARACTERS

The new compound characters with learned radicals in this chapter are 吃, 关, 伯, 知, 咖, 卖, 前, 客, 请, 啡, 喝, and 做.

Character	Basic meaning	No. of strokes	Stroke order	Radical	Meaning clue	Phonetic clue	Components	Structure
吃 chī	to eat	6	口 吇 吃	口	口	乞 qǐ	口 乞 (𠂉乙)	☐
关 (關) guān	to close	6	丷 ⺶ 关	丷丨			丷天	☐
*伯 bó	father's elder brother	7	亻 伯	亻	亻	白 bái	亻 白	☐
知 zhī	to know	8	𠂉 矢 知	口	口	矢 shǐ	矢 口	☐

Char-acter	Basic meaning	No. of strokes	Stroke order	Radical	Meaning clue	Phonetic clue	Compo-nents	Struc-ture
*咖 kā	coffee (咖啡)	8	口 叮 叻 咖	口	口	加 jiā	口 力 口	
卖 (賣) mài	to sell	8	十 卖	十		买	十 买 (宀头)	
*前 qián	front	9	丷 广 芦 肯 前 前	丷[1]			丷 一 月 刂	
客 kè	guest	9	宀 宀 宏 安 客	宀	宀	各 gè	宀 各 (夂口)	
请 (請) qǐng	to invite	10	讠 讠 讠 讠 请 请	讠	讠	青 qīng	讠 丰 月	
做 zuò	to do/ make	11	亻 什 估 估 做	亻	亻		亻 十 口 夂	
*啡 fēi	coffee (咖啡)	11	口 叮 吖 吖 吖 唎 啡 啡 啡	口	口	非 fēi	口 非	
喝 hē	to drink	12	口 叩 吗 喝 喝 喝	口	口	曷 hé	口 日 匃	

1. 丷 is a variant of radical 八.

RADICALS

The radicals of focus in this chapter are 冫, 忄/心, 夂, 氵, and 辶.

1. 冫

This radical is used as the left part in a compound character and it is used to indicate coldness or ice.

Character	Basic meaning	No. of strokes	Stroke order	Meaning clue	Phonetic clue	Compo-nents	Structure
冰 bīng	ice	6	冫 冰	冫 水		冫 水	

2. 忄/心

心 is the image of the heart in ancient Chinese. 心 *xīn* can be used as an independent character or as a radical to be put underneath a character. *Xīn* takes the form of

忄 when it used as the left part in a compound character. This radical means things or activities that are connected with a person's mind. The compound characters in this chapter that contain this radical are 忙, 快, 想, and 意.

Character	Basic meaning	No. of strokes	Stroke order	Meaning clue	Phonetic clue	Compo-nents	Structure
忙 máng	busy	6	丶 丷 忄 忄 忙 忙	忄, 亡 (wáng, death)	亡 wáng	忄 亡	⊟
快 kuài	quick	7	忄 忄 快	忄	夬 guài	忄 夬	⊟
想 xiǎng	to think, want	13	木 相 相 想 想 想	心 (xīn, heart)	相 xiāng	木 目 心	⊟
*意 yì	idea, wish, meaning	13	亠 立 立 音 意	心 (xīn, heart)		立 曰 心	☰

忙: When you are busy, your heart is dead.

3. 饣

As an independent character, this means "food" and is written as 食 *shí*. As a radical, it is used as the left part in a compound character and is written as 饣. It means "food" or things related to cuisine. The compound characters in this chapter that contain this radical are 饭, 馆, and 饿.

Character	Basic meaning	No. of strokes	Stroke order	Meaning clue	Phonetic clue	Compo-nents	Structure
饭 (飯) fàn	cooked rice, meal	7	丿 饣 饣 饣 饤 饭	饣	反 fǎn	饣 反	⊟
*馆 (館) guǎn	place for public use	11	饣 饣 饣 馆 馆 馆 馆	饣	官 guān	饣 官 (宀 目)	⊟
饿 (餓) è	hungry	10	饣 饿	饣	我 (usually indicates the sound *è* when used as a phonetic clue)	饣 我	⊟

4. 氵

This radical is used as the left part in a compound character and it means water or things related to water. The compound characters in this chapter that contain this radical are 汉, 没, and 酒.

Character	Basic meaning	No. of strokes	Stroke order	Meaning clue	Phonetic clue	Components	Structure
*汉 (漢) hàn	Chinese nationality, name of a river	5	丶 汀 汉	氵		氵 又	
没 méi	not	7	氵 氵 汐 没			氵 几 又)	
酒 jiǔ	wine, alcohol	10	氵 洒 洒 酒	氵	酉 yǒu	氵 酉	

* Note the difference between the right top part of 没 (几) and 几 in writing.

5. 辶

辶 is used in compound characters to indicate things related to a road or walking. The compound characters in this chapter that contain this radical are 还, 送, and 道.

Character	Basic meaning	No. of strokes	Stroke order	Meaning clue	Phonetic clue	Components	Structure
还 (還) hái	also, additionally	7	不 还 还 还			辶 不	
送 sòng	to give as a gift, to see someone off	9	关 送	关 (guān, close (gate))		辶 关 (丷 天)	
道 dào	principle, way	12	丷 丷 首 道 道	辶, 首 (shǒu, head)		辶 首 (丷 一 自)	

EXERCISES

CHARACTER EXERCISES

1. Add more strokes to each of the following characters to form a new character.

了 _____   水 _____   关 _____   小 _____

2. Find the independent characters you have learned hidden in each of the following characters.

客 _____   午 _____   关 _____   要 _____

3. In the blank below write the component common to all three given characters.

汉, 饭, 没 (   )   意, 喝, 得 (   )

你, 乐, 东 (   )   卖, 话, 支 (   )

4. Write the Pinyin for the following characters and put the phonetic element to that character in the blank.

卖: _____ (   )   字: _____ (   )

5. Add a radical to each of the following to make different characters.

(   ) + 不, 关 → (   ), (   )

(   ) + 反, 我, 官 → (   ), (   ), (   )

(   ) + 亡, 相, 夬 → (   ), (   ), (   )

6. Write as many characters you have learned as possible that use the 口 radical.

_____

_____

7. Correct the errors in the following characters.

冫水 _____   䜣 _____   快 _____

8. Circle the wrong character in each sentence and correct it in the brackets.

a. 王中书 yǒu 一 liàng 自行车, 可shì 他想冉买一 liàng。(　　　)

b. 毛 shūshu 做生意, 他 de diàn 卖很 duō 乐西。(　　　)

c. 中 guó cài 好吃, 可shì 太 nán 做了, 我们 qù 饭关吃吧。(　　　)

d. 我 jiāo 文文说汉语, 文文清我吃饭。(　　　)

e. 兰兰得卖一本词典, 可shì 她没 yǒu qián。(　　　)

9. Write the characters for the following Pinyin.

a. Qǐng kè, chīfàn bù kěyǐ méi jiǔ。

_____

b. Wǒ gēge hěn máng。

_____

VOCABULARY EXERCISES

1. Form as many words or phrases as possible by using the characters given below.

a. 吃 → _____

b. 喝 → _____

c. 饭 → _____

d. 好 → _____

e. 很 → _____

g. 客 → _____

h. 可 → _____

i. 知 → _____

j. 汉 → _____

k. 以 → _____

2. Link a character in the left column with a character in the right column to form a word and write down the word in the bracket. An example is already given.

冰	母	( )
午	啡	( )
生	必	( )
伯	西	( )
咖	意	( )
东	饭	( )
不	水	(冰水)

3. Find the word that is not in the same category as the other three words and write it in the brackets.

a. 饭馆, 冰水, 可乐, 酒   (   )

b. 妈妈, 伯母, 姐姐, 先生   (   )

c. 小说, 词典, 日文书, 小吃   (   )

STRUCTURE EXERCISES

1. Rearrange the elements of each of the entries to make a grammatical sentence.

a. 酒, 不, 王, 可以, 喝, 先生

→ _____

b. 生意, 以前, 不, 他, 做

→ _____

c. 汉语, 我, 说, 弟弟, 了, 会

→ _____

d. 好吃, 卖, 小吃, 饭馆儿, 很, 的

→ _____

e. 酒, 不, 只, 喝, 咖啡, 我, 喝, 日本

→ _____

2. Choose the appropriate character or words from the characters and words given immediately below and fill in the brackets.

$$\boxed{\text{不必　不行　还　再　太　想}}$$

a. 伯伯很 xǐhuan 喝酒, 他想 (　　　) 喝一 bēi 酒, 可 shì 没酒了。

b. 万文生 shì 我 de 伯伯, 他请客, 我们 (　　　) 客气。

c. 姐姐会做中 guó cài、日本 cài, (　　　) 会做 Xīn 西兰 cài。

d. (　　　) 饿了! 真 (　　　) 吃一 diǎn 儿东西。

e. 小万问妈妈可以买可乐吗? 他妈妈说, (　　　)！喝可乐不好。

3. Fill in the blanks with the most appropriate characters, using one character for each blank.

　　　王关乐家＿＿＿＿ ＿＿＿＿ yǒu 十个人: bàba、妈妈、一个哥哥、＿＿＿＿

个姐姐、两个弟弟、一个妹妹 hé 他。兄弟姐妹一半 shì nánde, 一＿＿＿＿ shì

女 de。王关乐 de 妈妈＿＿＿＿ de 日本小吃真好＿＿＿＿。大姐姐做 de 冰

咖啡＿＿＿＿很好＿＿＿＿。他们一家人 dōu 很客气, 很 xǐhuan 请客。王关

乐＿＿＿＿我 qù 他们家吃午饭。我送他妈妈＿＿＿＿ ＿＿＿＿东西＿＿＿＿?

4. Translate the following sentences into Chinese, using Chinese characters for learned words.

a. What would you like to drink?

_____

b. Please give me a bottle of beer.

_____

c. Mr. Wang was an owner of a bookstore, but he is no longer doing business now.

_____

d. I know what you like to eat. I'll treat you.

_____

e. The business in uncle's Japanese restaurant is brisk.

_____

f. I like having coffee, tea, and Cokes, but I don't like drinking.

_____

SUPPLEMENTARY READING

READING 1

文汉:　　<u>小兰</u>, 这 xiē <u>中</u> guó 小吃 shì 你做的吗?

小兰:　　Shì。

文汉:　　真好吃。

小兰:　　好吃 jiù duō 吃一 diǎnr。

文汉:　　真的? Nà, 我 jiù 不客气了。

小兰:　　没问 tí, néng 吃 duōshao jiù 吃 duōshao, bié 客气。

True or false questions

1. <u>小兰</u>做的<u>中</u> guó 小吃不好吃. (　　　)

2. <u>文汉</u>很 xǐhuan 吃<u>小兰</u>做的<u>中</u> guó 小吃. (　　　)

READING 2

　　我很 xǐhuan 喝冰水, 可 shì <u>中</u> guó 人说喝冰水不好。<u>中</u> guó de 饭馆儿不卖冰水, 也不 gěi 客人冰水。他们 gěi 客人<u>中</u> guó chá, <u>中</u> guó 人说喝<u>中</u> guó chá 好。我 de <u>Měiguó</u> 朋友说喝可乐好。你说呢?

Comprehension questions

1. 我很 xǐhuan 喝什么?

_____

2. 中 guó 饭馆儿 gěi 客人喝什么?

_____

CHARACTER PRACTICE

了	了							
午	午							
水	水							
气	气							
必	必							
乐	乐							
东	东							
吃	吃							

关	关							
伯	伯							
知	知							
咖	咖							
卖	卖							
前	前							
客	客							
请	请							
做	做							
啡	啡							
喝	喝							
冰	冰							
忙	忙							
快	快							

想	想							
意	意							
饭	饭							
馆	馆							
饿	饿							
汉	汉							
没	没							
酒	酒							
还	还							
送	送							
道	道							

8

TEXT

这是我 de 好朋友, 他 de 名字叫毛乐生。小毛是法国人。他很有意思, xǐ 欢买地道 de 法国东西。他 chuān de 那双法国皮 xié 很 guì, 四百 duō 块 qián 一双。我只买便宜 de 皮 xié, 我 de 旧皮 xié 只有八十块 qián 一双。有人说小毛很 cōng 明, 可是我说他真笨。你 kàn, 他 chuān 很 guì de 法国皮 xié, 可是没有 qián 买吃 de 东西了。他 xiàn 在不吃早饭了, 只喝牛奶, 午饭也不吃了, 只喝一 diǎn 儿汤。不吃饭真不容 yì。我问他饿不饿, 他说没问 tí。我真不明白, 他不 néng 不吃东西吧。我想请他吃晚饭。他很 xǐ 欢地道 de 法国东西, 可是不 xǐ 欢吃法国 cài。对了, 他 xǐ 欢吃中国 cài, 我请小毛去我叔叔 de 中国饭馆儿吃晚饭。小毛早饭 hé 午饭都没吃, 太饿了。他说那家饭馆儿做 de cài 太好吃了, 他 xiàn 在不饿了, 吃饱了。我叔叔还送小毛一支中国毛笔、一本中国地图呢。

生词 NEW WORDS

这	zhè	(Pr) this
是	shì	(V) be, is, am, are
朋友	péngyou	(N) friend
名字	míngzi	(N) name
叫	jiào	(V) be called, call
毛乐生	Máo Lèshēng	(N) a personal name
法国	Fǎguó	(PW) France
中国	Zhōngguó	(PW) China
有意思	yǒuyìsi	(SV) be interesting
xǐ 欢	xǐhuan	(V) like, prefer, enjoy, like to
地道	dìdao	(SV) be authentic
那	nà	(Pr) that
-双	-shuāng	(Cl) a pair of
皮 xié	píxié	(N) leather shoes (Cl -双)
四	sì	(Nu) four
-块	-kuài	(Cl) dollars
都	dōu	(Adv) in all cases
旧	jiù	(SV) be old (of objects, *not* living things)
有	yǒu	(V) have, has
有人	yǒu rén	(Ph) somebody
cōng 明	cōngming	(SV) be intelligent, be smart
可是	kěshì	(Conj) but, however
笨	bèn	(SV) be stupid
没(有)	méi(.yǒu)	(V) not have, has not
xiàn 在	xiànzài	(TW) presently, now
早饭	zǎofàn	(N) breakfast
牛奶	niúnǎi	(N) milk
汤	tāng	(N) soup
容 yì	róngyì	(SV) be easy
没问 tí	méi wèntí	(Ex) Not a problem.
明白	míngbai	(V) understand
吧	ba	(P) (indicates an assumption)
请	qǐng	(V) please, treat, hire, invite
晚饭	wǎnfàn	(N) supper
对	duì	(SV) be correct

对了	duì le	(Ex) by the way, it occurred to me that…
去	qù	(V) go to (a place)
叔叔	shūshu	(N) uncle (father's younger brother)
饱	bǎo	(SV) be full (from eating)
吃饱了	chībǎo le	(Ex) to be full (from eating)
毛笔	máobǐ	(N) writing brush (see Chapter 5)
地图	dìtú	(N) map (Cl -zhāng 张), atlas (Cl -本)
呢	ne	(P) (used at the end of sentences for emphasis)

COMPREHENSION QUESTIONS

1. Read the text of this chapter and answer the following questions.

a. Shéi 是我 de 好朋友?

_____

b. 他是 něi 国人?

_____

c. 他 xǐ 欢什么?

_____

d. 他 chuān 什么皮 xié?

_____

e. 小毛很有 qián, 是吗?

_____

f. 我 wèishénme ("why") 请小毛吃晚饭?

_____

g. 我们去 nǎ 儿吃晚饭?

_____

h. 小毛 xǐ 欢吃什么?

_____

i. 我叔叔送小毛什么?

_____

WRITING HELP

INDEPENDENT CHARACTERS

Character	Basic meaning	No. of strokes	Stroke order	Radical	Components	Structure
牛 niú	ox	4	ノ 二 牛	牛	牛	☐
白 bái	white, surname	5	ノ イ 白 白 白	白	白	☐
皮 pí	leather, skin	5	フ 厂 皮 皮	皮	皮	☐

COMPOUND CHARACTERS

The new compound characters with learned radicals in this chapter are 叫, 奶, 名, 汤, 吧, 这, 法, 饱, 思, and 容.

Character	Basic meaning	No. of strokes	Stroke order	Radical	Meaning clue	Phonetic clue	Components	Structure
叫 jiào	to call	5	口 叩 叫	口	口		口 丩	☐☐
奶 nǎi	milk, grandma*1	5	女 妁 奶	女	女	乃 nǎi	女 乃	☐☐
*名 míng	name	6	ノ ク タ 名	口	口		タ 口	☐☐
汤 (湯) tāng	soup	6	氵 汇 汤 汤	氵	氵	勿 (indicating sound of -ang)	氵 勿)	☐☐
吧 ba	(particle)	7	口 叮 叮 叩 吧	口	口	巴 bā	口 巴	☐☐
这 (這) zhè	this	7	文 这	辶			辶 文	☐☐
*法 fǎ	method, law	8	氵 泔 法	氵			氵 去	☐☐

Char-acter	Basic meaning	No. of strokes	Stroke order	Radical	Meaning clue	Phonetic clue	Compo-nents	Struc-ture
饱 (飽) bǎo	to have eaten one's fill	8	饣 饣 饣 饱	饣	饣	包 bāo	饣 包	⊟
*思 sī	to think	9	田 思	心	心		田 心	⊟
*容 róng	face, ap-pearance	10	宀 宀 宀 容	宀	宀, 口		宀 谷	⊟

容: To better remember this character, think of it as the facial features of a person with a hat on top, two eyebrows below it, and then two sides of a very bushy moustache, and finally a mouth at the bottom.

RADICALS

The radicals of focus in this chapter are 又, 阝, 口, 土, 日, 月, and 竹.

1. 又

As an independent character, 又 *yòu* means "again". As a radical, it indicates a hand. It is used in characters related to hands. The compound characters in this chapter that contain this radical are 双, 友, 对, 欢, and 叔.

Character	Basic meaning	No. of strokes	Stroke order	Meaning clue	Phonetic clue	Compo-nents	Structure
*双 (雙) shuāng	pair	4	又 双	又 (yòu, again), 又		又 又	⊟
*友 yǒu	friend, friendly	4	一 ナ 友	ナ (hand)	又 yòu	ナ 又	⊟
对 (對) duì	correct	5	又 又 对 对			又 寸	⊟
*欢 (歡) huān	happy	6	又 欢 欢			又 欠 (ﾉ人)	⊟
叔 shū	father's younger brother	8	上 朱 叔			上 小 又	⊟

2. 阝

阝 , as an image of an ear, can be used as either a right or left part of a character. In this chapter, 阝 is only used as a right-hand radical. The compound characters in this chapter that contain this radical are 那 and 都.

Character	Basic meaning	No. of strokes	Stroke order	Meaning clue	Phonetic clue	Compo-nents	Structure
那 nà	that	6	コ ヲ ヲ 月 月阝 那			月阝	▯▯
都 dōu	all	10	土 耂 者 都			者 (土 丿 日)阝	▯▯

3. 囗

This radical is found on the outside of a character to indicate enclosure, the border of a nation, a picture frame, etc. The compound characters in this chapter that contain this radical are 图, 国, and 四.

Character	Basic meaning	No. of strokes	Stroke order	Meaning clue	Phonetic clue	Compo-nents	Structure
图 (圖) tú	picture	8	冂 冈 冈 图 图	囗, 冬 (dōng, winter)		囗 冬 (夂 冫)	▢
国 (國) guó	country	8	冂 国 国 国	囗, 玉 (yù, jade), indicat-ing the emper-or's jade seal		囗 玉	▢
四 sì	four	5	冂 冂 四			囗 儿	▢

图: A winter scene in a frame.

4. 土

土 *tǔ* can be both an independent character and a radical. It means "earth" or "soil" as an independent character. As a radical, it is usually used to form characters relat-ed to the earth or soil. The compound characters in this chapter that contain this radical are 去, 地, 块, and 在.

Character	Basic meaning	No. of strokes	Stroke order	Meaning clue	Phonetic clue	Components	Structure
去 qù	to go (to a place)	5	土 去			土 厶	
地 dì	ground, land	6	一 十 土 地	土, 也		土 也	
*块 (塊) kuài	lump of earth	7	土 圠 圤 块 块	土	夬 guài	土 夬 (冂 大)	
在 zài	be present	6	一 ナ 才 才 在 在			才 土	

地: In classical Chinese, 地, 土 也 means "Earth is soil".

5. 日

日 can be both an independent character and a radical. The character 日 *rì* is the image of the sun. As a radical, it is used in characters related to the sun and time. The compound characters in this chapter that contain this radical are 旧, 早, 明, 是, and 晚.

Character	Basic meaning	No. of strokes	Stroke order	Meaning clue	Phonetic clue	Components	Structure
旧 (舊) jiù	old	5	丨 旧	日		丨 日	
早 zǎo	early, morning	6	日 早	日, 十		日 十	
*明 míng	bright, tomorrow	8	日 明	日, 月 (yuè, *moon*)		日 月	
是 shì	to be	9	日 旦 早 早 昰 是	日, 正 (zhèng, *correct*)		日 疋	
晚 wǎn	later, evening	12	日 日' 盯 昤 晚 睁 晚	日	免 miǎn	日 免 (⺈ 田 儿)	

早: It is like showing the sun (日) just above the trees—early morning.
是: Anything under the sun (日) is certain, correct (正). Now it means "to be".

6. 月

月 *yuè* means "moon" or "month" when it is an independent character. As a radical, 月 is used to form characters related to flesh, meat, or the moon. The compound characters in this chapter that contain this radical are 有 and 朋.

Character	Basic meaning	No. of strokes	Stroke order	Meaning clue	Phonetic clue	Components	Structure
有 yǒu	to have	6	𠂇 有	𠂇 (hand), 月		𠂇 月	
*朋 péng	friend	8	月 朋	月, 月 (two side by side)		月 月	

有: To have meat in hand is 有 "to have".

7. 竹

竹 can be both an independent character and a radical. As an independent character, 竹 *zhú* means "bamboo". As a radical, it is usually put on the top of the character to indicate a relationship to bamboo. The compound characters in this chapter that contain this radical are 笔 and 笨.

Character	Basic meaning	No. of strokes	Stroke order	Meaning clue	Phonetic clue	Components	Structure
笔 (筆) bǐ	pen	10	ノ ⺮ ⺮ ⺮ ⺮ ⺮ 笔	竹, 毛		⺮毛	
笨 bèn	stupid	11	⺮ 笨	竹	本	⺮ 本 (木 一)	

笔: Chinese ancient writing tool: a writing brush is made of a bamboo tube on the top with animal hair at the bottom.

笨: The bamboo radical indicating a blocked brain (stupidity), like the structure inside of bamboo.

EXERCISES

CHARACTER EXERCISES

1. Add one or more strokes to the character on the left side to form a new character that is also at least one stroke less than the character to its right.

一 (　　　) 土 (　　　) 玉 (　　　) 一 (　　　) 日 (　　　)

2. Find the independent characters you have learned hidden in the following characters.

笔 _____　　　容 _____　　　早 _____　　　明 _____

3. Add a different radical to the following to make different characters, then form a word or a sentence with the new character.

也 →　a: _____

　　　　b: _____

　　　　c: _____

4. Write in the brackets the component that is common to all of the following characters.

白, 晚, 明, 意, 都 → (　　　)　　　奶, 要, 好, 姓 → (　　　)

块, 法, 在, 地 → (　　　)　　　欢, 叔, 友, 对 → (　　　)

5. Write as many characters you have learned as possible that are vertically symmetrical, i.e. they can be turned left to right, without changing the meaning, e.g. 本.

---

6. Solve the character riddles.

a. 一半朋一半友: _____

b. 一口 bites off the tail of 牛: _____

c. Although it has many mouths, it has only one heart. If you want to guess what it is, you need to think it over: _____

7. Write as many characters you have learned as possible using the 氵 radical.

_____

8. Circle the wrong character in each sentence and correct it in the brackets.

a. 毛乐生是我 de 好明友, 他是个法国人。(   )

b. 汉文有一本叔叔送 de 中国池图。(   )

c. 日语很 nán, 一 diǎn 儿也不谷 yì 学。(   )

d. 会说日语 de 人不新会写汉字, 有 de 会, 有 de 不会。(   )

VOCABULARY EXERCISES

1. Complete the following sentences in Chinese characters.

a. Bàba de 哥哥是我 de_____。

b. Bàba 哥哥 de 太太是我 de _____。

c. Bàba de 弟弟是我 de _____。

d. 我是个女 hái 子, 我是我父母 de _____。

e. 我哥哥 hé 弟弟是我父母 de _____。

2. Find the word that is not in the same category as the other three words and write it in the brackets.

a. 牛奶, 汤, 咖啡, 饭馆   (   )

b. 毛笔, 地图, 皮 xié, 地道   (   )

c. 吃, 喝, 叫, 真   (   )

d. 早饭, 午饭, 晚饭, 好喝   (   )

3. Find a word from the text that has the opposite meaning of the underlined word in each sentence below. The word with the opposite meaning does not necessarily have to have the same number of characters as the underlined word.

a. 王太太 de 那双皮 xié 真 guì。(   )

b. 小毛说 cōng 明的人 yídìng 都会写汉字吧。(   )

c. 汉语很 nán 学。(   )

d. 他没吃午饭, 可是他说不饿。(   )

e. 我们去那家 xīn 饭馆儿吃晚饭吧。(   )

STRUCTURE EXERCISES

1. Write the correct classifier character to complete each of the following phrases.

三_____皮 xié　　两_____地图　　十_____qián　　一_____饭馆

2. Choose the appropriate character from the characters given immediately below and fill in the brackets. Some characters may be used more than once.

了　　吧　　呢

a. 他以前会做饭, xiàn 在不会做 (　　　)。

b. 这双<u>法国</u>皮 xié 要800块 qián (　　　), 真 guì!

c. 我 xǐ 欢吃地道 de <u>法国</u> cài, 你 (　　　)?

d. <u>小王</u>: 好 de 自行车不便宜 (　　　)。

　　<u>小文</u>: 对, 不便宜。

e. 快要吃晚饭(　　　), 可是我还不饿。

3. Rearrange the elements of each of the entries to make a grammatical sentence.

a. 一, 地图, de, 送, 我, 大, 他, <u>中国</u>, 本, 很

→ _____

b. <u>法国</u>, de, 地道, 太, 了, 不, 便宜, 东西

→ _____

c. 书, 好 kàn, 书, 有 de, 很, 有意思, 有 de, 不

→ _____

d. 你, 这, de, 朋友, 吧, 是, 名字

→ _____

4. Translate the following sentences into Chinese, using Chinese characters for learned words.

a. I would like to invite *Xiao Mao* to eat authentic Chinese cuisine.

_____

b. This dictionary is an old one, not a newly bought one.

_____

c. This novel is very interesting and I enjoy reading it very much.

_____

d. Not all Chinese food is difficult to cook. Some is easy to cook and some is difficult to cook.

_____

e. *Xiao Mao* likes to watch TV while having coffee.

_____

f. I presume you now understand.

_____

SUPPLEMENTARY READING

READING 1

Lǎobǎn: 买自行车吗?

万文生: 这 liàng 自行车 duōshao qián?

Lǎobǎn: 八百块 qián。

万文生: 六百, 行吗?

Lǎobǎn: 不行。七百吧!

万文生: 太 guì 了。两 liàng 一千二 zěnme yàng?

Lǎobǎn: 一千三吧!

万文生: 太 guì 了。不买了。

Lǎobǎn: 好吧! Jiù mài 你一千二。

万文生: Hǎo, gěi 你一千五。

Lǎobǎn: Zhǎo 你三百。

Comprehension questions

1. <u>万文生</u>买几 liàng 自行车?

_____

2. <u>万文生</u>买 de 自行车 duōshao qián 一 liàng?

_____

READING 2

买东西

　　我想买 píngguǒ。我问 lǎobǎn píngguǒ 一 jīn duōshao qián, 他说: "一块八毛五。" 他问我要几 jīn, 我说太 guì 了。我问他一块五毛一 jīn 卖不卖, 他说我得买五 jīn。我说: "好吧!" 我 gěi 他七块五。你说对不对?

True or false questions

1. 一 jīn píngguǒ 卖一块八毛五。(　　)
2. 七 jīn píngguǒ 卖七块五。(　　)

CHARACTER PRACTICE

牛	牛							
白	白							
皮	皮							
叫	叫							
奶	奶							
名	名							
汤	汤							
吧	吧							
这	这							
法	法							
饱	饱							
思	思							
容	容							

双	双								
友	友								
对	对								
欢	欢								
叔	叔								
那	那								
都	都								
图	图								
国	国								
去	去								
地	地								
块	块								
在	在								
旧	旧								

早	早							
明	明							
是	是							
晚	晚							
有	有							
朋	朋							
笔	笔							
笨	笨							

第九课

TEXT

　　城 lǐ 有家有名的大商 diàn。那家 diàn 卖很 duō 东西, lóu 上卖衣 fu hé 皮 xié, 那儿有衬衫、汗衫、wài 衣、内衣、毛衣 hé 牛仔 kù, 东西都很便宜。你看, 我 chuān 的这件毛衣好看吗? 就四十块 qián, 不 guì 吧。那儿卖的袜子 hé 皮 xié 也很好看。Lóu 下大门东边儿卖手 biǎo hé 眼 jìng。那儿的手 biǎo 不便宜, 一千 duō 块 qián 一块, 眼 jìng 也不便宜, 六百 duō 块 qián 一 fù。那家商 diàn 没有便宜的手 biǎo hé 眼 jìng, suǒ 以不要在那儿买手 biǎo, 也不要买眼 jìng。大门西边儿卖书、报、杂志、笔 hé 地图。大门前边儿卖吃的、喝的东西。你 想不想去那儿买东西? 你想喝冰牛奶还是喝可乐? 哎呀! 我忘了告诉你商 diàn 在什么地方。商 diàn 在北京Jiē, 不 nán 找。商 diàn 的老板姓方, 叫方宜思, 他 很高, 我认识他。他住我家的右边儿, 他的 fáng 子很大, 上边儿有四个 fáng- jiān, 下边儿有两个 fángjiān。方老板 hé 他的家人都很忙, 他们很 shǎo 在家。 我很 xǐ 欢去他的商 diàn 买东西。为什么呢? 因为他卖的东西很好呀。你知道 我 xiàn 在要去哪儿吗? 我要去方老板的商 diàn。你要 gēn 我一块儿去吗?

生词 NEW WORDS

城	chéng	(N) city, town
有	yǒu	(V) there is, there are
有名	yǒumíng	(SV) be famous
的	de	(P) indicates possession, used to join a modifying clause with the noun it modifies
商 diàn	shāngdiàn	(PW) shop, store (Cl -家)
lóu 上	lóushàng	(PW) upstairs
衣 fu	yīfu	(N) clothing (Cl -件)
那儿	nàr	(PW) there, that place
衬衫	chènshān	(N) shirt (Cl -件)
汗衫	hànshān	(N) T-shirt (Cl -件)
wài 衣	wàiyī	(N) jacket (Cl -件)
内衣	nèiyī	(N) underwear (Cl -件)
毛衣	máoyī	(N) sweater (Cl -件)
牛仔 kù	niúzǎikù	(N) denim jeans (Cl -*tiáo* 条)
看	kàn	(V) look, read, watch
-件	-jiàn	(Cl) (for clothing covering the upper half of the body, e.g. "shirt" and "jacket")
就	jiù	(Adv) only, just
袜子	wàzi	(N) socks (Cl -双 "pair", -*zhī* 只 "single")
lóu 下	lóuxià	(PW) downstairs
大门	dàmén	(N) main entrance
东边儿	dōng.biānr	(PS/PW) the east
手 biǎo	shǒubiǎo	(N) watch (Cl -块)
-块	-kuài	(Cl) a piece of (also used for "watch")
眼 jing	yǎnjìng	(N) eyeglasses (Cl -副)
六	liù	(Nu) six
没有	méi.yǒu	(V) there isn't, there aren't
在	zài	(CV) at, in
在	zài	(V) be located at, be present
西边儿	xī.biānr	(PS/PW) the west
报	bào	(N) newspaper
杂志	zázhì	(N) magazine (Cl -本 or -份)
笔	bǐ	(N) pen, writing instrument
前边儿	qián.biānr	(PS/PW) in front

还是	haíshi	(Conj) or
忘	wàng	(V) forget
地方	dìfang	(PW) place, location
北京	Běijīng	(PW) capital city of the People's Republic of China
北京 Jiē	Běijīng Jiē	(PW) name of a street
找	zhǎo	(V) to give change, to look for (something)
老板	lǎobǎn	(N) boss, owner
方宜思	Fāng Yísī	(N) a personal name
高	gāo	(SV) be tall or high
认识	rènshi	(V) be acquainted with
住	zhù	(V) reside
右边儿	yòu.biānr	(PS/PW) the right
fáng 子	fángzi	(N) house
上边儿	shàng.biānr	(PS) above
下边儿	xià.biānr	(PS/PW) below
家人	jiārén	(N) family members
为什么?	wèishénme?	(Adv) why?
因为……	yīn.wèi…	(Pat) because…
suǒ 以……	suǒyǐ…	(Pat) therefore…
呀	ya	(P) (tells listener s/he really should have known that)
哪儿	nǎr	(PW) where?
一块儿	yíkuàir	(Adv) together

COMPREHENSION QUESTIONS

1. Read the text of this chapter and answer the following questions.

a. 那家有名的商 diàn 在什么地方?

_____

b. 商 diàn 的 lóu 上卖什么?

_____

c. Lóu 下大门东边儿卖的手 biǎo 便宜吗?

_____

d. 商 diàn 的老板叫什么名字?

_____

e. 他住在哪儿?

_____

f. 什么地方卖书、报 hé 杂志?

_____

g. 大门的前边儿卖什么?

_____

h. 说说<u>方</u>老板的家。

_____

WRITING HELP

INDEPENDENT CHARACTERS

Character	Basic meaning	No. of strokes	Stroke order	Radical	Components	Structure
上 shàng	top	3	上	一	上	☐
下 xià	bottom	3	一丁下	一	下	☐
门 (門) mén	door	3	门	门	门	☐
为 (為) wèi	for	4	丶ソ为为	丶	为	☐
手 shǒu	hand	4	丿二三手	手	手	☐
方 fāng	square, surname	4	丶亠方	方	丶 万	☐
内 nèi	inside	4	丨冂内	冂	冂 人	☐
*衣 yī	clothes	6	亠亍衣	衣	衣	☐
老 lǎo	old	6	土耂老老	耂	土 丿 匕	☐

COMPOUND CHARACTERS

The new compound characters with learned radicals in this chapter are 认, 仔, 边, 右, 汗, 因, 件, 住, 识, 志, 忘, 城, and 哪.

Character	Basic meaning	No. of strokes	Stroke order	Radical	Meaning clue	Phonetic clue	Components	Structure
认 (認) rèn	to recognize	4	讠 认	讠	讠	人	讠 人	▯▯
*仔 zǎi	little boy, son	5	亻 子	亻	亻	子	亻 子	▯▯
边 (邊) biān	side	5	力 边	辶			辶 力	▯
*右 yòu	right	5	ナ 右	口	ナ		ナ 口	▯
汗 hàn	sweat	6	氵 汗 汗	氵	氵	干 gàn	氵 干	▯▯
因 yīn	because	6	口 因	口			口 大	▢
*件 jiàn	(a classifier)	6	亻 牛	亻			亻 牛	▯▯
住 zhù	to live	7	亻 亻 住 住 住	亻	亻	主 zhǔ	亻 主	▯▯
识 (識) shì	to know, to recognize	7	讠 识	讠	讠	只	讠 口 八	▯▯
*志 zhì	will, determination	7	士 志	心	心	士 shì	士 心	▭
忘 wàng	to forget	7	亡 忘	心	心	亡 wáng	亡 心	▭
城 chéng	city, town	9	士 圵 圵 坊 城 城 城	土	土	成 chéng	土 成	▯▯
哪 nǎ	where? which?	9	口 哪	口	口	那	口 尹 阝)	▯▯▯

右: To better remember 右, think of it as showing 𠂇, the image of a hand, taking food to mouth.

件: As a classifier, 件 is never used for 人 or 牛.

RADICALS

The new radicals of focus in this chapter are 丨, 亠, 扌, 木, 白, 礻, and 目.

1. 丨

What character have you learned using this radical?

Character	Basic meaning	No. of strokes	Stroke order	Meaning clue	Phonetic clue	Compo-nents	Structure
北 běi	north	5	丨 丬 丬 丬 北			丬 匕	⊟

2. 亠

This radical is put on top of a character to indicate coverage. The compound characters in this chapter that contain this radical are 六, 京, 高, 商, and 就.

Character	Basic meaning	No. of strokes	Stroke order	Meaning clue	Phonetic clue	Compo-nents	Structure
六 liù	six	4	亠 八			亠 八	⊟
*京 jīng	capital	8	亠 古 京			亠 口 小	⊟
高 gāo	tall, high, surname	10	亠 古 高 高			亠 口 冂 口	⊟
*商 shāng	com-merce, surname	11	亠 㐃 啇 商 商			亠 丷 冂 八 口	⊟
就 jiù	only, just	12	京 京 尌 就 就		尤 yóu	亠 口 小 尤	⊟

高: 高 is an image of a high tower or building.

3. 扌

As an independent character, it means "hand" and is written as 手. As a radical, it is used as the left part in a compound character and is written as 扌 to form characters of hand-related activities. The compound characters in this chapter that contain this radical are 报 and 找.

Character	Basic meaning	No. of strokes	Stroke order	Meaning clue	Phonetic clue	Components	Structure
报 (報) bào	newspaper	7	扌报	扌		扌反	▯▯
找 zhǎo	to look for	7	扌 扌 扌 找 找	扌		扌戈	▯▯

报: 又 indicates hand (see Chapter 8). To help you better remember this character, think of it as showing the opening of a newspaper with both hands.

找: Note the difference between the way 我 and 找 are written.

4. 木

木 *mù* is the image of a tree in ancient Chinese. As an independent character, it means "wood". As a radical, it can be put on the left, bottom, or right part of a character, indicating a relation to things associated with trees or wood. The compound characters in this chapter that contain this radical are 杂 and 板.

Character	Basic meaning	No. of strokes	Stroke order	Meaning clue	Phonetic clue	Components	Structure
杂 (雜) zá	multiple kinds, chaotic	6	九 杂	九, 木 (all kinds of wood)		九 木[1]	▭
板 bǎn	board, plank	8	木 板	木	反 fǎn	木 反	▯▯

1. 木 is a variant of the radical 木.

5. 白

白 can be both a radical and an independent character. With one additional stroke above the sun, this character (白 *bái* "white") / radical implies the white light of the sun.

Character	Basic meaning	No. of strokes	Stroke order	Meaning clue	Phonetic clue	Components	Structure
的 de	(particle)	8	白 白′ 的 的			白 勺 (勹丶)	▯▯

6. 衤

As an independent character it is written as 衣. As a radical it is used as the left-hand part in compound characters related to clothing. The compound characters in this chapter that contain this radical are 衬, 衫, and 袜.

Character	Basic meaning	No. of strokes	Stroke order	Meaning clue	Phonetic clue	Compo-nents	Structure
*衬 (襯) chèn	shirt	8	丶 亅 衤 衤 衤 衬	衤	寸 cùn	衤寸	
*衫 shān	upper garment	8	衤 衫	衤	三	衤彡	
*袜 (襪) wà	socks	10	衤 袜	衤, 末 (mò, end)		衤末	

7. 目

目 *mù* is the image of eyes in ancient Chinese. As an independent character it means "eye". When it is used as a radical, it is put at a character's left, right, or bottom, indicating a meaning related to eyes. The compound characters in this chapter that contain this radical are 看 and 眼.

Character	Basic meaning	No. of strokes	Stroke order	Meaning clue	Phonetic clue	Compo-nents	Structure
看 kàn[1]	to look	9	三 手 看	手, 目		手目	
眼 yǎn	eye	11	目 眼	目		目艮	

1. Please note that 看 is composed of a hand (手) shading the eyes (目) as one looks off into the distance.

EXERCISES

CHARACTER EXERCISES

1. Find the independent characters you have learned hidden in the following characters.

京 _____   件 _____

杂 _____   仔 _____

2. Write in the brackets the component that is common to all of the following characters.

报, 对, 皮, 友 → (   )   对, 得, 衬 → (   )

商, 容, 六, 识 → (   )   百, 的, 伯 → (   )

呢, 北, 老 → (   )

3. Add a different part inside of 囗 to form as many characters as you can.

_____

4. Write five characters you have learned which are of a top-bottom structure, e.g. 兄.

_____   _____   _____   _____   _____

5. Solve the character riddle below.

上字的下边儿, 下字的上边儿: _____.

6. Write as many characters you have learned as possible using the 心 radical.

_____

7. Rearrange the following characters in the ascending order of their number of strokes.

商, 吧, 必, 真, 车, 说, 字

→ _____

8. Circle the wrong character in each sentence and correct it in the brackets.

a. 大门前迈儿有卖小吃的, 你想去看看吗?   (   )

b. 这是诚 lǐ zuì 大的一家卖衣 fu 的商 diàn。   (   )

c. 他 xǐ 欢看书、看扳, 不 xǐ 欢看电 shì。   (   )

d. 你 chuān 的这件衬衫真好看, 哪儿买的?   (   )

e. 我的家在 <u>Shànghǎi</u>, 可shì 我不任在 <u>Shànghǎi</u>, 我在<u>北京</u> zū fáng 子任。

                                                 (   )

VOCABULARY EXERCISES

1. Write two characters in each group of homonyms, then form a word with each character.

a. shū: _____   c. huà: _____

    shū: _____   huà: _____

b. zài: _____   d. dì: _____

    zài: _____   dì: _____

2. Use the following characters to form as many words as possible.

a. 做 → _____

b. 有 → _____

c. 老 → _____

d. 客 → _____

e. 好 → _____

f. 地 → _____

3. Write the antonym of each of the following.

a. 西 → (   )   c. 大 → (   )

b. 上 → (   )   d. 饱 → (   )

4. **Form a few words or phrases with each of the following characters, paying attention to the pronunciations, meanings, and written forms of each pair.**

a.
{
我 → _____
找 → _____
}

b.
{
板 → _____
饭 → _____
}

c.
{
高 → _____
商 → _____
}

d.
{
京 → _____
就 → _____
}

5. **Find the word that is not in the same category as the other three words and write it in the brackets.**

a. 汗衫, 牛仔 kù, 内衣, 毛衣   (   )

b. 报, màn 画书, 笔, 杂志   (   )

c. 东边儿, 右边儿, 前边儿, 一块儿   (   )

d. 看, 呀, 找, 住   (   )

STRUCTURE EXERCISES

1. **Write the correct classifier character to complete each of the following phrases.**

一_____ 商 diàn   这_____衬衫

两_____袜子   那_____手 biǎo

六_____杂志   四_____毛衣

2. Following the example shown with *chuān* below, classify the nouns in the box according to the verbs that they can go with.

眼 jìng 衬衫 咖啡 手 biǎo wài 衣 牛仔 kù 小吃 汤 皮 xié 午饭

chuān (wear) 衬衫 _____

dài (wear) _____

喝 _____

吃 _____

3. Choose the appropriate word from the words given immediately below and fill in the brackets. Some words may be used more than once.

哪儿 还是 呀 在 一块儿 因为

a. <u>方宜思</u>不 gēn fùmǔ 住( )。

b. 那个商 diàn( )xuéxiào hé 饭馆儿 zhōngjiān。

c. <u>王中书</u>: 你为什么 zū zhèr 的 fángzi?

   <u>万文生</u>: ( )zhèr 的 fángzi 便宜( )。

d. 我想去买 zhāng zhuōzi。你知道( )有 jiājùdiàn 吗?

e. <u>王老板</u>太忙了, 很 shǎo( )家吃晚饭。

f. 你想去吃<u>中国</u> cài( )<u>法国</u> cài?

4. Rearrange the words below to form sentences. You may need to add some extra words in order to form a complete sentence.

a. 他说, 去, xiàn 在, 就

   → _____

b. 商 diàn, 有名的, 一家, 有, 城 lǐ

   → _____

c. 不容 yì, 找, 地图, 他, 没有

   → _____

d. <u>小王</u>, 手 biǎo, 想, 买

→ _____

e. 知道, 哪儿, 你, 商 diàn, 在, 吗?

→ _____

5. Connect the sentences from exercise 4 directly above into a short passage according to their meanings. Add some extra words if necessary.

_____

_____

_____

6. Complete the photo with the following information.

<u>王家兰</u>在右边儿。
<u>王家兰</u>的前边儿是<u>王太太</u>。
<u>王明志</u>在<u>王家兰</u>的 páng 边儿。
<u>王先生</u>在<u>王明志</u>的前边儿, <u>王太太</u> gēn <u>王明汉</u>的中 jiān。
<u>王先生</u> gēn <u>王国京</u>的中 jiān 是<u>王太太</u>。
<u>王</u>小弟在 bàba gēn 妈妈的前边儿。

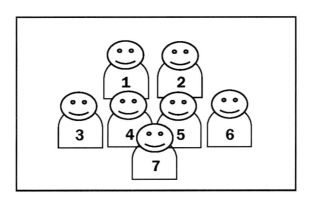

1: _____   5: _____

2: _____   6: _____

3: _____   7: _____

4: _____

7. Translate the following sentences into Chinese, using Chinese characters for learned words.

a. I haven't yet had an opportunity to be acquainted with my neighbor who is living upstairs.

_____

b. That shop is just on Beijing Street, very easy to find.

_____

c. Which store sells cheap spectacles (lit. "The eyeglasses of which store are cheaper")?

_____

d. Who is that girl in jeans on your right side?

_____

e. This bookstore sells books and also sells newspapers, magazines, and pens.

_____

SUPPLEMENTARY READING

READING 1

Lǎobǎn:	早! 你要什么?
高意兰:	我看看。这毛衣 duōshao qián?
Lǎobǎn:	四百八十块。
高意兰:	太 guì 了。
Lǎobǎn:	不 guì。
高意兰:	三百八十, 行吗?
Lǎobǎn:	不行。四百五十!
高意乐:	四百二十!
Lǎobǎn:	好吧, 好吧, 四百二十! 还要别的吗?
高意乐:	就要这个。谢谢。

这毛衣duōshǎo qián?

四百八十块。

Comprehension questions

1. 高意兰要什么?

_____

2. 高意兰买了什么?

_____

READING 2

没门儿

　　你们都知道门是什么意思。你们的家有 qián 门、hòu 门。可是, 你们知道 "没门儿" 是什么意思吗? 要是[1]你们都想去看 diànyǐng, 可是你们要我在家看门。你们说: "我们去看 diànyǐng, 你一个人在家看门。" 我说: "要我一个人在家看门, 没门儿。" 这儿的 "看门" 是什么意思? "没门儿" 呢? 是 fáng 子没有门的意思? 还是 "不行, 不可 néng[2]" 的意思?

---

1. 要是 "if"
2. 不可 néng "impossible"

Comprehension questions

1. "我们去看 diànyǐng, 你一个人在家看门。"这儿的"门"是什么意思?

   _____

2. "要我一个人在家看门, 没门儿。"这儿的"没门儿"是什么意思?

   _____

CHARACTER PRACTICE

上	上						
下	下						
门	门						
为	为						
手	手						
方	方						

内	内							
衣	衣							
老	老							
认	认							
仔	仔							
边	边							
右	右							
汗	汗							
因	因							
件	件							
住	住							
识	识							
志	志							
忘	忘							

城	城								
哪	哪								
北	北								
六	六								
京	京								
高	高								
商	商								
就	就								
报	报								
找	找								
杂	杂								
板	板								
的	的								
衬	衬								

衫	衫								
袜	袜								
看	看								
眼	眼								

10

第十课

TEXT

　　高小美是个住在中国的美国人。她住在上海 Lù, 她的家在书 diàn hé 咖啡 diàn 的中 jiān。以前她孩子小, 她在家 lǐ 很忙, suǒ 以没有机会学中文, 只会说英文, xiàn 在四个孩子都大了, 她 néng 去念书了。高太太以前什么汉字都不会 xiě, xiàn 在她是大学生了。她学两门课, 中文 hé 法文。中文不容易, 老 shī 上课都用汉语教, 中文书都是用中文 xiě 的。快要考试了, 她太忙了, 除了上课, 她哪儿都不去, 电 shì 不看了, 饭也不做了。大人、孩子都去她家后边儿的饭馆儿吃晚饭。除了中文以外, 她也要考法文。她说要看十几本书, 有的书是中文书, 有的书是法文书。

　　高太太有一个朋友叫王欢兰, 是女的。高太太的朋友 dāng 中, 就王欢兰是中国人。王小姐住在高太太家的北边儿, 高太太可以用汉语 gēn 王欢兰打电话, 用汉语 gēn 她说话。王欢兰也用汉语 gēn 高太太说话, 给她说中文故事。王欢兰会用毛笔 xiě 汉字, 她替高太太用毛笔给中文老 shī xiě 过中文信。高太太对欢兰也很好, 请她去中国饭馆儿吃饭。高太太没用过筷子, 王欢兰教她用筷子吃米饭。高太太没喝过中国茶, 王欢兰给她介绍中国茶。高太太给王欢兰做英国菜, 教她用刀子 hé 叉子吃牛肉。她们 xǐ 欢在一块儿笑着吃饭、喝茶。高太太想, 有一位中国朋友真好! 她考试一 dìng 没问 tí。真得谢谢王欢兰。

生词 NEW WORDS

高小美	Gāo Xiǎoměi	(N) a personal name
美国	Měiguó	(PW) America
上海	Shànghǎi	(PW) a city in Eastern China
书 diàn	shūdiàn	(PW) bookshop
中 jiān	zhōngjiān	(PS/PW) the middle (more concrete)
孩子	háizi	(N) child, youngster
机会	jīhuì	(N) opportunity
英文	Yīngwén	(N) English (language)
念书	niàn shū	(VO) study (academically)
大学生	dàxuésheng	(N) university student
学	xué	(V) study, learn
法文	Fǎwén	(N) French (language)
老 shī	lǎoshī	(N) teacher
上课	shàng kè	(VO) have class, attend class
用	yòng	(CV) using, by means of
用	yòng	(V) use
教	jiāo	(V) teach
考试	kǎoshì	(VO) take a test or examination
考试	kǎoshì	(N) test or examination
-门	-mén	(Cl) (for a course taken at school)
课	kè	(N) lesson, class, course
大人	dàrén	(N) adult

除了……以 　wài……	chúle…yǐwài…	(Pat) besides, except for
后边儿	hòu.biānr	(PS/PW) in back
有的……有的	yǒude…yǒude	(Pat) some…other
王欢兰	Wáng Huānlán	(N) a personal name
女的	nǚde	(N) woman, female
dāng 中	dāngzhōng	(PS/PW) the middle (more abstract)
小姐	xiǎojiě	(N) young lady, Miss
北边儿	běi.biānr	(PS/PW) the north
打电话	dǎ diànhuà	(VO) make a phone call
给	gěi	(CV) for, to
故事	gùshi	(N) story, narrative account
替	tì	(CV) in place of
-过	-guo	(P) (used after a verb to indicate an experience)
信	xìn	(N) letter (Cl -fēng 封)
对	duì	(CV) to, toward
筷子	kuàizi	(N) chopsticks (Cl -双)
米饭	mǐfàn	(N) cooked rice
介绍	jièshào	(V) introduce
茶	chá	(N) tea
英国	Yīngguó	(PW) England
菜	cài	(N) food, dishes
刀子	dāozi	(N) knife (Cl -bǎ 把)
叉子	chāzi	(N) fork (Cl -bǎ 把)
牛肉	niúròu	(N) beef
笑	xiào	(V) laugh, smile, laugh at
-着	-zhe	(P) (attached to verbs to indicate action in progress)
-位	wèi	(Cl) (polite, for persons)
一 dìng	yídìng	(Adv) definitely
问 tí	wèntí	(N) question
谢谢	xièxie	(Ex) thank you

COMPREHENSION QUESTIONS

1. Read the text of this chapter and answer the following questions.

a. 高太太叫什么名字? 她是哪国人?

_____

b. 他们家住哪儿?

_____

c. 她以前做什么? Xiàn 在呢?

_____

d. 她会说什么话?

_____

e. 高太太要考几门课? 考什么?

_____

f. Xiàn 在他们家人为什么都去饭馆儿吃晚饭?

_____

g. Shéi 是王欢兰? 她住哪儿?

_____

h. 说说王欢兰 hé 高太太的故事。

_____

i. 为什么高太太想她考试一 dìng 没问 tí? 你说呢?

_____

WRITING HELP

INDEPENDENT CHARACTERS

Character	Basic meaning	No. of strokes	Stroke order	Radical	Components	Structure
刀 dāo	knife	2	フ刀	刀	刀	☐
*叉 chā	fork	3	又叉	又	又、	☐
米 mǐ	rice	6	米	米	米	☐

COMPOUND CHARACTERS

The new compound characters with learned radicals in this chapter are 介, 打, 机, 考, 后, 位, 念, 事, 试, 信, 笑, 海, 课, 替, 谢, 筷, 除, and 过.

Character	Basic meaning	No. of strokes	Stroke order	Radical	Meaning clue	Phonetic clue	Components	Structure
*介 jiè	to introduce	4	人个介	人			人八	☐
打 dǎ	to hit	5	扌打	扌	扌, 丁 (ding, nail)		扌丁	☐
*机 (機) jī	machine	5	扌机	木	木	几	木几	☐
考 kǎo	to check	6	土耂耂考	十			耂丂	☐
*后 (後) hòu	later, after	6	一厂厂后	口			厂口	☐
*位 wèi	seat	7	亻亻伫位	亻	亻		亻立	☐
念 niàn	to read aloud, to study	8	人人今念	心	心		今心	☐

Character	Basic meaning	No. of strokes	Stroke order	Radical	Meaning clue	Phonetic clue	Components	Structure
事 shì	matter, affair	8	一 丆 写 写 事	一			一 口 ヨ 丿	▯
试 (試) shì	to try	8	讠 讠 讠 试 试	讠	讠	式 shì	讠 式	▯▯
信 xìn	letter	9	亻 亻 信 信 信	亻	亻, 言 (yán, speech)		亻 言	▯▯
笑 xiào	to laugh	10	⺮ 竺 笉 笑	竹	竹 (zhú, shape of smiling eyes)	夭 yāo	⺮1 夭	▭
海 hǎi	sea	10	氵 汇 海	氵	氵		氵 每	▯▯
课 (課) kè	lesson	10	讠 训 评 课	讠	讠		讠 田 木	▯▯
替 tì	for	12	二 夫 麸 替	日			夫夫1 日	▭
谢 (謝) xiè	to thank, surname	12	讠 讠 讠 讠 讱 讱 讱 谢	讠	讠, 身 (shēn, body), 寸 (cùn, inch)			▯▯▯
*筷 kuài	chop-sticks	13	⺮ 筷	竹	竹	快	⺮ 忄 夬	▱
过 (過) guò	to pass	6	寸 过	辶	辶		辶 寸	◲

打: Think of this as showing a hand striking a nail, hit—the action of hitting with a hand.

谢: This reminds you that one needs to bow (make your body shorter) to say thanks.

1. Note the differences in the way 天, 夭, and 夫 are written.

RADICALS

The radicals of focus in this chapter are 冂, 子, 艹, 纟, 攵, and 羊.

1. 冂

This radical means "border". The compound characters in this chapter that contain this radical are 用 and 肉.

Character	Basic meaning	No. of strokes	Stroke order	Meaning clue	Phonetic clue	Compo-nents	Structure
用 yòng	to use	5	冂 刀 月 用¹			冂丰	☐
肉 ròu	meat, flesh	6	冂 内 肉	人, 人		冂人人	☐

1. Note that the radical 冂 is written in a slightly different way in the character 用.

2. 子

This character, meaning "child", can function both as a character and as a radical. The compound characters in this chapter that contain this radical are 学 and 孩.

Character	Basic meaning	No. of strokes	Stroke order	Meaning clue	Phonetic clue	Compo-nents	Structure
学 (學) xué	to study	8	丶 丷 丷 兴 学	冖, 子		兴子	☐
*孩 hái	child	9	子 孑 孑 孩 孩	子	亥 hài	子亥	☐

学: A child holds a book with two hands studying under a cover.

3. 艹

艹 is the image of the shape of two shoots, meaning "grass". As a radical it is usually put at the top of a character to form characters related to plants. The compound characters in this chapter that contain this radical are 英, 茶, and 菜.

Character	Basic meaning	No. of strokes	Stroke order	Meaning clue	Phonetic clue	Compo-nents	Struct-ure
*英 yīng	flower	8	一 艹 艹 苫 英	艹	央 yāng	艹央	☐
茶 chá	tea	9	艹 艾 茶	艹, 人, 木		艹人木	☐
菜 cài	vegetable, dish (of food)	11	艹 艹 艹 苹 苹 菜	艹	采 cǎi	艹采	☐

茶: To help you remember this character, think of it as indicating people picking tea leaves among tea bushes.

4. 纟

This radical means "silk". The compound characters in this chapter that contain this radical are 绍 and 给.

Character	Basic meaning	No. of strokes	Stroke order	Meaning clue	Phonetic clue	Compo-nents	Structure
*绍 (紹) shào	to intro-duce (介绍)	8	ㄴ ㄠ 纟 纫 绍		召 zhāo	纟刀口	
给 (給) gěi	to give	9	纟 纠 纱 给	纟, 合 (hé, *together*)		纟 合 (人 一口)	

给: Think of it as indicating people putting hands together to present a gift of silk.

5. 攵

This can function both as a character, 文, meaning "culture" or "language", and as a radical with a similar meaning. It is usually found on the right-hand side of a compound character. The compound characters in this chapter that contain this radical are 故 and 教.

Character	Basic meaning	No. of strokes	Stroke order	Meaning clue	Phonetic clue	Compo-nents	Structure
*故 gù	story	9	十 古 故	古 (gǔ, old, ancient), 攵	古 gǔ	古攵	
教 jiāo	to teach	11	少 孝 教	攵	孝 xiào	少子攵	

6. 羊

羊 can be both a character and a radical. As an independent character (羊 yáng), it is an image of a goat. The compound characters in this chapter that contain this radical are 美 and 着.

Character	Basic meaning	No. of strokes	Stroke order	Meaning clue	Phonetic clue	Compo-nents	Structure
美 měi	beauty, beautiful	9	⸌ ⸜ 半 羊 美	羊, 大		羊大	
*着 (著) zhe	(particle)	11	⸌ 羊 着			羊目	

美: To help you remember this character, think of "beauty" in terms of a big sheep.

7. 阝

阝 , as an image of an ear, can be used as either a right or left part of a character. In this chapter, 阝 is only used as a left-hand radical. The compound character in this chapter that contains this radical is 除.

Character	Basic meaning	No. of strokes.	Stroke order	Meaning clue	Phonetic clue	Compo-nents	Structure
除 chú	to remove	9	阝 阝ᐟ 阝ᐟ 阝ᄼ 除 除			阝 余	⊟

EXERCISES

CHARACTER EXERCISES

1. **Delete one or two strokes from each of the following characters to form a new character.**

   叉 _____   肉 _____   学 _____

2. **Solve the character riddle below.**

   A person is among the grass and bushes: _____

3. **Write as many characters you have learned as possible using the 木 radical.**

   _____

4. **Write the common part of the following characters in the blank.**

   a. 茶, 课, 笨 → (   )   e. 得, 谢, 过 → (   )

   b. 除, 都, 那 → (   )   f. 因, 美, 太 → (   )

   c. 位, 肉, 给 → (   )   g. 眼, 着, 自 → (   )

   d. 学, 孩, 教 → (   )

5. Decompose each of the characters below into their respective components. Then combine these parts to form different characters, e.g. 木 (from 校) + 反 (from 饭) → 板.

思 汉 好 吗 考 有 忙 块 呢

_____ (from _____) + _____ (from _____) → _____

_____ (from _____) + _____ (from _____) → _____

_____ (from _____) + _____ (from _____) → _____

_____ (from _____) + _____ (from _____) → _____

_____ (from _____) + _____ (from _____) → _____

6. Circle the wrong character in each sentence and correct it in the brackets.

a. 她友三本好看的 màn 画。   (   )

b. 我姐姐 zuì xǐ 欢喝牛内汤。   (   )

c. 你 gēn 我一快儿去吧。   (   )

d. 快要考试了, 高太太要着十几本书。   (   )

e. 高太太对王欢兰说, 塧塧你教我 xiě 汉字。   (   )

f. 王老板 xiàn 在是大学生了, 除了孝试, 他还要做生意, 他太忙了。

(   )

VOCABULARY EXERCISES

1. How many words and phrases can you form using the following characters?

先, 子, 中, 女, 生, 国, 衣, 文, 学, 儿, 日

_____

2. Compare the following pairs of characters. Make words or phrases with each character.

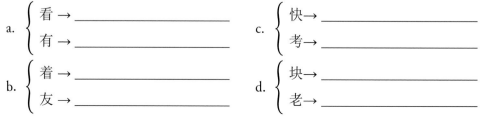

a.
{ 看 → _____
{ 有 → _____

b.
{ 着 → _____
{ 友 → _____

c.
{ 快→ _____
{ 考 → _____

d.
{ 块→ _____
{ 老 → _____

e. $\begin{cases} 只 \rightarrow \underline{\hspace{4cm}} \\ 万 \rightarrow \underline{\hspace{4cm}} \end{cases}$ g. $\begin{cases} 门 \rightarrow \underline{\hspace{4cm}} \\ 午 \rightarrow \underline{\hspace{4cm}} \end{cases}$

f. $\begin{cases} 兄 \rightarrow \underline{\hspace{4cm}} \\ 方 \rightarrow \underline{\hspace{4cm}} \end{cases}$ h. $\begin{cases} 们 \rightarrow \underline{\hspace{4cm}} \\ 牛 \rightarrow \underline{\hspace{4cm}} \end{cases}$

3. Give the antonyms to the following words.

a. 后 → (   )   d. 饱 → (   )

b. 那 → (   )   e. 上 → (   )

c. 买 → (   )   f. 孩子 → (   )

4. Solve the riddle below.

我是什么?

你们用我吃中国菜, 不用我吃英国菜。可以用我吃饭, 不可以用我喝茶。

我是_____。

5. Find the word that is not in the same category as the other three words and write it in the brackets.

a. 刀子, 孩子, 筷子, 叉子   (   )

b. 米饭, 汤, 茶, 牛奶   (   )

c. 上课, 念书, 考试, 故事   (   )

d. Xīn 西兰, 美国, 上海, 英国   (   )

STRUCTURE EXERCISES

1. Insert the word in brackets into the correct gap in the sentence.

a. Xiàn 在很 duō 人_____都_____用毛笔_____xiě 字了。(不)

b. 他_____shéi 的 qián_____不_____要。(都)

c. 除了茶, _____我_____xǐ 欢_____喝咖啡。(还)

d. 除了牛肉, 她_____都_____不想吃_____。(什么)

e. 王小姐在中国念书, 可是她_____还_____去_____过北京呢。(没有)

2. **Rearrange the elements of each of the entries to make a grammatical sentence.**

a. 吃, 是, 东西, 的, 都, 牛肉, 我, 米饭, ài, 菜, hé

→ _____

b. 上, 都, 他, 课, 没, 什么, 去

→ _____

c. 叉子, 不, 小文, 用, chǎo 饭, 会, 吃

→ _____

d. 你, 电话, shéi, 打, 给

→ _____

3. **Correct the following wrong characters, then make a sentence with the corrected ones.**

Incorrect	Correct	Make a sentence
会		
家		

4. **Complete the dialogue in Chinese characters.**

老板：　Nín 好! Nín 要吃什么?

客人：　_____

老板：　我们这儿中国 chǎo 菜、日本小吃、法国汤都有。我们的 Xīn 西兰牛肉 zuì 有名了。你 xǐ 欢什么?

客人：　_____

老板：　好。你用筷子还是用刀叉?

客人：　_____

5. **Fill in the blanks with the words provided in the box. There are more choices than there are blanks. Each word can only be used once.**

> 得　的　会　néng　在　也　中 jiān　dāng 中　gēn　都　右边儿

小明是我_____朋友。他家在我家_____小美家的_____。在我的朋

友_____, 就小明 _____说汉语。他_____会说日语。

6. **Choose the appropriate coverb from the words given immediately below to fill in the brackets for each sentence. Some words may be used more than once.**

用　对　gēn　替　给

a. 他 (　　　　) 我笑着, 什么也没说。

b. (　　　　) 毛笔 xiě 汉字不容 yì。

c. 他 (　　　　) 我 xiě 过信, 可是没 (　　　　) 我打过电话。

d. 没人 néng (　　　　) 你考试。

e. 小明 (　　　　) 他的中国朋友学中文。

f. 你会 (　　　　) 筷子吃中国菜吗?

SUPPLEMENTARY READING

READING 1

志高:　小欢, 我给你们介绍一下, 这是我的朋友方汉。

小欢:　方汉, 你好! 我叫小欢。

方汉:　小欢, 你好!

志高:　小欢是我的 línjū, 她是北京大学的学生。方汉也是大学生。

方汉:　我是大学生, 可是我只学两门课。你呢?

小欢:　我学五门。你学哪两门?

方汉:　中文 gēn 法文。

小欢:　你学中文! 你会用毛笔 xiě 汉字吗?

方汉:　我不会, 志高会, 可是我很想学。

小欢:　那, 志高, 你教我们, 行吗?

志高:　没问 tí。

Comprehension questions

1. 小欢学几门课?

_____

2. 方汉学几门课?

_____

3. 志高教不教小欢 hé 方汉写汉字?

_____

READING 2

没问 tí

　　中国人 xǐ 欢说"没问 tí"。你买的衣 fu 太大了, 你 gēn 商 diàn 的老板说: "这件衣 fu 太大了, 给我小的, 行吗?"老板说: "没问 tí。"在饭馆儿吃饭, 我 gēn 饭馆儿的老板说: "老板, 我不会用筷子, 给我刀叉, 行吗?"老板说: "没问 tí。" 吃饭前, 我 gēn 我的中国朋友小王说: "小王, 对不 qǐ, 我不吃饭了。"小王问: "为什么?"我说: "我没 qián。" 小王说: "没 qián? 没问 tí, 我这儿有。"吃饭后, 小王对我说: "哎呀! 有问 tí。"我问: "什么问 tí?"他说: "我也没 qián。"你也没 qián, 我想这真是个问 tí。

Comprehension questions

1. 吃饭前, 我 gēn 小王说: "我没 qián。" 小王说什么?

_____

2. 要是你的朋友 gēn 你说: "我没 qián", 你会对他说什么?

_____

_____

CHARACTER PRACTICE

刀	刀								
叉	叉								
米	米								
介	介								
打	打								
机	机								

考	考							
后	后							
连	连							
位	位							
念	念							
事	事							
试	试							
信	信							
笑	笑							
海	海							
课	课							
替	替							
谢	谢							
筷	筷							

用	用								
肉	肉								
英	英								
茶	茶								
菜	菜								
绍	绍								
给	给								
故	故								
教	教								
美	美								
着	着								
学	学								
孩	孩								

COMPLETE THE DIALOGUE

Complete the dialogue based on the information given.

A: 老板, _____?

B: 两块八毛 qián 一 jīn。 _____?

A: 两 jīn。

B: _____。

A: _____。

B: 好。 找你四毛。

FILL IN THE BLANK

Fill in each blank by choosing the most appropriate word from the alternatives provided in the box. You should not use any word more than once. There are more choices than blanks.

zuì 有 hé 还是 因为 没 dài 双 可是 个 再 太 卖 只 chuān

Zhāng 学 xǐ 欢_____好 kàn 的衣 fu hé 皮 xié, _____piàoliang 的
眼 jing _____手 biǎo。 他的衣 fu 都很 xīn, 也都很 guì。 Zhāng 学的皮
xié 不多, _____都很 guì。 他_____xǐ 欢 chuān 法国皮 xié 了。 他有
一_____很 piàoliang、很 guì 的法国皮 xié。 Zhāng 学的旧衣 fu 都给他弟弟
了, 因为他弟弟没 qián 买 xīn 衣 fu。 他弟弟也很 xǐ 欢他的那双法国皮 xié, 可是,
_____guì 了, 他不想给他弟弟。 _____他弟弟不做 shì, _____ài 看电
shì, suǒ 以没有 qián。 Zhāng 学不 ài 看电 shì, ài 做 shì, 他很_____qián。

TRANSLATION

Translate each of the following passages into Chinese. For characters you have not yet been taught, you may use *Hànyǔ Pīnyīn* romanization together with the tone marks.

1.

Across from my house is a clothing shop. The shirts, T-shirts, jackets, sweaters, and blue jeans that that clothing shop sells are all quite cheap. My mother likes the clothes that that shop sells very much because she likes cheap things. I don't like the clothes that that shop sells because that shop does not sell clothes made in France. I like authentic French things very much.

_____

_____

_____

_____

_____

_____

_____

_____

_____

_____

2.

Among their brothers and sisters, *Xiaomei* is the most clever/intelligent. *Xiaomei* likes to tell stories. All the children of Mrs. Wang (who lives) below them in the building say that the stories she tells are very interesting. *Xiaomei* is able to speak Chinese, English, French, and Korean. She likes to drink milk, and she also likes to eat apples. She doesn't like to buy expensive things.

_____

_____

_____

_____

_____

_____

_____

_____

_____

_____

3.

Miss Gao is my neighbor. She lives above me. Because she is rarely at home, we rarely have an opportunity to talk. I know that she sells shoes at a shoe shop downtown. That shoe shop is behind the school, between the bookshop and the Japanese restaurant.

_____

_____

_____

_____

_____

_____

_____

4.

There are 150 foreign students in our school; 85 are male. All of them are studying Chinese. *Zhang Mei* is their teacher. She also teaches them English. Not all of the students like writing Chinese characters, but they all like speaking Chinese. (Today) Teacher Zhang tells each of them to buy a Chinese dictionary, which is expensive. *Xiao Gui* has no money, but he has to get one. (Finally) his good friend gives him one.

_____

_____

_____

_____

_____

_____

_____

_____

_____

_____

5.

There are five people in my family: my father, mother, two younger brothers, and me. Both my father and my mother are high school teachers. Not all of my younger brothers are high school students.

My father likes to read books and newspapers. My mother only likes to read newspapers. She says, "Books are expensive, newspapers are cheap." I like to watch movies. One of my younger brothers likes to watch television; one of them does not like to watch television. Both of my brothers have Chinese friends. They say, "Can you give us a map of China?"

_____

_____

_____

_____

_____

_____

_____

_____

_____

_____

_____

_____

_____

_____

6.

a. I like eating Chinese food because it tastes very good.
b. There are people everywhere: at the school, outside the school, in front of the school, and at the back of the school.
c. I used to live in the city, but now I don't anymore.
d. Your book is not with me, it's with your brother.
e. My auntie and uncle do business together.

_____

_____

_____

_____

_____

_____

_____

7.

My father was an English language teacher before, but now he no longer is. Because he loves reading books and magazines, now he is working at my uncle's (father's older brother) bookshop.

My uncle is the owner of a bookshop, but he does not like to read (books) at all. He loves to cook. He can cook Chinese dishes and Japanese dishes. He also loves to drink beer. My father does not drink beer. He drinks coffee.

My uncle's bookshop is in the city. There is a Chinese restaurant on the left side of my uncle's bookshop. The owner of this Chinese restaurant is my aunt's best friend. My aunt loves to eat Chinese food, but she doesn't know how to cook it.

_____

_____

_____

_____

_____

_____

8.

My younger brother asked me, "Do you know where my magazine is?"

"Your magazine is on top of the work of fiction, underneath the dictionary," I said.

"Which brush pen is mine?"

"That one on the left is yours, that one on the right is mine."

"Wrong. These two are both old. Mine is new."

"On top of the bicycle to the front is a brush pen, have a look to see if it is yours or not."

"(Do you mean) the front of the bicycle?"

"No, it is the bicycle to the front."

"I had a look. This is also not mine."

"This one is not (yours) and that one is not (yours). I don't know where your brush pen is."

"Ai ya! I forget. I didn't buy a brush pen."

_____

_____

_____

_____

_____

_____

_____

_____

READING COMPREHENSION

Read each of the following passages and answer the questions that follow it.

1.

　　王先生一家人就住在我家后边儿。他的 fáng 子很大，Lóu 上有四个 fáng-jiān，lóu 下有两个 fángjiān。他们 fáng 子的东边儿是学 xiào，西边儿是商 diàn。

　　王先生是做生意的，他的 diàn 在前门大 Jiē。他的 diàn 卖很多东西，有衬衫、汗衫、毛衣、内衣、牛仔 kù、袜子、书、笔、报、杂志……Diàn 的 wài 边儿卖书报，lǐ.biānr 卖衣 fu。大门的 zuǒ 边儿卖女人的衣 fu，右边儿卖 nán 人的衣 fu。Zuǒ 边儿的前边儿卖 qún 子、女衬衫、毛衣和内衣，zuǒ 边儿的后边儿卖 kù 子、牛仔 kù hé 袜子。右边儿的前边儿卖 nán 衬衫 hé nán 汗衫，右边儿的后边儿只卖 kù 子。

　　王太太很少在家，因为她以前没有机会上大学，xiàn 在孩子大了，她 hé 她的孩子一块儿上大学。

Questions:

a. 王先生家住在哪儿？

_____

b. 王先生家一共有几个 fángjiān？

_____

c. 王先生卖什么？

_____

d. 王太太 xiàn 在做什么事？

_____

2.

我的名字叫 Zhāng 国 xǐ, 我是<u>中国</u>人。我太太是<u>英国</u>人。我的孩子, 一个叫 Zhāng 好, 一个叫 Zhāng Néng。他们都是中学生。<u>Zhāng 好</u>是哥哥, <u>Zhāng Néng</u> 是弟弟。哥哥会说中文, 也会说英文, 弟弟只会英文。

<u>Zhāng 好</u>有两 zhāng <u>英国</u>地图。他不 xǐ 欢看地图, 也不 xǐ 欢看电 shì, 他 xǐ 欢看电 yǐng。<u>Zhāng Néng</u> xǐ 欢看电 shì , 也 xǐ 欢看电 yǐng。<u>Zhāng 好</u>说 wài 国 电 yǐng 好看, <u>Zhāng Néng</u> 说<u>中国</u>电 yǐng 好看。

Questions:

a. <u>Zhāng 好</u>、<u>Zhāng Néng</u> 都 xǐ 欢看电 shì 吗?

_____

b. <u>Zhāng 国 xǐ</u> 姓什么? 他有几个孩子?

_____

c. <u>Zhāng Néng</u> 有几个哥哥?

_____

d. <u>Zhāng Néng</u> 的妈妈是哪国人?

_____

e. <u>Zhāng Néng</u> 的哥哥叫什么名字?

_____

f. <u>Zhāng 好</u>、<u>Zhāng Néng</u> 都说<u>中国</u>电 yǐng 好看吗?

_____

3. Read the following passage. Indicate whether the following five statements are true or false by circling the appropriate word.

我叫 Zhāng Liàng。我们家有六个人: bàba、妈妈、姐姐、哥哥、弟弟和我。 我 bàba 是老 shī, 在大学教法文。我妈妈也是老 shī, 在中学教日语。我姐姐在<u>北京</u> <u>大学</u>教英语。我哥哥在<u>美国</u>念大学, 学习法文和中文。我弟弟念中学。他 gēn bàba 学法文, gēn 妈妈学日语, gēn 我学汉语。他说学法文 zuì 容 yì, 学日语 zuì nán, 学汉 语不太 nán, 可是也不是很容 yì。

在我们四兄弟姐妹 dāng 中, 我弟弟 zuì cōng 明, suǒ 以 bàba 妈妈都很 ài 他。 在学 xiào lǐ, 因为他是个好学生, suǒ 以学 xiào lǐ 的老 shī 和同学都很 xǐ 欢 他。 他想去<u>中国</u>学习中文, 我 bàba 妈妈说没问 tí。

a. <u>Zhāng Liàng</u> 的父母住在<u>北京</u>。 对   不对

b. <u>Zhāng Liàng</u> 的姐姐是英语老 shī, 她在<u>中国</u>。 对   不对

c. Zhāng Liàng 和哥哥在一块儿学习汉语。   对   不对

d. Zhāng Liàng 的弟弟说学日语很不容 yì。   对   不对

e. Zhāng Liàng 的父母不想 Zhāng Liàng 的弟弟去中国学中文。   对   不对

4.

　　王国明的 bàba 是一家法国饭馆儿的老板。 他们家就在我家的右边儿。国明的父母就有国明一个孩子, 因为他父母很有 qián, suǒ 以他们给国明很 duō qián。

　　我叫大朋。 国明是我姐姐的 tóng 学, 也是我姐姐的好朋友, 他很 xǐ 欢 gēn 我姐姐去看电 yǐng。 我姐姐很 xǐ 欢买地道的法国东西, 可是地道的法国东西很 guì, 她是学生, 她没有 qián 买很 guì 的东西。 国明知道了, 他说: "没关 xi, 你没有 qián, 我有。 我买。"

　　我姐姐要买手 biǎo, 她 hé 国明去城 lǐ 的一家大商 diàn 看手 biǎo。 我姐姐很 xǐ 欢那家商 diàn 卖的一块手 biǎo, 那块手 biǎo 很好看, 可是要一千 duō 块 qián。 我姐姐说: "这家商 diàn 的手 biǎo 太 guì 了, 我们去对 miàn 那家 diàn 看看吧。" 国明说: "一千 duō 块 qián 一块法国手 biǎo 不 guì。 你看, 我的要两千 duō 块 qián。" 姐姐问卖手 biǎo 的 fúwùyuán: "有五百 duō 块 qián 的吗?" 卖手 biǎo 的那位 fúwùyuán 说: "对不 qǐ, 这是 zuì 便宜的了, 法国做的东西都很 guì。" 国明说: "没关 xi, 你 xǐ 欢, 我买。我给你。" 姐姐说: "真的吗? 那, xièxie 你了。"

　　在大商 diàn 的右边儿有一家法国 xiédiàn, 那儿卖的皮 xié 都很 guì, 都要五百 duō 块 qián 一双。 国明说: "小宜, 我们去看看。" 姐姐说: "我不去, 那儿卖的皮 xié 太 guì 了。" 国明知道姐姐 xǐ 欢法国做的东西, 他说: "没关 xi, 我们去看看。" 在 xiédiàn lǐ, 姐姐说: "国明, 你看, 那双皮 xié 真 piàoliang! 我很 xǐ 欢, 可是太 guì 了。" 国明说: "五百九十块 qián, 不 guì。 你 xǐ 欢, 我给你。" 那家 xiédiàn 的右边儿是一家法国饭馆儿, 国明不 xǐ 欢去那家法国饭馆儿吃饭, 他说: "那家饭馆儿卖的法国菜不地道。"

　　姐姐说国明真好, 真 cōng 明。 我不明白为什么国明 xǐ 欢我姐姐, 她不会做饭, xǐ 欢买东西。 你们一 dìng 说国明很笨, 对不对? 我说国明一 diǎn 儿都不笨, 他给我的东西不是法国做的, 是中国做的。 我问他为什么不给我 guì 的东西, 他说: "你不是小宜, 你是他弟弟。"我明白了, 因为他 xǐ 欢小宜。

Questions:

a. 王国明有几个兄弟姐妹? 他 bàba 做什么 shì?

_____

b. 小宜是 shéi? 她认识王国明吗? 小宜 xǐ 欢买什么?

_____

c. 为什么城 lǐ 那家大商 diàn 卖的手 biǎo 很 guì? 王国明给小宜的手 biǎo duōshao qián?

_____

d. 什么 diàn 在大商 diàn hé <u>法国</u>饭馆儿的中 jiān? 为什么<u>国明</u>不 xǐ 欢去那家<u>法国</u>饭馆儿吃饭?

_____

e. 为什么<u>大朋</u>说<u>国明</u>不笨? 为什么<u>国明</u>给<u>小宜</u>很 guì 的东西?

_____

5.

  <u>王汉生</u>是一家书 diàn 的老板, 他的书 diàn 在<u>大学 Jiē</u> 的眼 jìng diàn hé 咖啡 diàn 中 jiān。<u>王汉生</u>的书 diàn 卖英文书、法文书、中文书、日文书, 也卖中文、日文的杂志, 词典和法文杂志。这家书 diàn 很容 yì 找, 书很多, 学生买书还可以便宜一 diǎn 儿, 很多人 xǐ 欢去这家书 diàn 买书。

  <u>王汉生</u>的太太思兰是 <u>Xīn 西兰</u>人。她的中文很好, 在中学教中文 hé 英文。她会画<u>中国</u>画, 会 xiě 毛笔字, 也会做几个很地道的<u>中国</u>菜, 朋友们都说她做的<u>中国</u>菜好吃也好看。<u>王汉生</u>也会做<u>中国</u>菜, 可是他做的<u>中国</u>菜不好吃。<u>王汉生</u> zuì ài 吃太太做的<u>中国</u>菜。

  <u>王汉生</u> hé <u>思兰</u>有一个儿子、一个女儿。儿子<u>道乐</u>上中学, xǐ 欢喝<u>可口可乐</u>, 看电 yǐng。女儿<u>道宜</u>上小学, xǐ 欢看杂志。他们都 ài 吃<u>中国</u>小吃, 也 ài 学中文。<u>道乐</u>学中文, 因为他想看中文电 yǐng, 也想看中文小说。他会 xiě 四百个汉字了, <u>中国</u>饭馆儿的菜、茶 hé 酒的中文名字他都认识。他的<u>中国</u>朋友都说他的中文真不 cuò。女儿<u>道宜</u>学中文, 因为她想看中文 màn 画书。<u>道宜</u>说中文很 nánxiě, 可是很有意思。她要 bàba 送她一本中文词典, 她要 měi 天学两个汉字。

  <u>王汉生</u>住在书 diàn 的上边儿。他家只有三个 fángjiān, 都不大, 可是因为他们是住在有名的<u>大学 Jiē</u>, 他们住的 fáng 子很 guì。<u>王汉生</u> hé 他太太快有 dì 三个 hái 子了, 他们想卖他们的 fáng 子, 再买一个大的、ānjing 的、便宜 diǎn 儿的 fáng 子。他们不知道 dì 三个 hái 子是 nán 的还是女的。<u>道乐</u>想要一个妹妹, <u>道宜</u>想要一个弟弟。他们都会 ài 这个 hái 子!

According to the information given in the passage, identify the following five sentences as being either true or false by circling the appropriate word.

a. <u>王汉生</u>的书 diàn 卖英文杂志。   对 不对

b. <u>王汉生</u>的书 diàn 生意很好。   对 不对

c. <u>王汉生</u>和思兰会做地道的<u>中国</u>菜。 对 不对

d. <u>道乐</u>会 xiě 汉字。   对 不对

e. <u>王汉生</u>和<u>思兰</u>有三个儿子。   对 不对

Answer the following questions in Chinese characters; use Pinyin with original tone marks only if the character has not been learned. The answers should be in your own words based on the information in the text. Directly copying from the text will be penalized.

Questions:

a. 为什么很 duō 人 xǐ 欢去<u>王汉生</u>的书 diàn 买书?

   _____

b. <u>思兰</u>会什么 (请 xiě 三件<u>思兰</u>会的 shì)?

   _____

c. <u>道乐</u> hé <u>道宜</u>为什么学中文?

   _____

d. 为什么<u>王汉生</u>要卖他的 fáng 子?

   _____

e. <u>王汉生</u>要买什么 fáng 子?

   _____

11

第十一课

TEXT

　　白京以是我中学的同学, xiàn 在是北京大学的学生。他很 cōng 明, 功课很好, 可是他不会开车, 去哪儿都 qí 自行车。他说坐公共汽车很便宜, 可是车上人太多, 太不舒服了; 打的很方便, 也很舒服, 可是不便宜。Suǒ 以他去哪儿都 qí 车。

　　白京以晚上给我打电话, 问我在做什么, 我说我正在看书呢。他问我有 kòng 吗, 我说, 我有 kòng, 你 dào 我家来 liáoliao 天, 喝喝酒吧。他说太好了, 可是他不知道怎么来我家。 我告诉他我家在同心街, 同心街左边儿有个火车 zhàn, 从火车 zhàn 往左拐, 再往前一直走, 就是我家。我家右边儿有个小学, 左边儿有个图书馆, 图书馆的外边儿开着灯, 不 nán 找。白京以 qí 着车从这条街 dào 那条街问 lù, 没有人知道同心街在哪儿, suǒ 以白京以就不 qí 自行车了, 他坐 chū 租汽车来我家。我问他为什么不买一张地图, 拿着地图找 lù 就容 yì 了。他真笨, 一 diǎn 儿也不 cōng 明。

　　晚上, 我和白京以喝着中国酒 liáo 天, 吃着我太太给我们做的上海小吃和南京炒菜。白京以说因为有这么好吃的菜, 那么好喝的酒, suǒ 以他很 xǐ 欢来找我喝酒 liáo 天。

173

生词 NEW WORDS

白京以	Bái Jīngyǐ	(N) a personal name
中学	zhōngxué	(PW) high school
同学	tóngxué	(N) fellow student, classmate
大学	dàxué	(N) university
美思大学	Měisī Dàxué	(PW) name of a university
学生	xuésheng	(N) student
功课	gōngkè	(N) schoolwork, homework
开	kāi	(V) open, operate, drive (a car), turn on
车	chē	(N) vehicle (Cl -liàng 辆)
坐	zuò	(V) sit, ride, take (a means of transportation)
公共汽车	gōnggòng qìchē	(N) public bus
公 jiāo 车/公车	gōngjiāochē/gōngchē	(N) same as 公共汽车
多	duō	(SV) many, be abundant
舒服	shūfu	(SV) be comfortable
打的	dǎ dī	(VO) take a taxi (slang)
方便	fāngbiàn	(SV) be convenient
晚上	wǎnshang	(TW) in the evening
正(在)……(着) (呢)	zhèng(zài)…(zhe)(ne)	(Pat) right in the middle of…
有 kòng	yǒu kòng	(VO) have free time
来	lái	(V) come
liáo 天	liáotiān	(VO) chat
怎么	zěnme	(Adv) how? why?
同心街	Tóngxīn Jiē	(PW) a street name
左边儿	zuǒ.biānr	(PS/PW) the left
火车 zhàn	huǒchēzhàn	(PW) train station
从	cóng	(CV) from
往	wǎng	(CV) toward
前	qián	(PS/PW) in front
拐	guǎi	(V) turn
一直	yìzhí	(Adv) straight
走	zǒu	(V) walk, go, move along, leave
就	jiù	(Conj) then
小学	xiǎoxué	(PW) elementary school
图书馆	túshūguǎn	(PW) library

外边儿	wài.biānr	(PS/PW) outside
……着(呢)	…-zhe (ne)	(Pat) description of a state
灯	dēng	(N) lamp, lights
从……dào……	cóng…dào…	(Pat) from…to…
-条	-tiáo	(Cl) (for things that are seen as long, narrow, and flexible)
街	jiē	(N) street (Cl -tiáo 条)
问 lù	wèn lù	(VO) ask the way
chū 租(汽)车	chūzū (qì)chē	(N) taxi
拿	ná	(V) take, bring, pick up
和	hé	(Conj) and, with
南京	Nánjīng	(PW) a city in China
炒	chǎo	(V) stir fry
这么	zhème	(Adv) in this way, this
那么	nème (nàme)	(Adv) in that way, that

COMPREHENSION QUESTIONS

1. Read the text of this chapter and answer the following questions.

a. Shéi 是白京以?

_____

b. 为什么白京以不 xǐ 欢坐公 jiāo 车?

_____

c. 他 xǐ 欢打的吗? 为什么?

_____

d. 晚上 "我" 在家做什么?

_____

e. 白京以 知道 "我" 家在哪儿吗?

_____

f. 请告诉他怎么来 "我" 家。

_____

g. 为什么白京以坐 chū 租汽车来 "我" 家?

_____

h. 你说<u>白京以</u> cōng 明还是笨?

_____

i. 晚上, "我" 和<u>白京以</u>一块儿做什么?

_____

j. 为什么<u>白京以</u> xǐ 欢来 "我" 家?

_____

2. Draw a map of the neighborhood according to the passage.

同心街

WRITING HELP

INDEPENDENT CHARACTERS

Character	Basic meaning	No. of strokes	Stroke order	Radical	Components	Structure
心 xīn	heart	4	心	心	心	☐
开 (開) kāi	to open	4	二 于 开	一	开	☐
天 tiān	sky, day	4	二 天	大	一 大	☐
火 huǒ	fire	4	丶 丷 少 火	火	火	☐
正 zhèng	upright	5	一 丁 千 正 正	一	一 止	☐
来 (來) lái	to come	7	一 丷 丌 立 平 来 来	一	一 米	☐
走 zǒu	to walk, to go	7	土 走	走	土 止	☐

正: The character 正, with a total of five strokes, is used by Chinese as a tally marker for counting things. With each increase of one, the next stroke of the character is added in the stroke order shown above, until the full character is complete, at which point one starts writing a new 正. This method of tally counting is very similar to the | ‖ ⫼ ⦀ 𝍩 convention used in many English-speaking and European countries for tallying quantities in units of five.

COMPOUND CHARACTERS

The following are the new compound characters with learned radicals in this chapter: 公, 从, 同, 坐, 汽, 条, 服, 往, 拐, 直, 怎, 南, 拿, 街, and 舒.

Char-acter	Basic meaning	No. of strokes	Stroke order	Radical	Meaning clue	Phonetic clue	Compo-nents	Struc-ture
*公 gōng	public	4	八 公	八			八 厶	
从 (從) cóng	follow	4	人 从	人	人, 人		人 人	
*同 tóng	together	6	冂 冂 同	冂	一 , 口		冂 一 口	
坐 zuò	sit	7	人 从 坐	土	人, 人, 土 (tǔ, soil)		人 人 土	
汽 qì	steam	7	氵 汽	氵	氵	气	氵 气	
*条 (條) tiáo	(a clas-sifier)	7	丿 夂 夂 条	木	木		夂 木	
服 fú	cloth-ing*, obey	8	月 𦙵 肌 服	月	月 (yuè, flesh)		月 㞋	
往 wàng	toward	8	彳 往	彳	彳	王	彳 主	
拐 guǎi	to turn	8	扌 护 拐	扌	扌		扌 口 力	
直 zhí	straight	8	直	十			十 目	
*怎 zěn	how	9	丿 𠂉 𠂉 乍 乍 怎	心	心	乍 zhà	乍 心	
南 nán	south	9	十 冇 冇 南 南	十			十 冂 羊)	
拿 ná	to hold	10	八 𠆢 合 拿	人	合, 手		合 手	
街 jiē	street	12	彳 往 往 街	彳	彳 行		彳 土 土 丁	
*舒 shū	com-fort-able	12	人 𠂤 舍 舍 舒 舒 舒	人			舍 予	

同: Think of it as showing all the voices (口) in the room (冂) expressing unison (一): 同.

坐: Two persons sitting on the ground (土 "soil").

拿: Using a hand (手) to close (合 "close, shut") is the way to hold something.

RADICALS

The new radicals introduced in this chapter are 工, 夕, 火, and 禾.

1. 工

As a character, 工 *gōng* means "work". As a radical it can be used as various parts of a character to form a compound character. The compound characters in this chapter that contain this radical are 功 and 左.

Character	Basic meaning	No. of strokes	Stroke order	Meaning clue	Phonetic clue	Components	Structure
功 gōng	achieve-ment, merit	5	工 功	力 (lì, *strength*)	工 gōng	工 力	
左 zuǒ	left	5	一 ナ 左			ナ工)	

2. 夕

As a character, 夕 xī means "dusk". The compound characters in this chapter that contain this radical are 外 and 多.

Character	Basic meaning	No. of strokes	Stroke order	Meaning clue	Phonetic clue	Components	Structure
*外 wài	outside	5	夕 列 外	丨 (wall), 丶 (out-side)		夕 卜	
多 duō	many	6	夕 多	夕 + 夕 = more than one, many		夕 夕	

3. 火

As a character, 火 *huǒ* means "fire". As a radical, it is used in compound characters related to fire and light. The compound characters in this chapter that contain this radical are 灯 and 炒.

Character	Basic meaning	No. of strokes	Stroke order	Meaning clue	Phonetic clue	Compo- nents	Structure
灯 (燈) dēng	lamp	6	火 火⁻ 灯	火	丁 dīng	火丁	⊟
炒 chǎo	stir fry	8	火 炒	火	少 shǎo	火少	⊟

4. 禾

禾 *hé* can be a character meaning grain. As a radical, it is used as the left-hand part in compound characters. The compound characters in this chapter that contain this radical are 租 and 和.

Character	Basic meaning	No. of strokes	Stroke order	Meaning clue	Phonetic clue	Compo- nents	Structure
和 hé	and	8	丿 二 千 禾 禾 和			禾口	⊟
租 zū	to hire, to rent	10	禾 租			禾且	⊟

EXERCISES

CHARACTER EXERCISES

1. **Form new characters by using different components of the following characters, e.g. 工 (from 功) + ナ (from 有) → 左.**

租 右 服 她 炒 打

_____ (from _____) + _____ (from _____) → _____

_____ (from _____) + _____ (from _____) → _____

_____ (from _____) + _____ (from _____) → _____

_____ (from _____) + _____ (from _____) → _____

_____ (from _____) + _____ (from _____) → _____

2. **Add one or two strokes to each of the following characters to form a new character.**

直 _____   心 _____   住 _____   大 _____   白 _____

3. **Write as many of the characters you have learned as possible that can be divided into top and bottom parts, e.g. 怎.**

_____

4. **从 is constructed with two identical 人 characters. Can you write down other characters you have learned with a similar formation?**

_____

5. **Find the common component shared by the group.**

同, 和, 点, 拿, 拐 → (   )   同, 肉, 用 → (   )

南, 直, 车, 什 → (   )   拐, 为, 功 → (   )

去, 坐, 地, 老 → (   )   服, 叔, 皮 → (   )

6. **Solve the character riddles.**

a. 不左不右: _____

b. 你没有他有, 天没有地有: _____

c. 一口 bites off half of 多: _____

7. **How many words and phrases can you form with the following characters?**
开, 公, 功, 坐, 火, 上, 车, 课

_____

VOCABULARY EXERCISES

1. Write the Pinyin for the following characters, then form a word with each character.

a.
直 ( ) _____
住 ( ) _____

b.
真 ( ) _____
往 ( ) _____

c.
会 ( ) _____
公 ( ) _____

2. Form two different words for each of the following characters.

a. 电 → _____ _____   c. 车 → _____ _____

b. 学 → _____ _____   d. 馆 → _____ _____

3. Give the antonyms to the following words.

a. 来 → ( )   c. 左边儿 → ( )

b. 这么 → ( )   d. xiàn 在 → ( )

4. Find the word that is not in the same category as the other three words and write it in the brackets.

a. chū 租汽车, 公共汽车, 火车, 坐车   ( )

b. 大学, 同学, 中学, 小学   ( )

c. 便宜, 炒菜, 舒服, 方便   ( )

d. 一直走, 开车, 打的, qí 自行车   ( )

e. 喝酒, liáo 天, 吃菜, 功课   ( )

STRUCTURE EXERCISES

1. Rearrange the elements of each of the entries to make a grammatical sentence.
a. 去, 公共汽车, 得, 火车 zhàn, 大学, 从, 坐

→ _____

b. 着, 地图, 找, 难, 拿, 不, 了, 就

→ _____

c. dào, 你家, 怎么, 从, 图书馆, 走

→ _____

2. Choose the appropriate word from the words given immediately below to fill in the brackets in the dialogue. Some words may be used more than once.

> 从　去　dào　来　往　怎么　走　前边儿

小美：　晚上有 kòng 吗? (　　　) 我家吃饭 liáo 天吧。

小明：　好呀。可是我不知道 (　　　) 你家 (　　　) 走。

小美：　我家就在大学图书馆 (　　　) 的一条街上, (　　　) 图书馆大门

　　　　(　　　) 右拐, (　　　) 一条街就 néng (　　　) 我家。

小明：　(　　　) 大学 (　　　) 你家真方便。

3. You have invited your class for a dinner at your house. Write a paragraph in Chinese characters to describe how to go to your house.

_____

_____

_____

_____

_____

4. Translate the following sentences into Chinese, using Chinese characters for learned words.

a. She is in the middle of driving and can't talk to you.

_____

b. The light in elder brother's room is still on. He is still studying.

_____

c. To get from Shanghai to Nanjing, one can take a train and can also take a bus.

_____

d. He is wearing a pair of denim jeans and a pair of new leather shoes.

_____

e. Bái Jīngyǐ has always been doing very well in schoolwork from primary school to university.

_____

SUPPLEMENTARY READING

READING 1

高志明: 你好! 请问火车 zhàn 在哪儿?

行人[1]:   在前边。

高志明: 怎么走?

行人: 一直往前走, dào 了十字 lù 口往左拐就是了。

高志明: 谢谢你!

行人: 不用谢。

_____

1. 行人 "pedestrian"

Comprehension questions

1. <u>高志明</u>想去哪儿?

   _____

2. 请问, 去火车 zhàn 怎么走?

   _____

READING 2

成语[2]故事

　　汉语中有许多四个字的**成语**。有的成语的**背后**[3]有故事, 有的没有。"一日三秋""九牛一毛""月下老人"都是**成语**, 这些**成语**的**背后**都有故事。

Comprehension questions

1. 成语的背后都有故事吗?

   _____

2. 你知道"一日三秋""九牛一毛"的意思吗?

   _____

---

2. 成语 chéngyǔ (idiom)
3. 背后 bèihòu "behind"

CHARACTER PRACTICE

心	心								
开	开								
天	天								
火	火								
正	正								
来	来								
走	走								
公	公								
从	从								
同	同								
坐	坐								
汽	汽								
条	条								

服	服							
往	往							
拐	拐							
直	直							
怎	怎							
南	南							
拿	拿							
街	街							
舒	舒							
功	功							
左	左							
多	多							
外	外							
灯	灯							

炒	炒								
租	租								
和	和								

12

TEXT

　去年春天, 方美春和同学到北京来学汉语。 他们已经在英国学了一年的汉语了。以前, 他们谁也没有来过中国。他们要在北京上一年半的课, 明年秋天回家。除了星期六和星期日以外, 他们 měi 天都有课。上午的课从八点十分到十一点半, 下午一点三刻上课, 四点钟下课, 晚上还要做很多作业。他们最 ài 去图书馆做作业,因为那儿很安 jìng,同学们都很用功。

　到了星期六、星期日, 方美春和她的同学都很高兴, 因为他们可以在家 liáo 天、做饭, 也可以去看电 yǐng, 去商 diàn 买东西。以前方美春没有做过饭, 现在她会做很好吃的中国炒饭了。她 xǐ 欢请同学和老师来她这儿吃饭,朋友们都 ài 吃她做的中国炒饭。

上个月二十号星期天是<u>方美春</u>的生日, 她的 nán 朋友<u>海明</u>说因为是<u>美春</u>的生日, 别在家做饭了, 他要请美春和朋友们去一家好的饭馆儿吃晚饭。他说银行对面的那家 xīn 的<u>英国</u>饭馆儿里边儿很不错, 他想去那儿。<u>美春</u>说当然可以。不过, <u>英国</u>饭馆儿一定没有炒饭, <u>美春</u>拿了很多炒饭去饭馆儿。<u>美春</u>的同学、朋友差不多都来了。你知道一共来了多少人? 二十多个! 他们还请了<u>英国</u>老板一块儿来吃。<u>海明</u>说: "真不错, 我还没在<u>英国</u>饭馆儿吃过<u>中国</u>炒饭呢。"<u>英国</u>老板还说有 kòng 要 gēn <u>美春</u>学做<u>中国</u>炒饭。

生词 NEW WORDS

去年	qùnián	(TW) last year
春天	chūntiān	(TW) spring
方美春	Fāng Měichūn	(N) a personal name
到	dào	(CV) to
已经	yǐjīng	(Adv) already
了	le	(P) (indicates completed action)
年	-nián	(TD) year(s)
谁	shéi/shuí	(Pr) who
半	bàn	(NU) half, semi-
明年	míngnián	(TW) next year
秋天	qiūtiān	(TW) autumn, fall
回	huí	(V) return
除了……以外……	chúle…yǐwài…	(Pat) besides, except for
星期	xīngqī	(TW) week
星期日/天	Xīngqīrì/tiān	(TW) Sunday
上午	shàngwǔ	(TW) in the morning
-点	-diǎn	(Cl) (number) o'clock
-分	-fēn	(Cl) minute
下午	xiàwǔ	(TW) in the afternoon
-刻(钟)	-kè (zhōng)	(Cl) quarter hour, fifteen minutes
钟	zhōng	(N) clock, (time as measured in hours/minutes)
下课	xià kè	(VO) finish class
作业	zuòyè	(N) schoolwork, homework
最	zuì	(Adv) most
安 jìng	ānjìng	(SV) be peaceful and quiet

用功	yònggōng	(SV) be diligent
到	dào	(V) arrive
高兴	gāoxìng	(SV) be happy
电 yǐng	diànyǐng	(N) movie
饭	fàn	(N) meal, cooked rice, food, cuisine
现在	xiànzài	(TW) presently, now
老师	lǎoshī	(N) teacher
这儿, 这里	zhèr, zhèlǐ	(PW) here, this place
上(个)月	shàng(ge)yuè	(TW) last month
–号	-hào	(Cl) day of the month
生日	shēngrì	(N) birthday
海明	Hǎimíng	(N) a personal name
别	bié	(Conj) don't (imperative)
银行	yínháng	(PW) bank (financial institution)
对面	duìmiàn	(PW) side directly opposite
里边儿	lǐ.biānr	(PS/PW) inside
不错	búcuò	(SV) be pretty good
当然	dāngrán	(Adv) of course
不过	bú guò	(Conj) still, however
一定	yídìng	(Adv) definitely
差不多	chàbuduō	(Ex) almost, just about, good enough
多少?	duōshao?	(Q) How many? How much?
还……呢	hái… ne	(Pat) (continuation of an action)

COMPREHENSION QUESTIONS

1. Read the text of this chapter and answer the following questions.

a. 以前, 方美春和他的同学去过北京吗?

b. 他们在英国学了多 jiǔ 的中文?

c. 他们 měi 天都要上课吗?

d. 他们上午的课从几点到几点?

e. 下午几点下课?

f. 他们最 xǐ 欢去哪儿做作业?

g. 为什么到了星期六同学们都很高兴?

h. 方美春做的什么菜朋友们都 xǐ 欢吃?

i. 谁是方美春的 nán 朋友?

j. 请你告诉我方美春的生日。

k. 生日那天, 他们去哪儿吃饭了?

l. 海明和美春请了什么人吃生日晚饭?

m. 说说方美春生日的晚饭。

WRITING HELP

INDEPENDENT CHARACTERS

Character	Basic meaning	No. of strokes	Stroke order	Radical	Components	Structure
年 nián	year	6	ノ ⺅ ⺊ ⺉ 仨 年	ノ	年	☐
*已 yǐ¹	already	3	ㄱ コ 已	己	已	☐
月 yuè	month	4	月	月	月	☐
*业 (業) yè	line of business	5	｜ ｜｜ ｜｜｜ ⺟ 业	业	｜ ｜ 、 ノ 一)	☐
*里 (裏) lǐ	inside	7	日 里	里	田 土	☐

1. Please note that 已 is one of three characters that look remarkably similar, the other two being the 己 jǐ of 自己 zìjǐ "self" (taught in Chapter 19) and 巳 sì, the sixth of twelve units in one of the traditional systems of counting. These three characters differ in the degree of closure of the vertical, left-hand stroke of the upper box. The 已 of 已经 taught in this chapter has a halfway closed line, while the 己 jǐ of 自己 zìjǐ "self" taught in Chapter 19 lacks this left-hand line altogether, and the less commonly seen character 巳 has a completely closed box on top.

COMPOUND CHARACTERS

The following are the new compound characters with learned radicals in this chapter: 春, 经, 谁, 秋, 回, 星, 期, 钟, 作, 最, 安, 兴, 号, 面, 定, and 差.

Character	Basic meaning	No. of strokes	Stroke order	Radical	Meaning clue	Phonetic clue	Components	Structure
*春 chūn	spring	9	一 二 三 声 夫 春	日	日		夫 日	☐
经 (經) jīng	to go through	8	纟 纠 纺 经	纟		圣 jīng	纟 又 工	☐
谁 (誰) shéi	who	11	讠 讠 讠 讠 谁 谁	讠	讠		讠 亻 主	☐

Character	Basic meaning	No. of strokes	Stroke order	Radical	Meaning clue	Phonetic clue	Components	Structure
*秋 qiū	autumn	9	禾 秋	禾	禾 (hé, *grains*) 火		禾火	
回 huí	to return	6	冂 回 回	口			口口	
星 xīng	star	9	日 星	日	日	生	日生	
*期 qī	period	12	一 十 卄 丗 甘 甘 其 其 期	月	月	其 qí	其月	
钟 (鐘) zhōng	clock, surname	9	丿 𠂉 𠂊 钅 钟	钅	钅	中	钅中	
作 zuò	to do/ make	7	亻 作	亻	亻	乍 zhà	亻乍	
最 zuì	most	12	日 旦 𣅂 冒 冒 冣 最	日			日 耳 又	
安 ān	peace (ful)	6	宀 安	宀	宀, 女		宀 女	
*兴 (興) xìng	to prosper	6	丶 丷 ⺍ 쓰 兴	八			丷 一 八	
号 (號) hào	to call	5	口 吕 号	口	口		口丂	
面 miàn	side	9	一 𠂆 丙 而 而 面	一			丆 囬	
定 dìng	to decide	8	宀 定	宀	宀		宀疋	
差 chà	difference	9	羊 差	羊			羊工	

秋: Grains 禾 under the hot sun 火 mean they are ready for harvest and thus it is autumn = 秋.

安: The presence of a woman under the roof provides a sense of peace.

兴: Lots of things growing on the ground 一 with roots underneath 八 is prosperous.

RADICALS

The new radicals introduced in this chapter are 灬, 刂, 王, 钅, 小, and 巾.

1. 灬

灬 is used as the bottom part in compound characters to indicate fire or dots. The compound characters in this chapter that contain this radical are 点 and 然.

Character	Basic meaning	No. of strokes	Stroke order	Meaning clue	Phonetic clue	Compo-nents	Structure
点 (點) diǎn	dot	9	占 占 占 点 点	灬		占 灬	
*然 rán	to burn	12	丿 ク 夕 夕 外 狀 然	灬		夕 犬 灬	

2. 刂

刂 is a variant form of the character 刀 *dāo* "knife". As a radical it often is found on the right-hand part of a character, indicating "knife" or a related meaning. The compound characters in this chapter that contain this radical are 别, 刻, and 到.

Character	Basic meaning	No. of strokes	Stroke order	Meaning clue	Phonetic clue	Compo-nents	Structure
到 dào	to arrive	8	一 工 丞 至 到	至 (zhì, reach)		云 土 刂	
刻 kè	quarter of an hour, carve	8	一 亠 歺 亥 刻	刂		亥 刂	
别 bié	other, not	7	口 另 别	另 (lìng, another), 刂 (sep-arating one from another)		口 力 刂	

3. 王

王 as a character means "king". As a radical it is used in compound characters related to jade or something precious. The compound character in this chapter that contains this radical is 现.

Character	Basic meaning	No. of strokes	Stroke order	Meaning clue	Phonetic clue	Compo- nents	Structure
*现 (現) xiàn	now	8	王 现		见	王见	⊟

玩: It is a rich man's hobby to collect and play with jade.

4. 钅

As a character, this means "gold" and is written as 金 *jīn*. As a radical it is used as the left part in a compound character and is written as 钅 to form characters related to metal or money. The compound characters in this chapter that contain this radical are 钱 and 银.

Character	Basic meaning	No. of strokes	Stroke order	Meaning clue	Phonetic clue	Compo- nents	Structure
银 (銀) yín	silver	11	钅 银	钅		钅艮	⊟
错 (錯) cuò	error, mistake	13	钅 钅 钅 钅 钅 错	钅		钅昔	⊟

5. 小

This can also be used as a radical. The compound characters in this chapter that contain this radical are 少 and 当.

Character	Basic meaning	No. of strokes	Stroke order	Meaning clue	Phonetic clue	Compo- nents	Structure
少 shǎo	few	4	小 少		小	小丿	⊟
当 dāng	to under- take	6	丨 丷 丷 当			丷彐	⊟

6. 巾

巾 *jīn* "towel" can be used as a character as well as a radical. The compound characters in this chapter that contain this radical are 师, 希, and 常.

Character	Basic meaning	No. of strokes	Stroke order	Meaning clue	Phonetic clue	Compo- nents	Structure
*师 (師) shī	teacher	6	丨 丿 丿 师 师			刂一巾	⊟

EXERCISES

CHARACTER EXERCISES

1. **Find out the common component shared by the group.**

左, 经, 功, 差 → (   )   最, 对, 服, 皮 → (   )

兴, 公, 真, 期 → (   )   思, 里, 课 → (   )

2. **Form new characters by using different components of the following characters, e.g. 工 (from 功) + ナ (from 有) → 左.**

着 行 银 找 过 功 别

_____ (from _____) + _____ (from _____) → _____

_____ (from _____) + _____ (from _____) → _____

_____ (from _____) + _____ (from _____) → _____

_____ (from _____) + _____ (from _____) → _____

_____ (from _____) + _____ (from _____) → _____

3. **Write as many characters as possible that you have learned that can be divided into a left-hand part and a right-hand part, e.g. 谁.**

_____

4. **Circle the wrong character in each sentence and correct it in the brackets.**

a. 方美春有很多作业, 丛上午到下午, 她一直在做作业。 (   )

b. 他想知道淮以前去过美国。 (   )

c. 那家饭馆就在银行对面。 (   )

d. 七点了, 他已泾吃过饭了。 (   )

e. 朋友们都 ài 吃美春作的中国炒饭。 (   )

5. **Solve the character riddle below.**

大口吃小口: _____

VOCABULARY EXERCISES

1. Write the Pinyin for the following characters, then form a word with each character.

   a. $\begin{cases} 学\ (\quad\quad) \underline{\hspace{5cm}} \\ 作\ (\quad\quad) \underline{\hspace{5cm}} \end{cases}$

   b. $\begin{cases} 字\ (\quad\quad) \underline{\hspace{5cm}} \\ 做\ (\quad\quad) \underline{\hspace{5cm}} \end{cases}$

2. Link a character in the left column with a character in the right column to form a word and write down the word in the bracket. An example is already given.

星	兴	(星期)
春	日	( )
用	课	( )
高	师	( )
生	天	( )
下	功	( )
老	期	( )

3. Write the following time words in Chinese characters. Use Pinyin for characters that you have not yet learned.

2:00   \underline{\hspace{5cm}}

3:30   \underline{\hspace{5cm}}

6:15 AM   \underline{\hspace{5cm}}

7:45 PM   \underline{\hspace{5cm}}

June 30   \underline{\hspace{5cm}}

May 11   \underline{\hspace{5cm}}

September 7, 1949   \underline{\hspace{5cm}}

December 25, 2018   \underline{\hspace{5cm}}

4. What are the differences in meaning between the two?

a. $\begin{cases} 六月\rule{4cm}{0.4pt} \\ 六个月\rule{4cm}{0.4pt} \end{cases}$

b. $\begin{cases} 十一月\rule{4cm}{0.4pt} \\ 十一个月\rule{4cm}{0.4pt} \end{cases}$

c. $\begin{cases} 几月?\rule{4cm}{0.4pt} \\ 几个月?\rule{4cm}{0.4pt} \end{cases}$

5. Give the antonyms to the following words.

a. 这儿 → (   )   c. 上课 → (   )
b. 上午 → (   )   d. 外边儿 → (   )

STRUCTURE EXERCISES

1. Rearrange the elements of each of the entries to make a grammatical sentence.

a. 海明, 了, 二十, 看, 去年, 书, 本, 一共

→ \rule{10cm}{0.4pt}

b. 星期五, 同学们, 说, 作业, 老师, 没有, 高兴, 很, 都

→ \rule{10cm}{0.4pt}

c. 以外, 东西, 他, 电 yǐng, 也, 除了, 去, 看, 商 diàn, 买, xǐ 欢

→ \rule{10cm}{0.4pt}

d. 星期天, 最, 因为, 上课, 他, 星期天, 不用, 了, xǐ 欢

→ \rule{10cm}{0.4pt}

2. Choose the appropriate word from the words given immediately below and fill in the brackets. Some words may be used more than once.

没	在	还	呢	了

a. - 你 (   ) 住在北京吗?

   - 我 (   ) 住在北京 (   )。

b. 我哥哥在南京念 (   ) 两个月的书, 还要再念十个月 (   )。

c. - 你吃（　　　）午饭（　　　）吗?

- （　　　）（　　　）吃呢, 太忙了。我（　　　）（　　　）念英文呢, 你呢?

- 我也（　　　）吃呢, 我（　　　）不 饿。

3. Fill in the blanks to complete the following mini dialogues.

a. A: 你生日＿＿＿＿＿＿＿＿＿?
   B: 三月四号。

b. A: 你生日＿＿＿＿＿＿＿＿＿?
   B: 1998 年。

c. A: ＿＿＿＿＿＿＿＿＿上中文课?
   B: 我星期三和星期四上中文课。

d. A: ＿＿＿＿＿＿＿＿＿到学校?
   B: 8 点 50。

e. A: ＿＿＿＿＿＿＿＿＿去的北京?
   B: 去年秋天。

4. Choose any day of last week and write a paragraph in Chinese characters to describe what you did on that particular day.

_____

_____

_____

_____

5. Translate the following sentences into Chinese, using Chinese characters for learned words.

a. It's already 11 o'clock in the evening. He hasn't returned home yet.

_____

b. So far she has been reading books for several hours in the library.

_____

c. The exam is around the corner. At present *Meichun* (lit. the *Meichun* of the present) is most hardworking.

_____

d. My older sister has forgotten the name of the film she watched last week.

_____

e. He goes to the university to attend class on Monday, Wednesday, and Friday, and reads books at home on Tuesday and Thursday.

SUPPLEMENTARY READING

READING 1

高小春: 文海,你上哪儿去?

王文海: 上课。

高小春: 你几点上课?

王文海: 两点。

高小春: 现在几点?

王文海: 差十分两点。

高小春: 那,你快走吧!

王文海: 再见。

高小春: 再见。

Comprehension questions

1. 王文海几点上课?

2. 王文海 gēn 高小春说话的时候 (shíhou, "time") 是几点?

READING 2

没事(shì)儿

中国人常说"没事儿"。你 gēn 朋友说好七点在电 yǐng 院等他, 你七点半才到, 你说: "对不 qǐ, 我来晚了。" 他说: "没事儿。" 朋友请你到饭馆儿吃饭, 可是你忘了去。第二天你给朋友打电话, 你说: "对不 qǐ, 昨天晚上我忘了你请我吃饭这事儿。" 你朋友说: "没事儿。" 你们知道这里的两个"没事儿"是什么意思吗? 在这里, "没事儿"就是"没关系, 没什么"的意思。

Comprehension questions

1. 你 gēn 你的中国朋友说 "对不 qǐ", 他会对你说什么?

_____

2. "没事儿" 这句话是什么意思?

_____

CHARACTER PRACTICE

年	年							
己	己							
业	业							
月	月							
里	里							
春	春							
经	经							
谁	谁							
秋	秋							
回	回							
星	星							
期	期							
钟	钟							

作	作								
最	最								
安	安								
兴	兴								
号	号								
面	面								
定	定								
差	差								
点	点								
然	然								
到	到								
刻	刻								
别	别								
现	现								

银	银								
错	错								
少	少								
当	当								
师	师								

13

第十三课

TEXT

我最不 xǐ 欢看病了,看病要花很多钱,吃了药病也不一定会好。可是,今天上午我去医院看医生了。

昨天<u>白京以</u>来找我练习汉语和 liáo 天。晚饭的时候, 我们喝了很多酒,也吃了很多好吃的东西。晚上<u>白京以</u>走了以后, 我就 jué 得不舒服了, 我头疼、肚子疼,哪儿都不舒服。

我太太说: "不好了, 你病了! "她先给我喝了一点儿水, 然后再给我吃了一点儿药。可是, 我还是哪儿都不舒服。我想, 我以前常常喝酒, 一直没有不舒服, 今天怎么了? 我太太说, 我昨天喝了太多酒, 吃了太多东西, 是吃坏了, suǒ 以不舒服。她说: "今天太晚了, 你喝杯水, 休息吧。明天一定要去看我们认识的<u>高医生</u>。"

今天早上我还头疼呢。我吃了早饭就去看医生了。

我从我家前边儿的车 zhàn 坐公 jiāo 车去医院, 车上很挤, 没有地方坐。我在<u>北京街</u>下车, 医院在<u>中国银行</u>的左边儿。<u>高医生</u>是这家医院有名的医生。医院里看病的人很多, 我等了很久才开始看。<u>高医生</u>给我仔细地看了病以后, 说我没发烧, 我的病没大问 tí, 不用吃药, 回家休息休息就会好。他告诉我这几天不要吃肉, 也不要喝酒, 要多喝水。 以后喝酒以前要先吃一点儿东西, 不要饿着肚子喝酒。

我在家休息了一天, 第二天就好多了。我不知道<u>老白</u>是不是也病了, 我还没给他打电话呢。他 xiàn 在不在家,我得给他打手机。

生词 NEW WORDS

病	bìng	(N) illness, (V) be ill
看病	kàn bìng	(VO) to see a doctor
医生	yīshēng	(N) physician, doctor
看医生	kàn yīshēng	(VO) (same as 看病)
花	huā	(V) spend (money or time)
钱	qián	(N) money
药	yào	(N) medicine
吃药	chī yào	(VO) take medicine
今天	jīntiān	(TW) today
医院	yīyuàn	(PW) hospital
昨天	zuótiān	(TW) yesterday
练习	liànxí	(V/N) practice
……的时候	…de shíhou	(Part) at the time of…
……以后	…yǐhòu	(Pat) after…
就	jiù	(Conj) then (earlier than expected)
jué 得	juéde	(V) think, feel
头	tóu	(N) head
疼	téng	(V) feel pain
肚子	dùzi	(N) stomach
先	xiān	(Adv) first
一点儿	yìdiǎnr	(Q) a bit, a little
水	shuǐ	(N) water
然后	ránhòu	(Conj) and then…
再	zài	(Adv) and then
常常	chángcháng	(Adv) frequently, often
怎么了?	Zěnme le?	(Ex) What's going on? What's the matter?
吃坏了	Chīhuài le	(Ex) digestive problem from eating the wrong food
晚	wǎn	(SV) be late
一杯	-bēi	(Cl) cup/glass of
休息	xiūxi	(V) rest
明天	míngtiān	(TW) tomorrow
早上	zǎoshang	(TW) in the morning
车 zhàn	chēzhàn	(PW) bus stop

挤	jǐ	(SV) be crowded
北京街	Běijīng Jiē	(PW) name of a street
下	xià	(V) get off, disembark
下车	xià chē	(VO) get off a bus or train
等	děng	(V) wait
久	jiǔ	(SV) take/be a long time
才	cái	(Conj) then (later than expected)
开始	kāishǐ	(V) begin
仔 xì	zǐxì	(SV) be careful, be detailed
-地	-de	(P) (marks the manner in which a single instance of an action is carried out)
ADV 地 V	ADV de V	(Pat) (indicates single instance manner of an action)
发烧	fā shāo	(VO) have fever
不用	búyòng	(Aux) need not, not have to
以后	yǐhòu	(TW) afterward
......以前	...yǐqián	(Pat) before...
第-	dì-	(Pre) (indicates numerical order)
-天	-tiān	(TD) day(s)
好多了	hǎo duō le	(Ex) feel much better
手机	shǒujī	(N) cell phone

COMPREHENSION QUESTIONS

1. Read the text of this chapter and answer the following questions.

a. 我为什么最不喜欢去看医生？

b. 为什么我今天上午去看医生了？

c. 我哪儿不舒服？

d. 医院在哪儿？

e. 医生对我怎么说?

_____

f. <u>老白</u>不在家, 我怎么找他?

_____

2. Act out 我 and 我太太 in pairs.

3. In groups, draw a map of where the hospital is located.

4. In groups, make a list of 高医生's advice.

_____

_____

_____

_____

_____

5. In pairs, write a telephone conversation with <u>老白</u>, 问他怎么了. Then write
   the dialogue down, using as many Chinese characters as possible.

老白: _____

我: _____

老白: _____

我: _____

老白: _____

我: _____

老白: _____

我: _____

WRITING HELP

INDEPENDENT CHARACTERS

Character	Basic meaning	No. of strokes	Stroke order	Radical	Components	Structure
久 jiǔ	long time	3	ノ ク 久	ノ	ノ 入	☐
才 cái	then	3	一 十 才	一	才	☐

COMPOUND CHARACTERS

The following are the new compound characters with learned radicals in this chapter: 花, 钱, 药, 今, 院, 昨, 练, 时, 候, 肚, 常, 坏, 杯, 休, 息, 挤, 等, 始, 发, 烧, 第.

Char-acter	Basic meaning	No. of strokes	Stroke order	Radical	Meaning clue	Phonetic clue	Compo-nents	Struc-ture
花 huā	flower, to spend	7	艹 艻 花	艹	艹	化 huà	艹 化	
钱 (錢) qián	money, surname	10	𨥉 𨥉 钅 钱 钱 钱	钅	戋 (indi-cating "ian")		钅 戋	
药 (藥) yào	medi-cine	9	艹 芗 药	艹	艹	约 yuē	艹 纟 勺	
今 jīn	today	4	今	人			亼 丁	
院 yuàn	court-yard	9	阝 阣 陀 院	阝		元 yuán	阝 完	
*昨 zuó	yester-day	9	日 昨	日	日	乍 zhà	日 乍	
练 (練) liàn	to prac-tice	8	纟 纟 纩 绕 练 练	纟			纟 东	
时 (時) shí	time	7	日 时	日	日, 寸 (cùn, inch)		日 寸	
*候 hòu	to wait for	10	亻 个 伫 候	亻			亻 丨 工 矢	
*肚 dù	stomach	7	月 肚	月	月	土 tǔ	月 土	
常 cháng	often, surname	11	丨 丷 𢗳 𢆉 常	巾			𢆉 口 巾	

Char-acter	Basic meaning	No. of strokes	Stroke order	Radical	Meaning clue	Phonetic clue	Compo-nents	Struc-ture
坏 (壞) huài	bad	7	土 坏	土	土 (tǔ, soil)		土 不	
*杯 bēi	cup	8	木 杯	木	木		木 不	
*休 xiū	to rest	6	亻 休	亻	人,木 (a person leaning on a tree to rest)		人 木	
*息 xī	to rest	10	自 息	心	自, 心 (to concentrate your heart on yourself)		自 心	
挤 (擠) jǐ	crowded	9	扌 扩 挤 挤	扌	扌	齐 qí	扌 齐	
等 děng	to wait	12	竹 竺 等	竹			竹 土 寸	
*始 shǐ	begin-ning	8	女 如 始	女	女		女 厶 口	
发 (發) fā	to emit	5	丿 𠄌 发 𡴂 发	又			发	
烧 (燒) shāo	to cook	10	火 灯 灶 炒 烌 烧	火	火	尧 yáo	火 戈 兀	
*第 dì	order, grade	11	竹 第	竹			弟	竹 弟

杯: Neither a glass nor a cup is made of wood.
等: Waiting under the bamboo shade in front of a temple.

RADICALS

The new radicals introduced in this chapter are 匚, 疒, 大, and 乙.

1. 匚

This is used in compound characters as the left 3/4 enclosure. The compound character in this chapter that contains this radical is 医.

Character	Basic meaning	No. of strokes	Stroke order	Meaning clue	Phonetic clue	Components	Structure
*医 (醫) yī	medicine (profession)	7	一 匸 匸 匡 医 医			匚 矢	

2. 疒

This radical is used as the left-top semi-enclosure in the compound characters to indicate a meaning related to illness or disease. The compound characters in this chapter that contain this radical are 病 and 疼.

Character	Basic meaning	No. of strokes	Stroke order	Meaning clue	Phonetic clue	Components	Structure
病 bìng	ill, illness	10	丶 一 广 广 疒 疒 疒 病 病 病	疒	丙 bǐng	疒 丙	
疼 téng	painful	10	疒 疒 疼	疒	冬 dōng	疒 冬	

3. 大

This was originally introduced in Chapter 4 as an independent character meaning "big, large". The compound character in this chapter where this functions as a radical is 头.

Character	Basic meaning	No. of strokes	Stroke order	Meaning clue	Phonetic clue	Components	Structure
头 (頭) tóu	head	5	丶 丷 头	大		丷 大	

4. 乙

This is used in a handful of compound characters and sits on the right. The compound character in this chapter that contains this radical is 习.

Character	Basic meaning	No. of strokes	Stroke order	Meaning clue	Phonetic clue	Components	Structure
*习 (習) xí	to study	3	乛 乛 习			*习 (習) xí	☐

EXERCISES

CHARACTER EXERCISES

1. Find the independent characters you have learned hidden in the following characters.

头 _____ 　　　　晚 _____

常 _____ 　　　　杯 _____

2. Write in the brackets the component that is common to all of the following characters.

花, 北, 老, 呢 → (　　　)　　　公, 始, 到, 去 → (　　　)

肚, 教, 考, 坏 → (　　　)　　　药, 练, 经 → (　　　)

等, 过, 时, 得 → (　　　)

3. Form new characters by using different components of the following characters, e.g. 工 (from 功) + ナ (from 有) → 左.

钱　住　始　很　学　定

_____ (from _____) + _____ (from _____) → _____

_____ (from _____) + _____ (from _____) → _____

_____ (from _____) + _____ (from _____) → _____

_____ (from _____) + _____ (from _____) → _____

_____ (from _____) + _____ (from _____) → _____

4. Add a different part to 阝 to form as many characters as you can.

_____

5. Add a different part to 火 to form as many characters as you can.

_____

6. Circle the wrong character in each sentence and correct it in the brackets.

a. 我令天上午去医院看医生了。   (   )

b. 医生说我没发烧, 多体息就好。   (   )

c. 昨天我吃了晚饭以后就 jué 得不书服了。 (   )

d. 我吃了药, 弟二天肚子就不疼了。   (   )

e. - 你想喝冰水还是可乐?

   - 给我一坏冰水吧。   (   )

f. 白京以常常来我家练刁汉语。   (   )

7. Solve the character riddle.

有它(tā, "it") 就卖, 没它(tā, "it")就买: _____

VOCABULARY EXERCISES

1. Write two different characters next to the Pinyin in each group of homonyms, then form a word or phrase with each character.

a. { zài: _____
    { zài: _____

b. { yī: _____
    { yī: _____

c. { yào: _____
    { yào: _____

d. { míng: _____
    { míng: _____

2. Use each of the following characters to form as many words as possible.

a. 天 → _____

b. 看 → _____

c. 午 → _____

d. 车 → _____

3. Find the word that is not in the same category as the other three words and write it in the brackets.

a. 医院, 银行, 坐车, 图书馆　　（　　　　）

b. 医生, 老师, 学生, 机会　　（　　　　）

c. 有名, 发烧, 看病, 吃药　　（　　　　）

d. 昨天, 春天, 今天, 明天　　（　　　　）

e. 舒服, 仔 xì, 安 jìng, 然后　　（　　　　）

4. Link a character in the left column with a character in the right column to form a verb-object collocation and write down the collocation in the bracket. An example is already given.

炒	作业	(炒饭)
打	车	(　　　　)
看	钱	(　　　　)
下	药	(　　　　)
花	手机	(　　　　)
吃	医生	(　　　　)
做	饭	(　　　　)

STRUCTURE EXERCISES

1. Correct any error you find in each of the following sentences.

a. 我正在看了一本英文书。

→ _____

b. 他一个早上开车了。

→ _____

c. 他还不在吃午饭呢。

→ _____

d. 我吃饭了就去看你。

→ _____

e. 他们先到了学校, 才去银行。

→ _____

f. 他昨天就去北京呢。

→ _____

2. Insert the word in brackets in the correct position in the sentence.

a. 我不会汉语, 你用英文说我明白。(才)

_____

b. 我去中国就已经学了三年汉语了。(以前)

_____

c. 英国朋友来了, 我们就都说英文了。(以后)

_____

d. 妈妈对小明说: "你做了作业可以去看电 shì。"(就)

_____

e. 她去商 diàn 买了衣 fu 回家做饭。(先……然后……)

_____

3. Rearrange the elements of each of the entries to make a grammatical sentence.

a. 他, 十点, 开始, 到, 一直, 五点, 做, 做饭, 从

→ _____

b. 病, 在, 挤, 很多, 医院, 看, 很, 人, 等着

→ _____

c. 好多了, 我, 休息, 不过, 吃坏了, 昨天, 一天, 就

→ _____

d. 不, 怎么了, 哪儿, 今天, 不, jué 得, 知道, 他, 舒服, 都

→ _____

4. Translate the following sentences into Chinese, using Chinese characters for learned words.

a. Last autumn when I was in Nanjing, I ate a lot of Nanjing snacks.

_____

b. He likes to have a cup of coffee before breakfast.

_____

c. You can call me by mobile phone any time before 9:30 PM.

_____

d. After you get off at Beijing Street, then walk a little bit, and then you will reach my home.

_____

e. Fellow students are reading books and doing assignments quietly in the library.

_____

SUPPLEMENTARY READING

READING 1

打车

开 chū 租汽车的:　你好! 你去哪儿?

打车的:　　　　北京医院。

开 chū 租汽车的:　行, 上车吧!

打车的:　　　　谢谢。

开 chū 租汽车的:　Dào 了。十二块。

打车的:　　　　给你二十块。

开 chū 租汽车的:　你有两块钱吗? 我给你十块。

打车的:　　　　对不 qǐ, 我没有两块钱。

开 chū 租汽车的:　没事儿, 我找你八块。

打车的:　　　　谢谢。

Comprehension questions

1. 从上车的地方到<u>北京医院</u>打车要多 shao 钱?

_____

2. 打车的给开 chū 租汽车的多 shao 钱?

_____

READING 2

xǐ 欢喝酒的商人

有的人很 xǐ 欢喝酒, 也很会喝酒。他们喝 pí 酒, 也喝白酒。五六个人就 néng 喝四五十 píng pí 酒。很多人都说, 要是想 gēn 会喝酒人的做生意, 就得先学喝酒。Gēn 他们做生意, 他们请你喝酒, 你一定要喝。要是你不喝, 他们心里会想你不是真心想 gēn 他们做生意。

Comprehension questions

1. 要是想 gēn 会喝酒人的做生意, 就得先学什么?

_____

2. 要是你不喝, 他们会 gēn 你做生意吗?

_____

CHARACTER PRACTICE

久	久								
才	才								
花	花								
钱	钱								
药	药								
今	今								
院	院								
昨	昨								
练	练								
习	习								

时	时								
候	候								
头	头								
肚	肚								
常	常								
坏	坏								
杯	杯								
休	休								
息	息								
挤	挤								
等	等								
始	始								
发	发								
烧	烧								

第	第								
医	医								
然	然								
病	病								
疼	疼								

14

第十四课

TEXT

前天是星期六, 早上九点左右, <u>方美春</u>还没起床呢, 她的男朋友<u>海明</u>就给她打电话, <u>海明</u>说想请她去市中心看电 yǐng。他说他十点在市中心大商场的书店门口等她。从<u>方美春</u>住的地方去市中心的那个大商场差不多要一个钟头, 要是人多车挤的话, 就要一个多钟头。<u>方美春</u>起床以后, 没吃早饭就 chū 门了。

她先坐公 jiāo 车去市中心, 然后走 lù 去商场。下车的时候已经十点差五分了。她想: "哎呀, 我晚了, <u>海明</u>一定已经在商场门口等我了, 我得走得快一点儿。" 从车 zhàn 到商场, <u>美春</u>平常要走一刻钟, 那天她走得很快, 十点过五分她就到了。<u>海明</u>已经在那儿等了半天了, 他九点三刻就来了。

<u>海明</u>问<u>美春</u>想去哪儿, <u>美春</u>说: "看电 yǐng 以前, 我们先去 guàngguang 街吧。快冬天了, 我想买一条冬天 chuān 的裙子。" <u>海明</u>说: "好。" 商场里有很多好看的衣服, 有好多裙子, 什么颜 sè 的都有, 有红的、粉红的、灰的、黄的、浅蓝的、白的、深绿的。<u>海明</u>问<u>美春</u> xǐ 欢什么颜 sè 的, <u>美春</u>说: "这么多

颜 sè, 我不知道我 xǐ 欢什么了。" 海明说: "那你就一条一条 chuānchuan 吧,
看看你 chuān 哪一条最好看。" 美春 chuān 了好几条, 花了一个多钟头, 一条
也不 xǐ 欢。有的不好看, 有的太 guì。她说: "我饿了, 我没吃早饭, 现在快中午
了, 咱们去那个有名的韩国饭馆儿吃顿午饭吧。午饭以后去别的商场看看。"
海明说: "你一个人去吧, 我在前面的咖啡馆儿看书, 你买了裙子来找我。"

美春去了三家商店, 都没有她 xǐ 欢的裙子。她去咖啡馆儿找海明。海明
正喝着咖啡在看书, 他看书看得很快, 已经看了几十页了。他真不懂, 买一条
裙子怎么这么难。美春别的事都做得很快, 就是买东西 tè 别慢。

美春说: "我累了, 咱们回家吧。明天再来。" 海明不高兴地说: "我明天不
来了, 我要准备下星期的考试。我们今天 chū 门不是来买东西的, 也不是来
看书的, 而是来看电 yǐng 的。你要是不买裙子, 咱们今天就可以去看电 yǐng
了。你 jiāng 来买东西别找我, 还是找别人一块儿去吧。"

生词 NEW WORDS

前天	qiántiān	(TW) the day before yesterday
左右	zuǒyòu	(Adv) about, more or less
起床	qǐ chuáng	(VO) get out of bed, get up
男-	nán-	(Pre) male (human)
里	lǐ	(PS/PW) inside
市中心	shìzhōngxīn	(PW) city center, downtown
商场	shāngchǎng	(PW) market, bazaar
书店	shūdiàn	(PW) bookshop
钟头	zhōngtóu	(N) hour
要是 (的话) ……就	yàoshi (de huà)…jiù	(Pat) if…then
chū 门	chū mén	(VO) go out, leave home (for a bit)
差	chà	(V) lacking, less than
得	de	(P) (marks the manner or extent of an action)
(VO)V 得……	(VO)V de…	(Pat) (indicates customary manner or the extent of an action)
快	kuài	(SV) be fast, be quick
平常	píngcháng	(Adv) usually
过	guò	(V) surpassing, more than, pass by
半天	bàntiān	(TD) for a long time
guàng 街	guàng jiē	(VO) go window-shopping, stroll around the streets

冬天	dōngtiān	(TW) winter
裙子	qúnzi	(N) dress, skirt (Cl -条)
衣服	yīfu	(N) clothing (Cl -件)
好	hǎo	(Adv) quite, very
颜 sè	yánsè	(N) color
红	hóng	(SV) be red
粉红	fěnhóng	(SV) be pink
灰	huī	(SV) be gray
黄	huáng	(SV) be yellow
浅	qiǎn	(SV) be shallow, be light
蓝	lán	(SV) be blue
白	bái	(SV) be white
深	shēn	(SV) be deep, be dark, be profound
绿	lǜ	(SV) be green
那	nà	(Conj) in that case
看	kàn	(V) consider, be of the opinion
中午	zhōngwǔ	(TW) noon
咱们	zánmen	(Pr) we, us (inclusive of listener)
韩国	Hánguó	(PW) Korea
-顿	-dùn	(Cl) used with 饭 to mean "meal"
别的	biéde	(N) other
咖啡馆儿	kāfēiguǎnr	(PW) café
商店	shāngdiàn	(PW) shop, store (Cl -家)
在	zài	(Adv) be…ing
-页	-yè	(Cl) page
懂	dǒng	(V) understand
难	nán	(SV) be difficult
事	shì	(N) matter, affair
tè 别	tèbié	(SV) be special
慢	màn	(SV) be slow
累	lèi	(SV) be physically drained, be tired
准备	zhǔnbèi	(V) prepare
下星期	xiàxīngqī	(TW) next week
不是……(而)是	búshì…(ér)shì	(Pat) it's not…but rather
jiāng 来	jiānglái	(TW) in the future, future
还是	háishì	(Adv) still (best to…)
别人	bié.rén	(N) other people

COMPREHENSION QUESTIONS

1. Read the text of this chapter and then complete the following timetable according to the context.

Time 时间	Person 人	Action 做什么
9:00 AM		
9:45 AM		
9:55 AM		
10:05 AM		

2. Indicate if the following statements are true or false according to the text.

a. (   ) 美春想买一条裙子。

b. (   ) 海明知道美春 xǐ欢什么颜 sè。

c. (   ) 美春不 xǐ欢她 chuān 的那几条裙子。

d. (   ) 美春 xǐ欢吃日本菜。

e. (   ) 他们一块去咖啡馆儿喝茶。

f. (   ) 海明要买一本书。

g. (   ) 海明看书看得很慢。

h. (   ) 美春什么事都做得很快, 买东西也很快。

i. (   ) 海明明天没有事。

j. (   ) 海明今天很想跟美春一块儿去看电yǐng。

k. (   ) 因为美春买东西买得太慢, 海明 jiāng 来不要跟她去买东西了。

WRITING HELP

INDEPENDENT CHARACTERS

Character	Basic meaning	No. of strokes	Stroke order	Radical	Components	Structure
平 píng	flat	5	一 ㇀ 一 平 平	一	干丷	☐
*页 (頁) yè	page	6	页	页	页	☐
而 ér	but	6	一 丆 丙 而 而	一	而	☐

COMPOUND CHARACTERS

The followings are the new compound characters with learned radicals in this chapter: 场, 红, 灰, 浅, 咱, 难, 黄, 深, 绿, 韩, 裙, 蓝, 慢, 懂, 准, and 市.

Character	Basic meaning	No. of strokes	Stroke order	Radical	Meaning clue	Phonetic clue	Components	Structure
场 (場) chǎng	site, gathering place	6	土 场	土	土	昜 (indicating *ang*)	土昜	☐
红 (紅) hóng	red	6	纟 红	纟	纟	工 gōng	纟工	☐
灰 huī	gray	6	𠂇 𠂇 灰 灰	火	𠂇 (cover), 火		𠂇火	☐
浅 (淺) qiǎn	shallow	8	氵 氵 氵 浅 浅 浅	氵	氵	戋 (indicating *ian*)	氵戋	☐
咱 zán	I, me	9	口 咱	口			口自	☐
难 (難) nán	difficult	10	又 刈 𣥂 𣥂 难 难 难	又			又隹	☐

Char-acter	Basic meaning	No. of strokes	Stroke order	Radical	Meaning clue	Phonetic clue	Compo-nents	Struc-ture
黄 huáng	yellow, surname	11	卄 艹 꿨 昔 昔 莆 莆 黄	卄	卄		卄一由八	
深 shēn	deep	11	氵 氵 沪 沪 深	氵	氵	罙 (in-dicating en)	氵宀八木	
绿 (綠) lǜ	green	11	纟 纟 纟 纟 纤 纤 绿 绿 绿	纟		录 lù	纟录	
*韩 (韓) hán	Korea	12	一 十 六 古 古 吉 直 卓 卓 车 车 韩	十			十日十韦	
*裙 qún	skirt	12	礻 礻 衤 衤 衣 裙	衤	衤	君 jūn	衤尹口	
蓝 (藍) lán	blue	13	艹 艹 莁 莁 芐 萨 蔝 蓝	卄	卄	监 (in-dicating ian)	卄监	
慢 màn	slow	14	忄 忄 愠 慢	忄	忄	曼 màn	忄日四又	
懂 dǒng	to un-derstand	15	忄 忄 忄 忄 憧 懂	忄	忄	董 dǒng	忄艹重 (千里)	
准 zhǔn	allow, grant, permit	10	冫 隹	冫			冫隹	
*市 shì	market, city	5	亠 市	亠	亠		亠巾	

*监: Though this character is pronounced as *jiān* when it functions as an indepen-dent character, as a phonetic component it often indicates the *ian* sound.

RADICALS

The new radicals introduced in this chapter are 夂, 广, 田, 米, 页, and 走.

1. 夂

夂 *zhǐ* is a radical meaning "to retreat". The compound character in this chapter that contains this radical is 冬.

Character	Basic meaning	No. of strokes	Stroke order	Meaning clue	Phonetic clue	Components	Structure
*冬 dōng	winter	5	夂 冬			夂 丶丶	⊟

2. 广

广 *guǎng* as a character means "extensive". As a radical, it is used as the left half enclosure in a compound character. The compound characters in this chapter that contain this radical are 床 and 店.

Character	Basic meaning	No. of strokes	Stroke order	Meaning clue	Phonetic clue	Components	Structure
床 chuáng	bed	7	丶 亠 广 床	木		广 木	⊏
店 diàn	shop	8	广 庐 店		占 (zhàn, to occupy)	广 占	⊏

店: Think of a shop as occupying an enclosed space.

3. 田

田 *tián* as a character means "field". As a radical, it indicates field or hard work. The compound characters in this chapter that contain this radical are 男, 备, and 累.

Character	Basic meaning	No. of strokes	Stroke order	Meaning clue	Phonetic clue	Components	Structure
*男 nán	male	7	丿 口 曰 田 田 男	田, 力 (lì, strength)		田 力	⊟
备 (備) bèi	ready	8	夂 备			夂 田	⊟
累 lèi	tired	11	田 罒 罗 累 累	田, 糸 (silk)		田 糸	⊟

累: It is tiring work to raise silkworms in a field.

4. 米

This character can also be used as a radical in compound characters related to rice or things made of rice. The compound character in this chapter that contains this radical is 粉.

Character	Basic meaning	No. of strokes	Stroke order	Meaning clue	Phonetic clue	Components	Structure
粉 fěn	(rice) powder	10	米 粉	米	分	米分	▯▯

5. 页

This can also be used as a radical in compound characters. The compound characters in this chapter that contain this radical are 顿 and 颜.

Character	Basic meaning	No. of strokes	Stroke order	Meaning clue	Phonetic clue	Components	Structure
*顿 (頓) dùn	(classifier)	10	一 亡 屯 屯 顿		屯 tún	屯页	▯▯
*颜 (顏) yán	color	15	亠 产 产 颜		彦 yàn	彦页	▯▯

6. 走

This character can also be used as a radical in the compound characters indicating movement. The compound character that contains this radical is 起.

Character	Basic meaning	No. of strokes	Stroke order	Meaning clue	Phonetic clue	Components	Structure
起 qǐ	to get up	10	士 走 起 起 起	走	己 jǐ	走己	⌐_

EXERCISES

CHARACTER EXERCISES

1. **Find the independent characters you have learned hidden in the following characters.**

红 _____   慢 _____   粉 _____

顿 _____   灰 _____   店 _____

2. Add no more than two strokes to each of the following to form new characters.

贝 _____　　　巾 _____　　　干 _____　　　田 _____

佳 _____　　　亥 _____　　　木 _____　　　未 _____

3. Add a radical to each of the following to make different characters.

? + 也, 不, 匆 → (　　), (　　), (　　)

? + 土, 月, 反 → (　　), (　　), (　　)

? + 罙, 戈, 每, 气 → (　　), (　　), (　　), (　　)

? + 中, 艮, 戈, 昔 → (　　), (　　), (　　), (　　)

? + 君, 末, 寸, 乡 → (　　), (　　), (　　), (　　)

4. Form new characters by using different components of the following characters, e.g. 工 (from 功) + 𠂇 (from 有) → 左.

法　钱　息　场　点　床　备

_____ (from _____) + _____ (from _____) → _____

_____ (from _____) + _____ (from _____) → _____

_____ (from _____) + _____ (from _____) → _____

_____ (from _____) + _____ (from _____) → _____

_____ (from _____) + _____ (from _____) → _____

5. Circle the wrong character in each sentence and correct it in the brackets.

a. 我姐姐最 xǐ欢 chuān 篮 sè 和绿 sè 的裙子了。　　　　　　　　(　　　)

b. 他准备汉语考试准备了很久, 已经一个月没休息了。　　　(　　　)

c. 错了, 我想买的不是钱灰 sè 的外衣, 而是深灰色的。　　　(　　　)

d. 他中文学得不好, suǒ以作业做得 tè 别慢。　　　　　　　　(　　　)

e. 商场里有个不错的<u>韩国</u>咖啡馆。　　　　　　　　　　　　(　　　)

VOCABULARY EXERCISES

1. Write two different characters next to the Pinyin in each group of homonyms, then form a word or phrase with each character.

a.
   zuò (   ) _____
   zuò (   ) _____

b.
   wèi (   ) _____
   wèi (   ) _____

c.
   nán (   ) _____
   nán (   ) _____

2. Write the Pinyin for the following characters, then form a word with each character.

a. 而 (   ) _____

b. 面 (   ) _____

c. 慢 (   ) _____

3. Link a character in the left column with a character in the right column to form a verb-object collocation and write down the collocation in the bracket. An example is already given.

看	男朋友	(看病)
等	考试	( )
chū	街	( )
起	法文	( )
准备	床	( )
懂	门	( )
chuān	病	( )
guàng	裙子	( )

4. **Find the word that is not in the same category as the other three words and write it in the brackets.**

a. 粉, 白, 黄, 深   (   )

b. 冬天, 秋天, 半天, 春天   (   )

c. jiāng 来, 而是, 以前, 现在 (   )

d. 他, 咱们, 她们, 我们   (   )

e. 书店, 商场, 钟头, 咖啡馆   (   )

STRUCTURE EXERCISES

1. **Write the correct classifier character to complete each of the following phrases.**

一＿＿＿＿＿裙子   两＿＿＿＿＿饭   几十＿＿＿＿＿ (page) 书

那＿＿＿＿＿商店   一＿＿＿＿＿水   四＿＿＿＿＿衣服

2. **Complete the following sentences using the (VO)V-*de* pattern.**

a. 他说英文＿＿＿＿＿＿＿＿＿＿, 我不懂。

b. 法国菜, 他＿＿＿＿＿＿最＿＿＿＿＿＿, 我们都 xǐ 欢吃。

c. 小方很用功, 他说汉语＿＿＿＿＿＿＿＿＿＿。

d. 老王开车＿＿＿＿＿＿＿＿＿＿, 所以我们都不坐他的车。

3. **Choose the appropriate character from the characters given immediately below and fill in the brackets. Some characters may be used more than once.**

得   的   地

a. 他常常用功(   )忘了吃饭。

b. 要是下星期考试(   )话, 我星期六就不去 guàng 街了。

c. 她 xǐ 欢蓝 sè, suǒ 以她买(   )衣服都是蓝 sè (   )。

d. 医生给我 zǐ 细(   )看了病, 叫我以后喝酒别喝(   )太多。

e. 他说中文说(   )很地道, 地道(   )别人 yǐwéi 他是中国人。

f. 星期六的下午, 他在家里舒服(   )坐着, 喝着咖啡。

g. 他太累了, 回家(   )时候, 他走(   ) tè 别慢。

4. Translate the following sentences into Chinese, using Chinese characters for learned words.

a. If she had bought a skirt in the first store, she wouldn't have gone to other stores.

_____

b. Would it look good to wear a gray shirt together with blue denim jeans?

_____

c. If you can have some rest at home, then you don't need to take medicine.

_____

d. It is not that _Meichun_ doesn't like eating beef, but that the beef cooked by her mother is really not delicious.

_____

e. You need to prepare for a long time (when you) make a delicious supper, from buying food to cooking the food.

_____

SUPPLEMENTARY READING

READING 1

老板:　　怎么 yàng? 这衬衫行吗?

万小冬:　有点儿大。有小一点儿的吗?

老板:　　这件是中号的, 行吗?

万小冬:　我不 xǐ 欢黄色, 有别的颜 sè 的吗?

老板:　　还有浅蓝 sè 的。

万小冬:　给我看看。

老板:　　你看看。不错吧!

万小冬:　多少钱?

老板:　　六百五十块。

万小冬:　这么 guì! 便宜一点儿, 行吗? 五百块。

老板:　　不行, 最 shǎo 六百块。

万小冬:　好吧, 好吧, 给你六百块。

Comprehension questions

1. 万小冬要买什么?

2. 万小冬花了多少钱买了那件浅蓝 sè 的衬衫?

READING 2

这是学文给美春 xiě 的一 fēng 电子 yóu 件[1]。

美春:

　　下星期六是我的生日, 我想请你到北京饭馆吃晚饭。北京饭馆在城里, 你可以先坐火车到城里, 然后走 lù 去饭馆儿。火车 zhàn 对面是图书馆, 从图书馆那儿一直往前走, 到了银行那儿往左拐, 再往前走两条街, 北京饭馆就在 xié 店和牛仔 kù 店的中 jiān。你也可以打的去北京饭馆。打的很舒服, 也很方便, 可是很 guì。

　　我也请了王小兰。小兰 gāng 从英国回来, 我想你一定很想 gēn 她 liáo 天。除了小兰以外, 我还请了白京以和志明。白京以还是 xǐ 欢 qí 自行车, 他说从他家 qí 车到北京饭馆只要半个小时。对了, 志明是你的 línjū, 你 gēn 他一块儿来吧。

学文

8月21日

　　美春看了信就给志明打电话, 她问志明去不去。志明说: "当然去。可是我最不 xǐ 欢坐火车。我们坐 chū 租汽车去吧!"她说: "好呀!"

---

1. 电子 yóu 件 "email"

Comprehension questions

1. <u>学文</u>为什么请客? <u>学文</u>请了几个人? 他们是谁?

_____

2. Identify the location of the 北京饭馆 on the map below based on the information given in the above passage. Circle the correct answer.

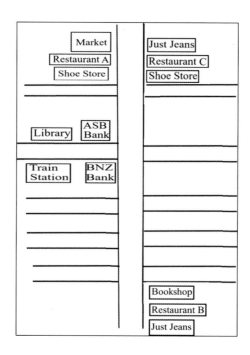

<u>北京饭馆</u>在哪儿?

a. Restaurant A   b. Restaurant B   c. Restaurant C

CHARACTER PRACTICE

平	平							
页	页							
而	而							
冬	冬							
场	场							
红	红							
灰	灰							
浅	浅							
咱	咱							
难	难							
黄	黄							
深	深							
绿	绿							

韩	韩								
蓝	蓝								
楼	楼								
慢	慢								
懂	懂								
床	床								
店	店								
男	男								
备	备								
累	累								
粉	粉								
顿	顿								
颜	颜								

准	准								
市	市								
起	起								

15

第十五课

TEXT

　　钱希平在城东住了七年了，后天要搬家了，因为从今年开始他在一个新的学校教书，这个学校在城南，从城东到城南开汽车要开一个半钟头。他们那儿夏天很热，冬天很冷，还常常下雪，春天不是刮风，就是下雨，出门很不方便。Měi 天来回的车票也要七八块钱，不便宜。钱希平的太太说，他们一定要搬去城南住。

　　钱希平的新家在城南一个公寓楼里，他们的公寓在三楼。新房子很大，有四个 wòshì、一个书房、一个客厅、一个饭厅，还有一个很大的厨房和两个厕所。公寓楼里有电梯，可是他们一家平常都不会去用，他家就在三楼，不必用电梯，用楼梯走上楼走下楼就可以了。城南的房子真是 guì，买这房子花了钱希平五十六万块钱。

　　要搬新家了，钱希平还要买好些家具。他的父母、哥哥、姐姐都想，他买了房子也许没钱了，所以大家要买几件家具送给他。下个月是钱希平 40 岁的生日，新的家具是送他的生日 lǐwù。家具都很好看，钱希平最 xǐ 欢的是他姐姐送的饭桌，是日本做的。

住进新家以后，钱希平上班下班都不用坐车了。孩子们上学，太太 guàng 街买东西也很方便。后边儿就是城里最高的<u>南山</u>，星期六、星期天还可以 dài 孩子们去爬山，孩子们都爱爬山。他早上不用很早起来，下午下班后，走 lù 一刻钟就可以到家了! 他太太做晚饭的时候，<u>钱希平</u>还可以 gēn 孩子们玩儿，huò 者休息休息。他晚上可以这么早回家，一家人都很高兴。

生词 NEW WORDS

钱希平	Qián Xīpíng	(N) a personal name
城东	chéngdōng	(PW) the east of a small city or town
后天	hòutiān	(TW) the day after tomorrow
要……了	yào…le	(Pat) about to…
搬家	bān jiā	(VO) move house, relocate
今年	jīnnián	(TW) this year
新	xīn	(SV) be new
学校	xuéxiào	(PW) school
南	nán	(PS) the south
城南	chéngnán	(PW) the south of a small city or town
汽车	qìchē	(N) automobile
夏天	xiàtiān	(TW) summer
热	rè	(SV) be hot
冷	lěng	(SV) be cold
下雪	xià xuě	(VO) snow
不是……就 是……	búshì…jiùshì…	(Pat) if not…then it's…
刮风	guā fēng	(VO) have wind gusts
下雨	xià yǔ	(VO) rain
车票	chēpiào	(N) bus ticket (Cl -zhāng 张)
搬	bān	(V) move (some large object)
公寓楼	gōngyù lóu	(PW) apartment building
公寓	gōngyù	(PW) apartment
-楼	-lóu	(Cl) floor
房子	fángzi	(N) house
书房	shūfáng	(PW) den, (private) library
客厅	kètīng	(PW) living room
饭厅	fàntīng	(PW) dining room
厨房	chúfáng	(PW) kitchen
厕所	cèsuǒ	(PW) toilet

电梯	diàntī	(N) elevator
楼梯	lóutī	(N) stairs
上	shàng	(V) go or come up
下	xià	(V) go or come down
是	shì	(Pat) (used to emphasize the doer, time or place of an action)
家具	jiājù	(N) furniture (Cl -件)
好看	hǎokàn	(SV) good-looking, have an interesting story
也许	yěxǔ	(Adv) perhaps
大家	dàjiā	(N) everyone
好些	hǎoxiē	(Q) several, many
所以……	suǒyǐ…	(Pat) therefore…
下个月	xiàgeyuè	(TW) next month
-岁	-suì	(Cl) age
饭桌/cān 桌	fànzhuō/cānzhuō	(N) dining table
是……的	shì…de	(Pat) (used to emphasize the doer, time or place of an action)
进	jìn	(V) enter
上班	shàng bān	(VO) go to work
下班	xià bān	(VO) finish work
上学	shàng xué	(VO) go to school
山	shān	(N) hill, mountain
爬山	pá shān	(VO) climb a mountain
爱	ài	(V) love
早	zǎo	(SV) be early
起来	qǐlai	(V) rise (up), get up
玩(儿)	wán(r)	(V) have fun, have a good time, enjoy oneself
huò 者	huòzhě	(Conj) or (in a statement)

COMPREHENSION QUESTIONS

1. **Read the text of this chapter and answer the following questions.**

a. 钱希平为什么要搬家?

b. 他的新家在哪儿? 说说他的新家。

_____

c. 谁送东西给<u>钱希平</u>? 送了些什么?

_____

d. <u>钱希平</u>最 xǐ 欢的是什么?

_____

e. 搬进新家后, <u>钱希平</u>的太太做晚饭的时候, 他做什么?

_____

WRITING HELP

INDEPENDENT CHARACTERS

Character	Basic meaning	No. of strokes	Stroke order	Radical	Components	Structure
山 shān	mountain	3	丨 山 山	山	山	☐
风 (風) fēng	wind	4	丿 几 凤 风	风	几乂	☐
雨 yǔ	rain	8	一 厂 币 雨 雨 雨 雨	雨	雨	☐

COMPOUND CHARACTERS

The following are the new compound characters with learned radicals in this chapter: 夏, 许, 冷, 进, 刮, 具, 者, 校, 热, 桌, 班, 梯, 寓, 搬, 希, 楼, and 玩.

Character	Basic meaning	No. of strokes	Stroke order	Radical	Meaning clue	Phonetic clue	Components	Structure
*夏 xià	summer	10	百 夏	夂			丆目夂	☰
许 (許) xǔ	to permit	6	讠 许	讠	讠	午	讠午	▯▯

Char-acter	Basic meaning	No. of strokes	Stroke order	Radical	Meaning clue	Phonetic clue	Compo-nents	Struc-ture
冷 lěng	cold	7	冫 冷 冷	冫	冫	令 lìng	冫 令	
进 (進) jìn	to enter	7	一 二 丰 井 进	辶	辶	井 jǐng	辶 井	
刮 guā	to scrape	8	千 舌 刮	刂	刂		舌 刂	
*具 jù	tool	8	具	八			目 廾	
*者 zhě	this	8	者	日			耂 日	
*校 xiào	school	10	木 杧 校	木	木	交 jiāo	木 亠 父	
热 (熱) rè	hot	10	扌 执 执 执 热 热 热	灬	灬		扌 丸 灬	
*桌 zhuō	table	10	丶 卜 卣 桌	木	木	卓 zhuó	卜 日 木	
班 bān	class, team	10	王 王 玡 班	王			王 刂 王	
*梯 tī	ladder	11	木 梯	木	木	弟	木 弟	
*寓 yù	resi-dence	12	宀 宀 宀 宫 宫 宫 寓 寓 寓	宀	宀	禹 yù	宀 禺	
搬 bān	to move	13	扌 扩 扪 拘 拘 拘 搬	扌	扌	般 bān	扌 舟 殳	
*希 xī	to expect	7	丿 乂 ⺈ 产 产 希 希	巾			乂 布	
楼 (樓) lóu	build, floor	13	木 杧 杧 材 材 楼 楼	木	木	娄 lóu	木 米 女	
玩 wán	to play	8	王 玒 玩	王		元 yuán	王 元	

RADICALS

The new radicals introduced in this chapter are 厂, 山, 斤, 户, 爪, 西, and 雨.

1. 厂

厂 *chǎng* "factory" can be used as a character as well as a radical. As a radical, it is used as the left semi-enclosure in compound characters, indicating the cover. The compound characters in this chapter that contain this radical are 厅, 厕, and 厨.

Character	Basic meaning	No. of strokes	Stroke order	Meaning clue	Phonetic clue	Compo-nents	Structure
*厅 (廳) tīng	hall	4	一 厂 厅	厂	丁 dīng	厂 丁	
*厕 (廁) cè	toilet	8	厂 厕 厕	厂	则 zé	厂 贝 刂	
*厨 (廚) chú	kitchen	12	厂 厂 后 后 厇 厨	厂, 豆 (dòu, bean)		厂 豆 寸	

2. 山

This can also be used as a radical in compound characters indicating hills or mountains. The compound characters in this chapter that contain this radical are 出 and 岁.

Character	Basic meaning	No. of strokes	Stroke order	Meaning clue	Phonetic clue	Compo-nents	Structure
出 chū	to go out	5	ㄴ 屮 中 出 出	山,山		山 山	
*岁 (歲) suì	year, age	6	丨 屵 山 岁	山 (as old as a hill)		山 夕	

出: Primitive man lived in caves among the mountains. When he wanted to go out, he needed to get out of the mountain.

3. 斤

As a character (*jīn*), this is a Chinese unit of weight (≈ 0.5 kilogram). It means "axe" when it is used as a radical. The compound character in this chapter that contains this radical is 新.

Character	Basic meaning	No. of strokes	Stroke order	Meaning clue	Phonetic clue	Components	Structure
新 xīn	new	13	亠　亣　立　亲　新		亲 qīn	立 木 斤	

4. 户

As an independent character *hù* means "door" or "family". The compound characters in this chapter that contain this radical are 所 and 房.

Character	Basic meaning	No. of strokes	Stroke order	Meaning clue	Phonetic clue	Components	Structure
*所 suǒ	hall	8	厂　戶　所	户 (hù, house)		户 斤	
房 fáng	house, room	8	户　房	户 (hù, house)	方	户 方	

5. 爪

As a character, 爪 *zhuǎ* means "paw". As a radical it can either be written as 爪, in which case it is found to the left of the compound character, or it can be written as 爫, in which case it is found on the top of the compound character. The compound characters in this chapter that contain this radical are 爬 and 爱.

Character	Basic meaning	No. of strokes	Stroke order	Meaning clue	Phonetic clue	Components	Structure
爬 pá	to crawl	8	丿　厂　爪　爬	爪	巴 bā	爪 巴	
爱 (愛) ài	to love	10	丿　丷　丷　丷　爫　爱	友		爫 冖 友	

6. 西

This character can also be used as a radical in compound characters. The compound character in this chapter that contains this radical is 票.

Character	Basic meaning	No. of strokes	Stroke order	Meaning clue	Phonetic clue	Components	Structure
票 piào	ticket	11	西　覀　票	示 (shì, to show)		西 示	

7. 雨

雨 can also be used as a radical in compound characters indicating rain-related weather words. The compound character in this chapter that contains this radical is 雪.

Character	Basic meaning	No. of strokes	Stroke order	Meaning clue	Phonetic clue	Components	Structure
雪 xuě	snow	11	雫 雪 雪 雪	雨		雨 彐	⊟

EXERCISES

CHARACTER EXERCISES

1. **Find the independent characters you have learned hidden in the following characters.**

许 _____   冷 _____   爱 _____   班 _____

票 _____   楼 _____   房 _____   雪 _____

2. **Write in the brackets the component that is common to all of the following characters.**

搬, 爱, 难 → (   )   男, 备, 累 → (   )

师, 希, 常 → (   )   别, 厕, 刮 → (   )

楼, 姓, 要 → (   )   厅, 灯, 打 → (   )

厨, 得, 时 → (   )

3. **Form new characters by using different components of the following characters, e.g. 工 (from 功) + ナ (from 有) → 左.**

| 外　孩　梯　出　筷　许　刮 |

_____ (from _____) + _____ (from _____) → _____

_____ (from _____) + _____ (from _____) → _____

_____ (from _____) + _____ (from _____) → _____

_____ (from _____) + _____ (from _____) → _____

_____ (from _____) + _____ (from _____) → _____

4. Write two characters containing 氵, then form a word or a phrase with each character.

a. (　　　) _____

b. (　　　) _____

5. Write four characters that have the same structure as 厅 where the radical is a left-top semi-enclosure.

_____

6. Write as many characters as possible that are made up of two components resembling each other.

_____

7. Solve the character riddle.

有一半, 又有一半: _____

VOCABULARY EXERCISES

1. Combine a character from column A with one from column B, and then write the word in brackets. No character can be used more than one time.

A	B	
刮	山	(　　　　　　)
公	雨	(　　　　　　)
下	桌	(　　　　　　)
厕	班	(　　　　　　)
家	许	(　　　　　　)
爬	风	(　　　　　　)
搬	梯	(　　　　　　)
饭	家	(　　　　　　)
上	具	(　　　　　　)
也	所	(　　　　　　)
楼	寓	(　　　　　　)

2. How many words and phrases can you form with the following characters?

a. 公 → _____

b. 所 → _____

3. Write two different characters next to the Pinyin in the following set of homonyms, then form a word or phrase with each character.

a.
$\begin{cases} \text{ér (} \quad \text{)} \\ \text{ér (} \quad \text{)} \end{cases}$
   _____
   _____

b.
$\begin{cases} \text{bān (} \quad \text{)} \\ \text{bān (} \quad \text{)} \end{cases}$
   _____
   _____

c.
$\begin{cases} \text{xīn (} \quad \text{)} \\ \text{xīn (} \quad \text{)} \end{cases}$
   _____
   _____

d.
$\begin{cases} \text{xiào (} \quad \text{)} \\ \text{xiào (} \quad \text{)} \end{cases}$
   _____
   _____

4. Add a radical to the following to form a new character, then use it in a word or phrase.

主 → (   ) _____

5. Write down the antonym of each of the following words, then transcribe the new words into Pinyin.

a. 旧 → (   ) _____

b. 慢 → (   ) _____

c. 冷 → (   ) _____

d. 进 → (   ) _____

e. 南 → (   ) _____

f. 难 → (   ) _____

g. 晚 → (   ) _____

h. 上班 → (   ) _____

6. **Find the word that is not in the same category as the other three words and write it in the brackets.**

a. 风, 雪, 雨, 山　　　　　(　　　)

b. 后天, 昨天, 冬天, 前天　(　　　)

c. 书房, 客厅, 家具, 厕所　(　　　)

d. 好看, 好些, 好喝, 好做　(　　　)

e. 上班, 上学, 上边儿, 上课　(　　　)

STRUCTURE EXERCISES

1. **Fill in each blank by choosing the most appropriate word or phrase from the alternatives provided in the box. You must not use any word or phrase more than once. There are more choices than blanks.**

a.

| 常常　得　会　可以　可是　从　往　到 |
| 了　已经　以前　以后　告诉　知道　就 |

　　昨天中午<u>王乐</u>来找我喝酒, 我们喝_____很多酒, 当然, 也吃了很多好吃的

东西。昨天晚上, 我_____不舒服了。我太太说: "不好了, 你病了!"她给我喝了

很多杯水, 给我吃了药, _____一点儿也没有用。我想: "我_____酒都好好的,

今天怎么了?"我坐在床上才好一点儿。我太太说我中午喝太多酒, 吃太多东西

了。她说我今天什么都不 néng 吃, 只_____吃米饭、喝水。我不想吃米饭, 就

喝了一点儿汤。_____了晚上, 我只好去看医生了。

b.

做	作业	后面	男	半	搬	客厅	去	和
来	huò	者	而是	进	出	以后	休息	

钱希平在我家楼上住了两年, 明天上午十点_____他要_____家了。

他是我的好朋友。他的新 fáng 子有一个大_____, 还有一个书 fáng, 孩子们

下课_____, 就可以在那里写_____。新家的_____就是山, 星期天还可

以_____孩子们_____爬山, _____ 在家_____。住_____新 fáng

子, 钱希平一家一定很高兴。

2. **Choose the appropriate verbs from the verbs given immediately below and fill in the brackets. Some verbs may be used more than once.**

上	下	来	去	进	出	过	回	到	走	开	起

A: (开门) 请 (　　)。这是我的新公寓。

B: 你的新公寓真不错。

A: 是呀, 从这儿 (　　) 学校很方便。

B: 你平常 (　　) lù (　　) 学校吗?

A: 是的, 现在 (　　) 班 (　　) 班都不用坐车了。我早上八点半 (　　) (　　),

　　九点 (　　) 十分 (　　) 门, (　　) 一刻钟就 (　　) 学校了。

B: 真方便呀! 我 měi 天得 (　　) 车去 (　　) 班, 早上开 (　　) (　　) 要一刻

　　钟, 晚上回来的时候车多, 开 (　　) (　　) 要半小时。

3. Translate the following sentences into Chinese, using Chinese characters for learned words.

a. I forgot where his apartment was. He lives on the fourth or the fifth floor.

_____

b. If *Qián Xīpíng* is not driving, then he is taking a bus. He seldom walks.

_____

c. It was last month that I moved house. My parents and friends bought me a lot of furniture.

_____

d. She loves cooking, so the kitchen at home is her favorite place.

_____

e. It is not that he loves taking the stairs but that there is no lift in his apartment building.

_____

SUPPLEMENTARY READING

READING 1

小平：　学文, 听说你搬家了。

学文：　是呀! 我在城里买了一个公寓。

小平：　在几楼?

学文：　十楼。

小平：　你住这么高呀!

学文：　有电梯, 上下楼都很方便。

小平：　我在中国住的公寓就没电梯。

学文：　你住几楼?

小平：　六楼。

学文：　六楼! 天天都要走楼梯, 那一定很不方便。

小平：　可不是。

Comprehension questions

1. <u>学文</u>为什么搬家?

_____

2. <u>小平</u>在<u>中国</u>的时候, 为什么天天都要走楼梯?

_____

READING 2

《家 ▪ 春 ▪ 秋》

　　《家》《春》《秋》这三本小说是<u>中国</u>一位很有名的作家[1]xiě的。这位作家在<u>上海</u>和<u>南京</u>上中学, 在<u>法国</u>上大学。从 1929 年到 1937 年 xiě 了很多很有名的小说,《家》这本小说也是在那时候xiě 的。他从1938 年到1940 年 xiě 了《春》和《秋》这两本小说。《家》《春》《秋》这三本小说 xiě 的是高家人的故事。很多人都 xǐ 欢看这位作家xiě 的小说。

_____

1. 这位作家的名字叫 Bā Jīn (<u>巴金</u>, 1904–2005)。

Comprehension questions

1. 《家》这本小说是在什么时候 xiě 的?《春》和《秋》呢?

   _____

2. 《家》《春》《秋》这三本小说 xiě 的是谁家的故事?

   _____

CHARACTER PRACTICE

山	山							
风	风							
雨	雨							
许	许							
冷	冷							
进	进							
刮	刮							
具	具							
者	者							
校	校							

热	热							
桌	桌							
班	班							
梯	梯							
寓	寓							
搬	搬							
厅	厅							
厕	厕							
厨	厨							
出	出							
岁	岁							
所	所							
新	新							
爬	爬							

爱	爱							
票	票							
雪	雪							
楼	楼							
玩	玩							
希	希							
房	房							
夏	夏							

TRANSLATION

Translate each of the following sentences into Chinese. For characters you have not yet been taught, you may use *Hànyǔ Pīnyīn* romanization together with the tone marks.

1.

I like to eat Chinese food. I also like to use chopsticks to eat it (Chinese food). I have a lot of Chinese friends. However, I can't speak Chinese. I would like to study Chinese. I asked *Xiao Ming* to introduce me to a Chinese teacher. *Xiao Ming* said that Teacher Wang is quite good (lit. "very not bad"). He is quite polite and very good to students. *Xiao Ming* said that he has Teacher Wang's mobile phone number.

I phoned Teacher Wang. Teacher Wang said it wasn't a problem. Teacher Wang lives on Beijing Street. To the left of his home is a primary school; to the right is a bookshop. It is not difficult to find. After finishing dinner I went to find Teacher Wang. I studied a few Chinese characters with Teacher Wang. Teacher Wang said that I am quite clever.

_____

_____

_____

_____

2.

My younger brother is the owner of a bookshop. His bookshop is in the city center. He used to live with our parents. He bought an apartment in the city center last month. He moved to his new apartment last week. His new apartment is rather small; there is only one bedroom. But it is very convenient for him to stroll around the streets and shop and to go to work.

It normally takes him half an hour to walk from his apartment to his bookshop. But it takes him just ten minutes (*fēn zhōng* 分钟) to bike there. He cycles pretty quickly. He likes to go to the department store opposite his apartment to shop. He bought his girlfriend a purple T-shirt and dark blue jeans yesterday.

_____

_____

_____

_____

_____

_____

_____

_____

_____

_____

_____

3.

This morning *Wang Wen* phoned me. He said he was ill. He had a headache and a stomachache, and beyond this he had a bit of a fever. He was thinking of going to the hospital to see a doctor. He asked me how to go to the hospital from the university library. I said, "Go straight ahead from the university library, when you get to the bank turn left, go another two blocks and you're there." In the afternoon I went to his house to see him. I asked him what the doctor said. He said the doctor said that in addition to taking medicine he also needed to drink more water and rest more.

_____

_____

_____

_____

_____

_____

_____

_____

4.

The weather the day before yesterday and yesterday was bad. If it wasn't snowing, then it was windy. Going to work or school or strolling the streets was all very inconvenient. Today's weather is a bit better. Just as I was thinking about going out on the street to buy a dining table, my younger sister rang me. She said that she has been waiting for me for "half a day" at the bus stop in front of the China Furniture Store in the south of the city. She asked me why I still hadn't come. I said, "*Ai ya!* Sorry, I forgot. I'm coming now."

_____

_____

_____

_____

_____

_____

_____

_____

READING COMPREHENSION

Read the following passage and answer the questions that follow it.

Zhāng学不会开车, 他去哪儿都 qí 自行车。他说坐公共汽车很便宜, 可是车上人太多, 太不舒 fu 了, 坐 chūzū 汽车很舒服, 可是太 guì 了, 所以他去哪儿都 qí 车。

我 gēn Zhāng学都 xǐ 欢 pí 酒。Zhāng学要来我家 gēn 我一块儿喝酒。我家在南京街, 南京街在北京街的 páng 边儿。Zhāng学不知道怎么来我家, 他从城东边儿 qí 车到城西边儿, 从这条街到那条街, 就是没有我那条街。他给我打电话, 我问他: "你在哪儿? " 他说: "我在图书馆对面的车 zhàn。" 我说: "你往左拐, 再往前走, 到了银行往右拐, 再走一点儿, 我家就在银行后面。"

Read the above passage carefully and identify the following five statements as being either true or false:

a. Zhāng学不打的, 因为打的太 guì 了。　　　　对　　　不对

b. Zhāng学 qí 自行车到我家。　　　　对　　　不对

c. Zhāng学来我家做功课。　　　　对　　　不对

d. Zhāng学住在南京街。　　　　对　　　不对

e. Zhāng学在图书馆对面的车 zhàn 给我打电话。　　　对　　　不对

第十六课

TEXT

　　钱希平搬进新家以后请了二十多个朋友去他家吃饭。他太太忙了三天,做了十几个菜。钱希平还买了很多酒,有白酒、红酒跟米酒,当然还有名 pái 儿的啤酒。两个孩子也跑来跑去地搬东西。钱希平有一个男孩子、一个女孩子。男孩子十三岁了,去年刚上中学。女孩今年才八岁,是小学生。下午五点左右,客人们都来了。希平的老同学黄家深一进门就大 shēng 地说: "啊, 希平, 你真不错, 能住上这么好的房子! 我不知道什么时候才能有这么多钱买得起这么好的房子呢。孩子们呢? 来, 来, 来, 这是给你们的。" 家深 měi 次来都给孩子们带来他们 xǐ 欢的东西, 跟他们玩儿。这次他给孩子们一人一本小说。孩子们也很 xǐ 欢家深。因为家深 dài 眼镜,所以孩子们叫他眼镜叔叔。

　　钱希平请客人们吃他太太做的菜。钱太太做的菜很地道, 好些菜在饭馆里都吃不着呢。大家也喝了不少酒。家深太 xǐ 欢喝酒了。那天, 客人当中他喝得最多了, 筷子都拿不住了。他太太对他说: "你喝得不少了, 你不能再喝了。" 可是他说: "没关系! 我还喝得下好几杯酒呢! 你看, 我的眼睛还能看

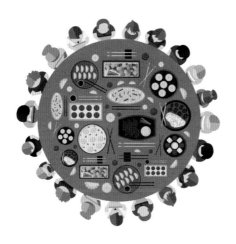

得很清楚, 看得见桌子上的菜, 我的耳朵还能听得很清楚你们在讲什么。来, 来, 喝酒! 喝酒! 好酒啊!" 钱希平说: "对, 对, 对! 大家慢慢儿吃, 多吃点儿, 多喝点儿, 别客气。我们的邻 jū 出门去了, 不在家, 吵一点儿没关系。"

　　二十几个朋友吃吃喝喝, 吃完饭又 liáo 天, 到半夜才高兴地回家去睡觉。可是第二天早上谁都起不来了, 家深睡醒起来已经下午两点了。

生词 NEW WORDS

跟	gēn	(Conj) and (usually joins nouns)
名 pái 儿	míngpáir	(N) famous brand, nameplate
啤酒	píjiǔ	(N) beer
跑	pǎo	(V) run
V 来 V 去	V+lái+V+qù	(Pat) indicates a thorough repetition
女-	nǚ-	(Pre) female (human)
刚	gāng	(TW) just, just now
小学生	xiǎoxuésheng	(N) elementary school pupil
老	lǎo	(SV) be old (usually of person or living things for a long time)
黄家深	Huáng Jiāshēn	(N) a personal name
一……就……	yī…jiù…	(Pat) as soon as
门	mén	(N) door
大 shēng	dà shēng	(Adv) loud
啊	à	(P) (indicates sudden realization)
能	néng	(Aux) can
-上	-shàng	(VC) come/go up
-起	-qǐ	(VC) afford to
-次	-cì	(VCL) times
带	dài	(V) take or bring along, lead around
跟	gēn	(CV) (together) with
又	yòu	(Adv) once again
给	gěi	(V) give, give to
眼镜	yǎnjìng	(N) eyeglasses (Cl -*fù* 副)
-着	-zháo	(VC) successfully complete
当中	dāngzhōng	(PS/PW) the middle (more abstract)
-住	-zhù	(VC) make secure or firm
少	shǎo	(SV) lack, be deficient, lose, be missing
没关系	méi guānxi	(Ex) Never mind. It doesn't matter.
-下	-xià	(VC) come/go down

眼睛	yǎnjing	(N) eye
清楚	qīngchu	(SV) be clear
-见	-jiàn	(VC) perceive
桌子	zhuōzi	(N) table
耳朵	ěrduo	(N) ear
听	tīng	(V) listen
讲	jiǎng	(V) speak, say
啊	a	(P) (tells listener s/he really should have known that)
邻 jū	línjū	(N) neighbor
吵	chǎo	(SV) be noisy
-完	-wán	(VC) finish, complete
半夜	bànyè	(N) midnight
睡觉	shuì jiào	(VO) sleep, "go to bed"
-来	-lái	(VC) come
睡	shuì	(V) sleep
醒	xǐng	(V) wake (up)
-醒	-xǐng	(VC) wake (up)

COMPREHENSION QUESTIONS

1. **Read the text of this chapter and find the following grammatical categories in the text.**

a. Resultative complements (action + result)

_____

_____

_____

b. Verbs (including stative verbs and auxiliary verbs)

verbs: _____

_____

_____

_____

_____

stative verbs: _____

_____

auxiliary verbs: _____

c. Circle each 了, and then classify its function and meaning.
to indicate a completed action: _____

_____

to indicate a change of status/situation: _____

_____

_____

to emphasize the extreme or excessive degree of a stative verb that is being intensified by the adverb *zuì* "most", *tài* "too", or *bù shǎo* "very many":

_____

_____

2. Answer the following questions.

a. 钱希平为什么请他的朋友去他家吃饭?

_____

b. 那天有多少朋友到钱希平家里吃饭?

_____

c. 他太太忙了几天? 准备了多少菜?

_____

d. 钱希平买了什么酒?

_____

e. 钱希平有几个孩子? 他们几岁了?

_____

f. 黄家深送什么东西给钱希平的孩子?

_____

g. 孩子们为什么叫黄家深 眼镜叔叔呢?

_____

h. 钱太太的菜做得好不好?

_____

i. 家深为什么筷子都拿不住了?

_____

j. 黄家深 jué 得自己喝没喝太多酒? 你怎么知道?

_____

k. 为什么钱希平说吵一点儿没关系?

_____

l. 朋友们什么时候回家?

_____

m. 为什么他们第二天早上都起不来了?

_____

n. 家深第二天几点才睡醒?

_____

WRITING HELP

INDEPENDENT CHARACTERS

Character	Basic meaning	No. of strokes	Stroke order	Radical	Components	Structure
又 yòu	again	2	フ 又	又	又	☐
*耳 ěr	ear	6	一 丆 丌 闬 盯 耳	耳	耳	☐
*系 xì	be related to	7	一 玄 系	丿	丿 糸	☰

COMPOUND CHARACTERS

The following are the new compound characters with learned radicals in this chapter: 听, 刚, 次, 朵, 讲, 邻, 吵, 完, 夜, 带, 啊, 能, 啤, 清, 睛, 楚, 睡, and 镜.

Character	Basic meaning	No. of strokes	Stroke order	Radical	Meaning clue	Phonetic clue	Components	Structure
听 (聽) tīng	to listen	7	口 听	口	口	斤 jīn	口 斤	
刚 (剛) gāng	just now	6	冂 冈 刚	刂		冈 gāng	冈 刂	
次 cì	times	6	冫 汄 次	冫			冫 欠	
*朵 duǒ	(classifier)	6	几 朵	木	木		几 木	
讲 (講) jiǎng	to talk	6	讠 讲	讠	讠	井 jǐng	讠 井	
*邻 (鄰) lín	next to	7	今 令 邻	阝		令 lìng	令 阝	
吵 chǎo	noise	7	口 吵	口	口	少	口 少	
完 wán	finish	7	完	宀		元 yuán	宀 元	
夜 yè	night	8	亠 亠 疒 夜 夜 夜	亠	夕 (xī, dusk)		亠 亻, 夕	
带 dài	to bring	9	一 十 艹 艹 芇 带	巾			卅 冖 巾	
啊 á	(particle)	10	口 呀 啊	口	口	阿 a	口 阿	
能 néng	can	10	厶 肖 能 能	月			厶 月 匕 匕	
*啤 pí	beer (啤酒)	11	口 咱 啤 啤	口	口	卑 bēi	口 白 千	
清 qīng	clear	11	氵 清	氵	氵	青 qīng	氵 青	

Char-acter	Basic meaning	No. of strokes	Stroke order	Radical	Meaning clue	Phonetic clue	Compo-nents	Struc-ture
*睛 jīng	eye	13	目　睛	目	目	青 qīng	目 青	
*楚 chǔ	clear	13	木　林　埜　楚	木			木 木 疋	
睡 shuì	to sleep	13	目 目ˊ 目ˊ 肝 肝 眶 睡 睡 睡	目	目	垂 chuí	目 垂	
*镜 (鏡) jìng	mirror	16	钅 钅ʼ 镐 镜	钅	钅	竟 jìng	钅 立日儿	

RADICALS

The new radicals introduced in this chapter are 见, 酉, and 足.

1. 见

见 can also be used as a radical in compound characters indicating eye or sight. The compound character in this chapter that contains this radical is 觉.

Character	Basic meaning	No. of strokes	Stroke order	Meaning clue	Phonetic clue	Compo-nents	Structure
*觉 (覺) jiào	to sleep	9	兴　觉	见		兴 见	

2. 酉

As a character, 酉 *yǒu* means "liquor". As a radical, it is often used in compound characters indicating related meanings. The compound character in this chapter that contains this radical is 醒.

Character	Basic meaning	No. of strokes	Stroke order	Meaning clue	Phonetic clue	Compo-nents	Structure
醒 xǐng	to wake up	16	酉　酊　醒	酉	星	酉日生	

3. 足

This character can be both a character and a radical. As a character, it means "foot" and is written as 足 *zú*. As a radical, it is written as ⻊ and used as the left-hand part of a compound character to form characters related to foot activities or with a meaning of foot. The compound characters in this chapter that contain this radical are 跑 and 跟.

Character	Basic meaning	No. of strokes	Stroke order	Meaning clue	Phonetic clue	Compo-nents	Structure
跑 pǎo	to run	12	口 𝌆 𝌆 𝌆 𝌆 跑	足	包 bāo	足包	▯
跟 gēn	with	13	𝌆 跟	足	艮 gěn	𝌆 艮	▯

EXERCISES

CHARACTER EXERCISES

1. Find the independent characters you have learned hidden in the following characters.

邻 _____   吵 _____   觉 _____   醒 _____

房 _____   朵 _____   就 _____   啊 _____

2. Add a radical to each of the following to make different characters.

? + 令, 完, 者, 余 → (   ), (   ), (   ), (   )

? + 冈, 舌, 亥, 另 → (   ), (   ), (   ), (   )

? + 元, 女, 各, 谷 → (   ), (   ), (   ), (   )

? + 竟, 昔, 戈, 中 → (   ), (   ), (   ), (   )

? + 欠, 水, 令 → (   ), (   ), (   )

3. Form new characters by using different components of the following characters, e.g. 工 (from 功) + 𠂇 (from 有) → 左.

讲　清　灰　觉　很　醒　吵　跑　字

_____ (from _____) + _____ (from _____) → _____

_____ (from _____) + _____ (from _____) → _____

_____ (from _____) + _____ (from _____) → _____

_____ (from _____) + _____ (from _____) → _____

_____ (from _____) + _____ (from _____) → _____

4. How many words and phrases can you form with the following characters?

a. 起 → _____

b. 半 → _____

c. 名 → _____

5. Circle each of the following characters that contains both a meaning clue and a phonetic clue.

耳	啊	睡	朵	清	镜	睛	吵	讲	次
完	邻	能	夜	楚	带	醒	觉	系	又

6. Write as many learned characters as possible containing the components of 小.

_____

7. Circle the wrong character(s) in each sentence and make the correction(s) in the brackets.

a. 钱希平忘了带眼睛了, 所以看不青楚书上的字。 (   ) (   )

b. 钱希平的太太下午一进们就开始准备晚饭, 一直忙到晚上。 (   )

c. 希平叫他的儿子别砲, 慢慢地走。 (   )

d. 饭馆里边儿很炒, 我听不见朋友说话。 (   )

e. 家深的太太对他说: "你喝得太多了!" 他说: "没关糸! 明天是星期六,

不用上班!" (   )

8. Solve the character riddle.

听说一半多一点: _____

VOCABULARY EXERCISES

1. Write the Pinyin for the following characters, then form a word or phrase with each character.

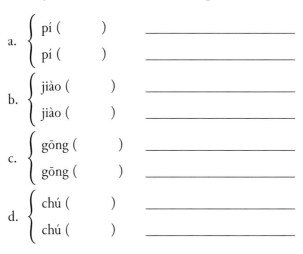

a. ⎰ 炒 (   )   _____
   ⎱ 吵 (   )   _____

b. ⎰ 请 (   )   _____
   ⎱ 清 (   )   _____

2. Write two different characters next to the Pinyin in each group of homonyms, then form a word or phrase with each character.

a. ⎰ pí (   )   _____
   ⎱ pí (   )   _____

b. ⎰ jiào (   )   _____
   ⎱ jiào (   )   _____

c. ⎰ gōng (   )   _____
   ⎱ gōng (   )   _____

d. ⎰ chú (   )   _____
   ⎱ chú (   )   _____

3. Combine a character from column A with one from column B, and then write the word in the brackets. No character can be used more than one time.

A	B	
眼	朵	( )
半	中	( )
桌	夜	( )
名	pái	( )
老	醒	( )
当	镜	( )
耳	子	( )
睡	师	( )

4. **Find the word that is not in the same category as the other three words and write it in the brackets.**

a. 眼睛, 头, 耳朵, 衣服　　（　　　）　　d. 能, 刚, 可以, 得　　　　（　　　）

b. 听, 讲, 跟, 看　　　　　　（　　　）　　e. 睡觉, 爬山, 搬家, 清楚 （　　　）

c. 病, 跑, 走, 拐　　　　　　（　　　）

5. **Give the antonyms to the following words.**

a. 安 jìng → （　　　）　　c. 女孩子 → （　　　）　　e. 起床 → （　　　）

b. 少 → （　　　）　　　　　d. 快 → （　　　）

STRUCTURE EXERCISES

1. **Write the correct classifier character to complete each of the following phrases.**

一_____酒　　　　　这_____咖啡馆　　　　三_____家具

两_____饭　　　　　四_____水　　　　　　那_____街

2. **Fill in each of the blanks with the proper resultative verb complement or its negative form.**

a. 小王的家你找_____吗?

b. 要是我看_____他, 叫他来找你。

c. 好吧, 你们一块儿来我家吃晚饭吧。我买了很多菜, 一个人吃_____。
大家来吃吧。

d. 医院里有很多人, 他到的时候已经很晚了, 今天一定看_____医生了。

e. 家深说他买_____房子, 只能先 zū 房子住。

f. 饭馆里太吵了, 他听_____坐在对面的朋友说什么。

g. 吃_____晚饭以后, 他又跑去了图书馆去念书。

3. Choose the appropriate words from the words given immediately below and fill in the brackets.

又   再   常常   平常   左右

a. 这 fù 眼镜不太贵, 就五百块 (　　　　　)。

b. 钱希平 (　　　　　) 八点起床, 九点出门去上班, 可是他今天不舒服, 很晚才起来。

c. 我没听清楚, 请 (　　　　　) 说一次。

d. 这里的夏天很热, 还 (　　　　　) 刮风下雨。

e. 他 (　　　　　) 讲了一 biàn 那个有意思的故事。

SUPPLEMENTARY READING

READING 1

白开水

　　我 xǐ 欢到我家对面的那家<u>中国</u>饭馆儿吃牛肉炒饭, 喝<u>中国</u>茶。<u>王</u>医生知道了就对我说, 吃牛肉的时候最好不要喝茶。今天我又去那家饭馆儿吃牛肉炒饭。我跟老板说: "我不要喝茶, 请给我热水。" 老板听了半天, 还是不知道我要什么。我又说: "你看, 那是茶, 是热的。我要水, 热的水。" 老板听懂了, 他说: "哦, 你要白开水。" 我明白了, 在<u>中国</u>饭馆儿里, 热的水不叫热水, 叫白开水。

Comprehension questions

1. 吃牛肉炒饭的时候, 我为什么不要喝茶?

_____

2. 吃牛肉炒饭的时候, 我不要喝茶, 我喝什么?

_____

READING 2

头疼

　　以前有一个叫美欢的女孩子, 她常常去看医生。Měi 一次去看医生, 她都跟医生说她头疼。有一天, 她又去看医生了。医生想了一想, 对她说: "你太忙了, 家里的事能做的就做, 做不了的就别做了。"

　　几天后, 美欢的妈妈来了。她对医生说: "我的头真疼。"医生给她看病了, 医生对她说: "你太累了, 家里的事能做的就做吧, 做不了的就别做了。"

　　过了几个星期, 医生在饭馆儿看到美欢和她妈妈。医生对她们说: "你们的头还疼吗?" 美欢说: "我和妈妈的头都不疼了。可是, 现在我 bàba 的头疼了。"

Comprehension questions

1. 美欢为什么常常去看医生?

_____

2. 美欢的 bàba 为什么头疼?

_____

CHARACTER PRACTICE

又	又								
耳	耳								
系	系								
听	听								
刚	刚								
次	次								
朵	朵								
讲	讲								
邻	邻								
吵	吵								
完	完								
夜	夜								
带	带								

啊	啊								
能	能								
啤	啤								
清	清								
晴	晴								
楚	楚								
睡	睡								
镜	镜								
觉	觉								
醒	醒								
跑	跑								
跟	跟								

第十七课

TEXT

　　商先生是 Xīn 西兰的华人。他六十岁才开始学汉语。他很用功, 不过, 他老是学不好, 记不住生词。他说一个星期要记五十多个生词太多, 太难了。十多、二十岁的人都记不了这么多生词, 他怎么能记得住呢!

　　他早上起来, 又是记生词, 又是写汉字。他把他学过的汉字都仔细地写在纸上, 他一有 kòng 儿就拿出来看。他还把汉字放在他床边儿的书桌上, 睡觉以前看几遍, 睡醒了又看一下。他说只要 měi 天学, 他就一定能把汉语学好, 能把生词记住。

　　商先生想明年去中国看他九十多岁的阿姨, 他已经有五十年没看到他阿姨了。

　　商先生家里, 这儿是汉字, 那儿也是汉字。他太太跟他的朋友说, 她看不懂汉字, 一看到汉字就生气, 家里楼上楼下的房间里都是汉字, 真气死人! 去

年, 她也开始学汉语了。商先生和商太太一块儿去图书馆借书还书。不到半年的时间, 他们已经会说好多汉语, 会写好多汉字了。他们还学会了包饺子。他们想来想去, 为什么要等到明年才去中国呢? 现在就去吧! 现在是秋天, 北京很凉快。到了中国可以好好儿练习练习汉语, 吃现成的中国饺子了。

上个月, 商先生和商太太带了一个放着他们所有的汉语书和别的行李的大箱子到中国去了。

他们下了飞机, 商先生用汉语跟机场的小姐说话。他 jǐn 张极了, 小姐听不懂他说的汉语。商先生就用铅笔在一张纸上写: "找想卖中国自酒, 你这儿有买吗?" 那小姐看了半天还是看不懂他的意思。你知道为什么吗? 商先生把 "我" 字写成了 "找" 字, 把 "白" 字写成 "自" 字, 还把 "买" 字写成 "卖" 字, 把 "卖" 字写成 "买" 字了。你想, 小姐能看懂商先生写的是什么吗?

生词 NEW WORDS

商先生	Shāng xiānsheng	(N) Mr. Shang
华人	Huárén	(N) person of Chinese ethnicity
老	lǎo	(Adv) always, invariably
-好	-hǎo	(VC) satisfactorily complete
记	jì	(V) remember
-了	-liǎo	(VC) able to
又……又……	yòu…yòu…	(P) both…and…
写	xiě	(V) write
写字	xiě zì	(VO) write
把	bǎ	(CV) take
仔细	zǐxì	(SV) be careful, be detailed
纸	zhǐ	(N) paper (Cl -张)
放	fàng	(V) put, place
床边儿	chuángbianr	(PS/PW) next to bed
书桌	shūzhuō	(N) desk
-遍	-biàn	(VCL) times
……一下	…yíxià	(Adv) a bit (after a verb)
只要	zhǐyào	(Conj) All you need to do is…
阿姨	āyí	(N) aunt (mother's sister)
-到	-dào	(VC) (reach a point)
-懂	-dǒng	(VC) understand
生气	shēngqì	(SV) be angry
楼上	lóushàng	(PS/PW) upstairs

楼下	lóuxià	(PS/PW) downstairs
房间	fángjiān	(N) room (of house; Cl -个, 间)
-死	-sǐ	(VC) (indicates extremeness of state)
真气死人!	Zhēn qìsǐ rén!	(Ex) How infuriating!
借	jiè	(V) borrow, lend
还	huán	(V) return (something)
时间	shíjiān	(N) time
-会	-huì	(VC) master
包	bāo	(V) wrap
饺子	jiǎozi	(N) "Chinese ravioli", "Chinese dump-ling"
凉快	liángkuài	(SV) be (comfortably) cool (said of air temperature)
好好儿	hǎohaor	(Adv) earnestly, all out
现成	xiànchéng	(Atr.) ready-made
所有的	suǒyǒude	(N) every-, all of something
行李	xínglǐ	(N) luggage (Cl -件)
箱子	xiāngzi	(N) (large) box, trunk, chest
飞机	fēijī	(N) airplane
(飞)机场	(fēi)jīchǎng	(PW) airport
说话	shuōhuà	(VO) speak
jǐn 张	jǐnzhāng	(SV) be nervous, be tense
……极了	…jíle	(Adv) extremely
铅笔	qiānbǐ	(N) pencil
-张	-zhāng	(Cl) (for flat objects like tables, paper, paintings)
意思	yìsi	(N) meaning
-成	-chéng	(VC) (indicates transformation)

COMPREHENSION QUESTIONS

1. **Read the text of this chapter and for each statement below indicate whether it is true or false.**

a. (　　　　) <u>商</u>先生六十六岁才开始学汉语。

b. (　　　　) 他很用功, 不过, 他老是学不好, 记不住生词。

c. (　　　　) 他说一个星期要记一百五十个生词太多了。

d. (　　　) 他 měi 天晚上睡觉前记生词, 写汉字。

e. (　　　) 他把他学过的汉字和生词都仔细地写在书上, měi 天早上都拿出来看。

f. (　　　) 他还把写好的汉字放在书桌上, 睡觉以前看几遍, 睡醒了再看一下。

g. (　　　) 他说只要 měi 天学, 他一定能把汉语学好。

h. (　　　) 商先生想明年去中国看他九十多岁的妈妈。

i. (　　　) 他已经有四十年没看到他妈妈了。

j. (　　　) 商太太很不 xǐ 欢家里都是汉字。

k. (　　　) 商太太也学习汉语了, 可是, 她只会说汉语, 不会写汉字。

l. (　　　) 他们很 xǐ 欢吃饺子, 可是不会包。

m. (　　　) 他们明年要去中国。

n. (　　　) 他们要去中国学汉语, 吃中国饺子。

o. (　　　) 他们带了他们所有的衣服去中国。

p. (　　　) 他们坐飞机去中国。

q. (　　　) 在飞机上, 商先生用汉语跟一位小姐练习汉语。

r. (　　　) 小姐听不懂他的话, 也看不懂他写的汉字。

2. Answer the following questions.

a. 商先生什么时候开始学汉语?

_____

b. 他为什么学不好, 记不住生词?

_____

c. 商先生怎么记生词?

_____

d. 他们明年想去哪儿? 做什么? 为什么?

_____

e. 商太太跟商先生的朋友说什么?

_____

f. 她为什么生气?

_____

g. 商太太什么时候开始学汉语?

_____

h. 他们一块儿去哪儿? 做什么?

_____

i. 不到半年的时间, 他们学会了什么?

_____

j. 他们什么时候要去中国? 为什么?

_____

k. 大箱子里有什么?

_____

l. 商先生用汉语跟谁说话?

_____

m. 为什么机场的小姐听不懂他的汉语?

_____

n. 为什么机场的小姐看不懂商先生写的是什么?

_____

WRITING HELP

INDEPENDENT CHARACTERS

Character	Basic meaning	No. of strokes	Stroke order	Radical	Components	Structure
飞 (飛) fēi	to fly	3	㇆ 飞 飞	乙	飞	☐
死 sǐ	death	6	一 歹 死	歹	歹 匕	☐
成 chéng	to suc-ceed	6	一 厂 厂 成 成 成	戈	戊 丁	⊓

COMPOUND CHARACTERS

The following are the new compound characters with learned radicals in this chapter: 记, 华, 把, 纸, 阿, 李, 极, 细, 放, 姨, 饺, 借, 凉, 铅, 遍, and 箱.

Character	Basic meaning	No. of strokes	Stroke order	Radical	Meaning clue	Phonetic clue	Components	Structure
记 (記) jì	to remember	5	讠 记 记 记	讠	讠	己 jǐ	讠 己	
*华 (華) huá	China	6	化 华	十		化 huà	化 十	
把 bǎ	to hold*	7	扌 把	扌	扌	巴 bā	扌 巴	
纸 (紙) zhǐ	paper	7	纟 纟 纤 纸 纸	纟	纟	氏 shì	纟 氏	
阿 ā	(particle)	7	阝 阿	阝			阝 可	
李 lǐ	plum, surname	7	木 李	木	木		木 子	
极 jí	extreme	7	朩 朸 极 极	木		及 jí	木 及	
细 (細) xì	fine, slender	8	纟 细	纟	纟		纟 田	
放 fàng	to put	8	方 放	攵		方	方 攵	
姨 yí	aunt	9	女 妡 妡 姇 姇 姨 姨	女	女	夷 yí	女 夷	
*饺 (餃) jiǎo	dumpling	9	饣 饬 饺	饣	饣	交 jiāo	饣 交	
借 jiè	to borrow, to lend	10	亻 亻 什 併 併 借	亻	亻		亻 昔 日	
凉 liáng	cool	10	冫 凉	冫	冫		冫 京	

Char-acter	Basic meaning	No. of strokes	Stroke order	Radical	Meaning clue	Phonetic clue	Compo-nents	Struc-ture
铅 (鉛) qiān	lead	10	钅 钌 铅	钅	钅		钅 几 口	
*遍 biàn	times	12	户 户 启 扁 扁 遍	辶		扁 biǎn	辶 扁	
*箱 xiāng	box	15	竹 笁 箱	竹	竹	相 xiāng	竹 木 目	

RADICALS

The new radicals introduced in this chapter are 冖, 勹, 门, and 弓.

1. 冖

This radical is used as the top part of a compound character. The compound character in this chapter that contains this radical is 写.

Character	Basic meaning	No. of strokes	Stroke order	Meaning clue	Phonetic clue	Compo-nents	Structure
写 (寫) xiě	to write	5	冖 冖 写 写			冖 与	

2. 勹

This radical encloses the top and right-hand sides of a compound character. The compound character in this chapter that contains this radical is 包.

Character	Basic meaning	No. of strokes	Stroke order	Meaning clue	Phonetic clue	Compo-nents	Structure
包 bāo	to wrap	5	丿 勹 勺 匇 包	勹	勹 bāo	勹 巳	

3. 门

门 can be both a character and a radical. As a radical, it is used to form characters related to the meaning of "door". The compound character in this chapter that contains this radical is 间.

Character	Basic meaning	No. of strokes	Stroke order	Meaning clue	Phonetic clue	Components	Structure
*间 (間) jiān	gap	7	门 间	门,日 (seeing the sun through an open door)		门 日	⊓

4. 弓

弓 means *gōng*, "bow" as a character. The compound character in this chapter that contains this radical is 张.

Character	Basic meaning	No. of strokes	Stroke order	Meaning clue	Phonetic clue	Components	Structure
张 (張) zhāng	(classifier)*, surname	8	ㄱ ㄱ 弓 弓´ 弘 张 张	弓	长 zhǎng/ cháng	弓长	⊓

EXERCISES

CHARACTER EXERCISES

1. **Find the independent characters you have learned hidden in the following characters.**

阿 _____   李 _____   凉 _____   间 _____

放 _____   铅 _____   华 _____   能 _____

2. **Write in the brackets the component that is common to all of the following characters.**

李, 床, 板, 杂 → (   )   成, 我, 找 → (   )

死, 老, 能, 华 → (   )   遍, 房, 所 → (   )

朵, 铅, 风, 机 → (   )   箱, 睡, 着 → (   )

都, 阿, 除 → (   )

3. Form new characters by using different components of the following characters, etc., e.g. 工 (from 功) + ナ (from 有) → 左.

跟　饱　铅　浅　想　筷　男

_____ (from _____) + _____ (from _____) → _____

_____ (from _____) + _____ (from _____) → _____

_____ (from _____) + _____ (from _____) → _____

_____ (from _____) + _____ (from _____) → _____

_____ (from _____) + _____ (from _____) → _____

4. Form five characters each using each of the following components.

a. 田 → _____

b. 扌 → _____

c. 木 → _____

d. 纟 → _____

e. 竹 → _____

f. 钅 → _____

g. 辶 → _____

5. Circle the misused characters in the following sentences and write the correct ones.

a. 他们 一快儿去学校介书。→ _____

b. 谢啊姨坐气车来找家。→ _____

c. 多吃点吵牛内把。→ _____

VOCABULARY EXERCISES

1. Combine a character from column A with one from column B, and then write the word in brackets. No character can be used more than one time.

A	B	
饺	气	( )
飞	思	( )
仔	桌	( )
书	快	( )
意	李	( )
凉	机	( )
生	细	( )
行	子	( )

2. Write the characters corresponding to the Pinyin and containing the following radicals, then form a word or phrase with each of the characters.

a. 纟 { zhǐ (   ) _____
       xì (   ) _____

b. 钅 { qiān (   ) _____
       qián (   ) _____

c. 昔 { jiè (   ) _____
       cuò (   ) _____

3. Write two different characters next to the Pinyin in each group of homonyms, then form a word or phrase with each character.

a. { zhǐ (   ) _____
     zhǐ (   ) _____

b. { chéng (   ) _____
     chéng (   ) _____

c. $\begin{cases} \text{lĭ} (\quad) \quad \underline{\hspace{5cm}} \\ \text{lì} (\quad) \quad \underline{\hspace{5cm}} \end{cases}$

d. $\begin{cases} \text{yí} (\quad) \quad \underline{\hspace{5cm}} \\ \text{yí} (\quad) \quad \underline{\hspace{5cm}} \end{cases}$

4. Each of the following characters is a polyphone (i.e. a character that has more than one pronunciation). Write two different Pinyin spellings for each character in the brackets and then for each spelling form a word or phrase with it using Chinese characters.

a. 还 $\begin{cases} (\quad) \underline{\hspace{5cm}} \\ (\quad) \underline{\hspace{5cm}} \end{cases}$

b. 得 $\begin{cases} (\quad) \underline{\hspace{5cm}} \\ (\quad) \underline{\hspace{5cm}} \end{cases}$

c. 仔 $\begin{cases} (\quad) \underline{\hspace{5cm}} \\ (\quad) \underline{\hspace{5cm}} \end{cases}$

d. 行 $\begin{cases} (\quad) \underline{\hspace{5cm}} \\ (\quad) \underline{\hspace{5cm}} \end{cases}$

5. Find the word that is not in the same category as the other three words and write it in the brackets.

a. 书桌, 灯, 厨房, 床 ( )

b. 飞机, 汽车, 公 jiāo 车, 机场 ( )

c. 写字, 现成, 看书, 说话 ( )

d. 铅笔, 饺子, 牛肉, 炒饭 ( )

e. 阿姨, 华人, 叔叔, 伯伯 ( )

f. 白酒, 红酒, 啤酒, 喝酒 ( )

6. Give the antonyms to the following words.

a. 楼上 → ( )   c. 凉快 → ( )

b. 借 → ( )   d. 睡 → ( )

STRUCTURE EXERCISES

1. Write the correct classifier character to complete each of the following phrases.

看几_____   九十多_____的阿姨   四_____房间

一_____纸   十二_____饺子   十多_____生词

2. Fill in the blanks to complete each of the following sentences.

a. 这个菜又_____又_____, 以后我们别 diǎn 这个
菜了。

b. 坐公 jiāo 车又_____又_____, 所以我 měi 天坐
车去上班。

c. 这门课又_____又_____, 我很 xǐ 欢。

d. 快要考试了, 他又_____又_____, 要看很多书
准备考试。

e. 我的姐姐 (也) _____, 我也_____。

f. 哥哥写的中文字 (也) _____, 弟弟写的也_____。

3. Fill in the brackets with the proper verb complement or its potential form.

a. 包饺子很容易, 他很快就学_____了。

b. 商先生听_____汉语, 也看_____汉字。

c. 他喝多了, 连筷子都拿_____了。

d. 商先生把 "我" 字写_____了 "找" 字, 所以机场的小姐看_____。

e. 家华一直住在英国, 已经有十年没看_____他的阿姨了。

f. 他想了半天才把要说的话想_____了。

4. Translate the following sentences into Chinese, using Chinese characters for learned words.

a. He spent all of his money on the house.

_____

b. Riding on an airplane for a day made me exhausted.

_____

c. He had too much luggage to fit into one suitcase. I lent him my suitcase.

_____

d. Can you wait a second for me? I'll be back very soon.

_____

e. He has seven or eight boxes of books. After he finished moving the books, he was both tired and hungry.

_____

WRITING EXERCISES

1. Write a short paragraph about 商先生是怎么学汉语的.

_____

_____

_____

_____

_____

_____

_____

_____

_____

2. 要是你去中国, 你要带什么? Make a list.

_____

_____

_____

_____

_____

_____

SUPPLEMENTARY READING

READING 1

四 hé 院

　　人们说起四 hé 院就会想起北京。什么是四 hé 院呢? 四 hé 院是北京一千年前就有的房子。四 hé 院的中心¹ 是院子, 院子的四面都有房子, 所以叫四 hé 院。住在四 hé 院北边房子的是家中的老人, 大儿子住在东边儿, 二儿子住在西边儿, 女儿住在后院。四 hé 院很 tè 别, 你去北京的时候应该去看一下。

Comprehension questions

1. 北京什么时候开始就有四 hé 院?

_____

2. 四 hé 院的四面有什么?

_____

---

1. 中心 "center"

READING 2

三毛

　　三毛 (1943–1991) 是一位很有名的女作家。三毛从小就 xǐ 欢看书。她看的第一本书是张乐平画和写的小人书[2]，那时候她才三岁。三毛英文名字叫 Echo，她的名字不叫三毛，三毛是她的笔名。因为她很 xǐ 欢张乐平画的三毛的故事，所以在她开始写作以后，就用三毛这个笔名。三毛去过很多国家，她懂得好几个国家的语言。

Comprehension questions

1. 三毛是谁? 三毛从小就 xǐ 欢做什么?

_____

2. 三毛为什么用三毛这个笔名?

_____

_____

2. 小人书 "picture story book"; 那本小人书叫《三毛 liúlàng 记》

CHARACTER PRACTICE

飞	飞							
死	死							
成	成							
记	记							
华	华							
把	把							
纸	纸							
阿	阿							
李	李							
极	极							
细	细							
放	放							
姨	姨							

饺	饺							
借	借							
凉	凉							
铅	铅							
遍	遍							
箱	箱							
间	间							
写	写							
包	包							
张	张							

TEXT

　我住在南京路，南京路很安静，一点儿都不吵，也不热闹，连商店也不多。我们家对面有一家小小的卖衣服的商店。那家商店的两个老板，一个姓常，一个姓张，我们叫他们常伯伯和张伯伯。我有空儿常常去那儿玩儿。

　常伯伯又高又瘦，他以前住在黄河北边。张伯伯没有常伯伯高，他不胖也不瘦。张伯伯以前住在长江的南边儿，他说长江比黄河长，常伯伯说长江跟黄河一样长。我说："我知道，我们老师说长江比黄河长。"张伯伯听了很高兴。

　常伯伯和张伯伯都五十多岁了。他们对做生意不太有兴趣，对做衣服很有兴趣，店里的衣服都是他们做的。他们店里卖的衣服又舒服又便宜，只是不够时 máo。他们说别的店卖的衣服虽然时 máo，可是比他们的几乎贵两倍，有钱的人才买得起。

我父母都是老师, 他们的薪水不是很高, 可是上个月的考试我的成绩 tè 别好, 他们给我买了两条名 pái 儿的牛仔裤。我现在穿的这条裤子比<u>常</u>伯伯店里最贵的裤子贵三分之一。<u>张</u>伯伯问我为什么不在他们店里买裤子。我说我穿的这条裤子跟他们店里卖的完全不同, 我的裤子又时 máo 又是名 pái 儿的。我现在穿的这条还不是最贵的, 我还有一条比这条更贵呢!

生词 NEW WORDS

路	lù	(N) road (Cl -条)
南京路	Nánjīng Lù	(PW) name of a street
安静	ānjìng	(SV) be peaceful and quiet
热闹	rènao	(SV) be bustling
连……都/也……	lián…dōu/yě…	(Pat) even…
常伯伯	Cháng bóbo	(N) Uncle Chang
张伯伯	Zhāng bóbo	(N) Uncle Zhang
有空儿	yǒu kòngr	(VO) have free time
瘦	shòu	(SV) be thin, be lean
黄河	Huánghé	(PW) the Yellow River
胖	pàng	(SV) be fat (of humans)
长江	Chángjiāng	(PW) the Yangtze River
比	bǐ	(CV) compared to
长	cháng	(SV) be long
一样	yíyàng	(Adv) similarly
做生意	zuò shēngyi	(VO) engage in commerce
兴趣	xìngqù	(N) interest (in something)
够	gòu	(V) be enough, sufficient, adequate
时 máo	shímáo	(SV) be fashionable
虽然……可是……	suīrán…kěshì…	(Pat) although…, however…
几乎	jīhū	(Adv) almost, nearly
贵	guì	(V) be expensive
–倍	-bèi	(Cl) -fold, number + times
薪水	xīnshuǐ	(N) salary
成绩	chéngjì	(N) grades, result, achievement
牛仔裤	niúzǎikù	(N) denim jeans (Cl -条)
裤子	kùzi	(N) pants, trousers (Cl -条)
穿	chuān	(V) wear, put on (clothing)

Y 分之 X	Y fēn zhī X	(Pat) (indicates X/Y fractions)
完全	wánquán	(Adv) completely
不同	bùtóng	(SV) be different
更	gèng	(Adv) even more

COMPREHENSION QUESTIONS

1. **Read the text of this chapter and for each statement below indicate whether it is true or false.**

a. (　　　) 常伯伯和张伯伯差不多一样大。

b. (　　　) 他们对做生意 tè 别有兴趣。

c. (　　　) 他们店里卖的东西很便宜。

d. (　　　) 别的店卖的衣服又时 máo 又便宜。

e. (　　　) 上个月我考试的成绩很好, 我的父母买了 lǐwù 送给我。

f. (　　　) 我名 pái 儿的裤子比常伯伯店里的裤子贵得多。

g. (　　　) 我穿的裤子跟常伯伯店里卖的不一样。

2. **Ask each other the following questions about the above text, then sketch the answers below.**

a. 商店在哪儿? 我家在哪儿?

b. 我认识的张伯伯和常伯伯.

c. 张伯伯和<u>棠</u>伯伯以前住在哪儿?

WRITING HELP

INDEPENDENT CHARACTERS

Character	Basic meaning	No. of strokes	Stroke order	Radical	Components	Structure
*之 zhī	的	3	丶 亠 之	丶	之	☐
长 (長) cháng	long	5	丿 二 乚 长	丿	长	☐
乎 hū	(particle)	5	丿 丷 口 丘 乎	丿	乎	☐

COMPOUND CHARACTERS

The following are the new compound characters with learned radicals in this chapter: 江, 全, 更, 闹, 河, 胖, 虽, 样, 倍, 够, 绩, 裤, 路, 瘦, 趣, 薪, and 连.

Character	Basic meaning	No. of strokes	Stroke order	Radical	Meaning clue	Phonetic clue	Components	Structure
江 jiāng	river, surname	6	氵 氵 江 江	氵	氵		氵 工	☐
全 quán	whole	6	人 全	人			人 王	☐
更 gèng	even	7	一 丆 冃 冃 百 更 更	一			一 日 乂)	☐
闹 (鬧) nào	noise	8	门 闩 闹	门	门, 市		门 市	☐

Char-acter	Basic meaning	No. of strokes	Stroke order	Radical	Meaning clue	Phonetic clue	Compo-nents	Struc-ture
河 hé	river	8	氵 河	氵	氵	可	氵可	
胖 pàng	fat	9	月 胖	月	月	半	月 半	
虽 (雖) suī	al-though	9	口 口 吕 吊 虽	口			口 虫	
*样 (樣) yàng	shape	10	木 样	木		羊 yáng	木 羊	
*倍 bèi	double	10	亻 佗 倍	亻			亻 立 口	
够 gòu	enough	11	句 够	夕	句 (jù, sentence), 多 (many sentences are enough)		句 夕 夕	
*绩 (績) jì	to accom-plish	11	纟 纟 纟 结 结 绩	纟			纟 责	
*裤 (褲) kù	trousers	12	衤 衤 衤 裤	衤	衤	库 kù	衤 广 车	
路 lù	road	13	𧾷 𧾷 𧾷 𧾷 足 路	足	足		𧾷 各 (夂口)	
瘦 shòu	skinny	14	广 疒 疒 疒 疒 疒 疒 痩 瘦	疒	疒	叟 sǒu	疒 叟	
*趣 qù	to call	15	走 趄 趣	走		取 qǔ	走 耳 又	
*薪 xīn	salary (from "fire-wood")	16	艹 薪	艹	艹	新	艹 亲 斤	
连 (連) lián	to con-nect	7	车 连	辶			辶 车	

闹: It is better remembered as a market (市 shì) inside the door = noisy 闹.

RADICALS

The new radicals introduced in this chapter are 贝, 比 ,穴, and 青.

1. 贝

贝 *bèi* as a character means "shell". As shells were used in earliest times in China as money, 贝 is used as a radical to indicate money or precious things. The compound character in this chapter that contains this radical is 贵.

Character	Basic meaning	No. of strokes	Stroke order	Meaning clue	Phonetic clue	Components	Structure
贵 (貴) guì	expensive, precious	9	口 中 虫 贵 贵	贝		中 一 贝	

2. 比

比 can be a character and a radical.

Character	Basic meaning	No. of strokes	Stroke order	Meaning clue	Phonetic clue	Components	Structure
比 bǐ	to compare	4	一 乜 比 比			乜 匕	

3. 穴

As an independent character, 穴 *xué* means "cave, hole". As a radical, it is used in some compound characters indicating related meanings. The compound characters in this chapter that contain this radical are 空 and 穿.

Character	Basic meaning	No. of strokes	Stroke order	Meaning clue	Phonetic clue	Components	Structure
空 kòng	empty	8	宀 穴 空	穴 (hole)	工 gōng	宀 八 工	
穿 chuān	to wear	9	穴 宊 宊 穿 穿			穴 牙	

4. 青

青 as a character means "glassy green". The compound character in this chapter that contains this radical is 静. Some characters learned before also contain this component as well. What are they?

Character	Basic meaning	No. of strokes	Stroke order	Meaning clue	Phonetic clue	Compo-nents	Structure
静 (靜) jìng	quiet	14	青 青 靑 靗 靜 静 静		青 qīng	青 争	▢

EXERCISES

CHARACTER EXERCISES

1. Find the independent characters you have learned hidden in the following characters.

江 _____   全 _____   闹 _____   河 _____

胖 _____   够 _____   裤 _____   薪 _____

2. Write in brackets the component that is common to each set of characters below.

更, 替, 最, 电 → (   )   路, 冬, 夏, 夜 → (   )

胖, 静, 有, 服 → (   )   趣, 叔, 报, 难 → (   )

样, 美, 差, 着 → (   )   薪, 诉, 听, 所 → (   )

够, 外, 名, 岁 → (   )   闹, 常, 带 → (   )

绩, 顿, 贵, 颜 → (   )

3. Form new characters by using different components of the following characters, e.g. 工 (from 功) + ナ (from 有) → 左.

┌─────────────────────────────┐
│ 空 深 绩 阿 今 静 现 │
└─────────────────────────────┘

_____ (from _____) + _____ (from _____) → _____

_____ (from _____) + _____ (from _____) → _____

_____ (from _____) + _____ (from _____) → _____

_____ (from _____) + _____ (from _____) → _____

_____ (from _____) + _____ (from _____) → _____

4. Form three or four characters each using each of the following components.

a. 王 → _____

b. 目 → _____

c. 人 → _____

d. 又 → _____

e. 页 → _____

5. Circle the wrong character in each sentence and make the correction in the brackets provided.

a. 在家里做饭吃比在外边儿吃饭几乎便宜一半。   (   )

b. 他跟我一佯 xǐ 欢上中文课。   (   )

c. <u>黄家深</u>的新水不是很高, 还买不起房子。   (   )

d. 他以前住的地方太吵了, 晚上睡不着, 所以就搬

     到了一个安镜的地方住。   (   )

e. 坐飞机比坐火车贵一蓓, 可是飞机又快又方便。   (   )

VOCABULARY EXERCISES

1. Combine a character from column A with one from column B, and then write the word in brackets. No character can be used more than one time.

A	B	
虽	乎	( )
成	绩	( )
热	静	( )
兴	全	( )
薪	闹	( )
安	然	( )
完	水	( )
几	趣	( )

2. Write the characters corresponding to the Pinyin and containing the following radicals, then form a word or phrase with each of the characters.

a. 氵 $\begin{cases} \text{jiāng (} \qquad \text{)} \rule{8cm}{0.4pt} \\ \text{hé} \quad \text{(} \qquad \text{)} \rule{8cm}{0.4pt} \end{cases}$

b. 疒 $\begin{cases} \text{bìng (} \qquad \text{)} \rule{8cm}{0.4pt} \\ \text{shòu (} \qquad \text{)} \rule{8cm}{0.4pt} \end{cases}$

c. 宀 $\begin{cases} \text{kòng (} \qquad \text{)} \rule{8cm}{0.4pt} \\ \text{chuān (} \qquad \text{)} \rule{8cm}{0.4pt} \end{cases}$

3. Write two different characters next to the Pinyin in each group of homonyms, then form a word or phrase with each character.

a. $\begin{cases} \text{jìng (} \qquad \text{)} \rule{7cm}{0.4pt} \\ \text{jìng (} \qquad \text{)} \rule{7cm}{0.4pt} \end{cases}$

b. $\begin{cases} \text{hé (} \qquad \text{)} \rule{7cm}{0.4pt} \\ \text{hé (} \qquad \text{)} \rule{7cm}{0.4pt} \end{cases}$

c. $\begin{cases} \text{zhī (} \qquad \text{)} \rule{7cm}{0.4pt} \\ \text{zhī (} \qquad \text{)} \rule{7cm}{0.4pt} \end{cases}$

d. $\begin{cases} \text{bǐ (} \qquad \text{)} \rule{7cm}{0.4pt} \\ \text{bǐ (} \qquad \text{)} \rule{7cm}{0.4pt} \end{cases}$

e. $\begin{cases} \text{xīn (} \qquad \text{)} \rule{7cm}{0.4pt} \\ \text{xīn (} \qquad \text{)} \rule{7cm}{0.4pt} \end{cases}$

f. $\begin{cases} \text{qù (} \qquad \text{)} \rule{7cm}{0.4pt} \\ \text{qù (} \qquad \text{)} \rule{7cm}{0.4pt} \end{cases}$

4. Find the word that is not in the same category as the other three words and write it in the brackets provided.

a. 北京, 黄河, 南京, 上海   (   )

b. 袜子, 裤子, 饺子, 裙子   (   )

c. 瘦, 高, 胖, 够   (   )

d. 时 máo, 便宜, 舒服, 生意   (   )

5. Give the antonym for each of the following words.

a. 胖 → (   )   c. 便宜 → (   )

b. 热闹 → (   )   d. 一样 → (   )

6. List as many words in each category as possible.

a. Clothing items:

_____

b. Food items:

_____

c. Stationery:

_____

d. Beverages (including water):

_____

STRUCTURE EXERCISES

1. **Fill in the blanks to complete each of the following sentences using the pattern 虽然……可是……**

a. 你虽然不借我钱, _____。

b. 棠伯伯店里的衣服虽然不时 máo, _____。

c. 我父母_____, 可是还是给我买了名 pái 儿的牛仔裤。

d. _____, 可是我的成绩 tè 别好。

e. 这家卖衣服的商店_____, _____。

2. **Solve the riddle.**

我的兄弟姐妹四个人当中, 哥哥比弟弟高一点儿, 姐姐没有妹妹那么高, 弟弟不比姐姐高, 也不跟姐姐一样高。

兄弟姐妹中谁最 ǎi? _____

3. Translate the following sentences into Chinese, using Chinese characters for learned words.

a. He is even more interested in making clothes than in doing business.

_____

b. Although the food in this restaurant is twice as expensive as in other restaurants, the food here is not as delicious.

_____

c. He was so busy that he didn't even have time to eat.

_____

d. There are still 10 days to go for this month. He has already spent three-fourths of the money and is about to run out of money to buy food.

_____

e. Learning Chinese is totally different from learning English and it's hard to say that learning Chinese is more difficult than learning English.

_____

WRITING EXERCISE

1. **Write a short paragraph about a place where you have lived before or you are currently living.**

_____

_____

_____

_____

_____

_____

_____

_____

_____

SUPPLEMENTARY READING

READING 1

大山

　　你们知道谁是 Mark Rowswell 吗? Mark Rowswell 的中文名字叫<u>大山</u>,他是<u>加拿大</u>[1]人。1988年他去<u>中国</u>, 他在<u>北京大学</u>念书。他在<u>北京</u>的时候, 因为常常上电 shì 说笑话, 所以人人都知道他的名字。<u>大山</u>说中文说得非常好。要是你只听他说话, 不看他的脸, 你一定想他是<u>中国</u>人。<u>大山</u>的 bàba 的 bàba 也住过<u>中国</u>。他 bàba 的 bàba 是医生, 1922年他在<u>中国</u>的一家医院做事。因为地方的名字不同了, <u>大山</u>找了十年才找到那家医院。<u>大山</u>虽然是外国人, 但<u>中国</u>的报纸说他不是外人。

Comprehension questions

1. 谁是<u>大山</u>? 为什么他在<u>中国</u>很有名?

　　_____

2. <u>大山</u>为什么花了这么多时间才找到他 bàba 的 bàba 工作的那家医院?

　　_____

3. 为什么<u>中国</u>的报纸说<u>大山</u>不是外人?

　　_____

---

1. 加拿大 Jiānádà "Canada"

READING 2

小人之过也，必文

　　2000 多年前的中文跟现在的很不一样。"小人之过也，必文" 这句话是 2000 年前写的。你知道这句话是什么意思吗？"小人之过也，必文" 的意思是 "小人做错了事，一定不想给别人知道"。这里 "过" 是 "做错了的事" 的意思，"之" 就是 "的"，"文" 是 "不要给别人知道"。虽然 "小人书" 是 "小孩子看的书"，可是 "小人" 不是 "小孩子" 的意思。这里 "小人" 说的是 "不好的人"，不好的人常常做坏事。

Comprehension questions

1. "小人之过也，必文" 是什么意思？

_____

2. "小人之过也，必文"，这里的 "小人" 是什么意思？

_____

CHARACTER PRACTICE

之	之							
长	长							
乎	乎							
江	江							
全	全							
更	更							
闹	闹							
河	河							
胖	胖							
虽	虽							
样	样							
倍	倍							
够	长							

绩	绩								
裤	裤								
路	路								
瘦	瘦								
趣	趣								
薪	薪								
连	连								
贵	贵								
比	比								
空	空								
穿	穿								
静	静								

19

第十九课

TEXT

　　钟名然今年二月从北京来新西兰学英语。来了新西兰以后，他就住在我家。钟名然很用功，这几个月，他英语已经说得很不错了。因为天天念书很 jǐn 张，所以哪儿都没去玩儿。

　　考完试以后，他比较有空儿，想轻松一下。他听说雪山城的风景很好看，很想到那儿去旅游，就给同学谢里打电话。谢里是法国人，他在雪山城找了个假期工作。他说他可以带钟名然去雪山城玩，钟名然听了很高兴。

　　七月，新西兰是冬天，雪山城很冷，他们得多带几件衣服去。可不是吗？电 shì 上说，雪山城那儿下大雪呢，路上都是白 sè 的，就是穿上两件毛衣、一件外衣也许还不够暖和呢! 钟名然越看越冷，马上去商店又买了一件外衣。

　　雪山城 lí 我家很远，一共有700多公里，中间还有一条大河。你知道坐火车到雪山城要多久吗? 至少得要六个小时，真不近。那儿比我们这儿冷得多了。虽然不刮大风，可是会下雪。雪山城的风景 tè 别好看，很多外国人都 xǐ 欢去那儿旅游。

钟名然和谢里到了雪山城,出了火车站就坐出租车去饭店。车站 lí 饭店不远,可是路上的车很多,好多学生假期都来这儿玩,堵车堵得很利害,他们很晚才到饭店。第二天,钟名然很早就起来了,可是谢里晚上跟他朋友去喝酒了,所以睡得比较晚。钟名然想谢里可能早上起不来了,就自己出去玩儿了。谢里醒了以后找不到钟名然很着急,他穿上外衣马上就去找钟名然。他知道钟名然最爱吃西瓜,就到饭店附近的水果摊去找钟名然。看! 钟名然正在水果摊旁边儿仔细地挑着西瓜呢!

生词 NEW WORDS

钟名然	Zhōng Míngrán	(N) a personal name
新西兰	Xīnxīlán	(PW) New Zealand
英语	Yīngyǔ	(N) English (language)
天天	tiāntiān	(Pat) (Cl-Cl) every...
听说	tīngshuō	(V) hear it said that...
雪山城	Xuěshānchéng	(PW) Snowy Mountain Town
风景	fēngjǐng	(N) scenery
旅游	lǚyóu	(V) tour
比较	bǐjiào	(Adv) comparatively
轻松	qīngsōng	(SV) be relaxed
谢里	Xiè Lǐ	(N) a personal name
假期	jiàqī	(TW) vacation, holiday period
工作	gōngzuò	(N) job
可不是吗?	Kě búshi ma?	(Ex) Isn't that so?
外衣	wàiyī	(N) jacket (Cl -件)
暖和	nuǎnhuo	(SV) be (comfortably) warm (said of weather)
越......越......	yuè...yuè...	(Pat) more and more
马上	mǎshàng	(Adv) right away
远	yuǎn	(SV) be far
公里	gōnglǐ	(Cl) kilometers
中间	zhōngjiān	(PS) the middle
河	hé	(N) river (Cl -条)
火车	huǒchē	(N) train
多久?	duō jiǔ?	(QW) how long?
至少	zhìshǎo	(Adv) at the very least
小时	xiǎoshí	(N) hour

近	jìn	(SV) be near
风	fēng	(N) wind
出	chū	(V) go/come out
火车站	huǒchēzhàn	(PW) train station
出租(汽)车	chūzū (qì)chē	(N) taxi
饭店	fàndiàn	(PW) restaurant, hotel
车站	chēzhàn	(PW) (train/bus) station
堵车	dǔ chē	(VO) jam up (of traffic)
利害[1]	lìhai	(SV) be formidable, be fierce
可能	kěnéng	(Adv) possibly
自己	zìjǐ	(Pr) self
着急	zháojí	(SV) be anxious
西瓜	xīguā	(N) watermelon
附近	fùjìn	(PW) vicinity
水果摊	shuǐguǒtān	(PW) fruit stall
旁边儿	páng.biānr	(PS/PW) the side
挑	tiāo	(V) choose, select

1. Sometimes *lìhai* is written as 厉害.

COMPREHENSION QUESTIONS

1. Read the text of this chapter and answer the following questions.

a. 钟名然是哪国人?

_____

b. 他为什么来新西兰?

_____

c. 他住哪儿?

_____

d. 他为什么没有去别的地方玩儿?

_____

e. 考完试以后, 他想去哪儿玩?

_____

f. 为什么?

_____

g. 他给谁打电话?

_____

h. <u>谢里</u>是谁?

_____

i. <u>谢里</u>怎么说?

_____

j. <u>雪山城</u>的天气 (tiānqì, "weather") 怎么样?

_____

k. <u>钟名然</u>看了电 shì 以后做了什么?

_____

l. "我"家 lí <u>雪山城</u>有多远?

_____

m. 那儿的风景怎么样? 谁 xǐ 欢去那儿?

_____

n. <u>钟名然</u>怎么去饭店?

_____

o. 那天晚上<u>钟名然</u>做了什么?

_____

p. 第二天早上<u>谢里</u>为什么很着急?

_____

q. <u>钟名然</u>去哪儿了? 在做什么?

_____

2. **Write a telephone conversation between 钟名然 and 谢里, discussing the plan to visit 雪山城. Write the conversation using as many Chinese characters as possible.**

钟名然: _____

_____

谢里: _____

_____

钟名然: _____

谢里: _____

钟名然: _____

谢里: _____

钟名然: _____

谢里: _____

WRITING HELP

INDEPENDENT CHARACTERS

Character	Basic meaning	No. of strokes	Stroke order	Radical	Compo-nents	Structure
*工 gōng	work	3	一 丁 工	工	工	☐
马 (馬) mǎ	horse	3	丆 马 马	马	马	☐
*己 jǐ[1]	oneself	3	𠃌 コ 己	己	己	☐
瓜 guā	melon	5	厂 瓜 瓜	瓜	瓜	☐
至 zhì	until	6	一 工 至 至 至 至	土	至	☐

1. See Chapter 12 for a comparison of the subtle contrast in appearance between 已 yǐ introduced in Chapter 12 and 己 jǐ introduced here.

COMPOUND CHARACTERS

The following are the new compound characters with learned radicals in this chapter: 利, 远, 近, 附, 松, 果, 急, 挑, 害, 假, 堵, 景, 游, 越, 暖, and 摊.

Char-acter	Basic meaning	No. of strokes	Stroke order	Radical	Meaning clue	Phonetic clue	Compo-nents	Struc-ture
利 lì	benefit	7	禾 利	刂	刂		禾 刂	
远 (遠) yuǎn	far	7	二 テ 元 远	辶	辶	元 yuán	辶 元	
近 jìn	near	7	斤 近	辶	辶	斤 jīn	辶 斤	
附 fù	to attach	7	阝 阝 附	阝		付 fù	阝 亻 寸	
松 sōng	pine tree, relaxed*	8	木 松	木	木	公	木 公	
*果 guǒ	fruit	8	曰 果	木	田, 木 (a tree grows in the field)		木 田	
急 jí	to hurry	9	勹 勻 勻 急 急	心	心		勹 彐 心	
挑 tiāo	to pick	9	扌 扌 扌 扎 挑 挑	扌		兆 iao[1]	扌 兆	
害 hài	to harm	10	宀 宀 宔 宔 害	宀			宀 丰 口	
假 jià	holiday	11	亻 仴 仴 仴 仴 假	亻	亻	叚 jiǎ	亻 叚	
堵 dǔ	to block up	11	土 堵	土	土		土 者	
*景 jǐng	scenery	12	曰 景	日	日	京	日 京	

Char-acter	Basic meaning	No. of strokes	Stroke order	Radical	Meaning clue	Phonetic clue	Compo-nents	Struc-ture
游 (遊) yóu	to swim	12	氵 氵 汸 游	氵	氵	斿 yóu	氵 方 ⺈ 子	⊟⊟⊟
越 yuè	to cross	12	走 走 赻 赻 越 越	走	走	戉 yuè	走 戉	
暖 nuǎn	warm	13	旷 旷 旷 旷 旷 暖	日	日	爰 yuán	日 爰	
*摊 (攤) tān	stall, stand (com-mercial)	13	扌 扫 摊	扌	扌	难	扌 又 隹	⊟⊟⊟

1. 兆: This character is pronounced as *zhào* when it functions as an independent character, but as a phonetic component it often indicates the *iao* sound.

RADICALS

The new radicals introduced in this chapter are 车, 方, and 立.

1. 车

When this character functions as a radical in a compound character it usually is found to its left. The compound characters in this chapter containing this radical are 轻 and 较.

Character	Basic meaning	No. of strokes	Stroke order	Meaning clue	Phonetic clue	Compo-nents	Structure
轻 (輕) qīng	light (not heavy)	9	车 轻		圣 jīng	车 圣	⊟
较 (較) jiào	to com-pare	10	车 轲 较		交 jiāo	车 交	⊟

2. 方

方 *fāng* as a character means "square, direction". It can be used in compound characters related to its original meaning. The compound characters in this chapter that contains this radical are 旁 and 旅.

Character	Basic meaning	No. of strokes	Stroke order	Meaning clue	Phonetic clue	Compo-nents	Structure
*旁 páng	beside	10	亠 亠 亠 旁	方	方	亠 冖 方	⊟
*旅 lǚ	to travel, trip	10	方 方 方 旅 旅 旅	方		方 ㇒ 氏	⊟

3. 立

立 can be used as a character as well as a radical. As a character it means to stand (立 *lì*). When it is used as a radical in compound characters, it indicates a related meaning. The compound character in this chapter containing this radical is 站.

Character	Basic meaning	No. of strokes	Stroke order	Meaning clue	Phonetic clue	Compo-nents	Structure
站 zhàn	to stand	10	立 站	立	占 zhàn	立 占	⊟

站: This is also a station where people stand around waiting.

EXERCISES

CHARACTER EXERCISES

1. **Find the independent characters you have learned hidden in the following characters.**

松 _____   堵 _____   景 _____   游 _____

摊 _____   轻 _____   害 _____   暖 _____

2. Write in brackets the component that is common to each set of characters below.

至, 场, 老, 坐 → (　　　　)　　　　旅, 游, 旁, 房 → (　　　　　)

急, 当, 雪 → (　　　　)　　　　站, 点, 店 → (　　　　)

附, 厨, 得, 衬 → (　　　　)　　　　假, 难, 趣, 瘦 → (　　　　)

近, 诉, 薪 → (　　　　)　　　　准, 摊, 谁 → (　　　　)

3. Form new characters by using different components of the following characters, e.g. 工 (from 功) + 广 (from 有) → 左.

> 利　完　进　急　咱　所

_____ (from _____) + _____ (from _____) → _____

_____ (from _____) + _____ (from _____) → _____

_____ (from _____) + _____ (from _____) → _____

_____ (from _____) + _____ (from _____) → _____

4. How many words and phrases can you form using the following characters?

a. 风 → _____

b. 可 → _____

c. 西 → _____

d. 车 → _____

5. Form four characters each using each of the following components.

a. 月 → _____

b. 衤 → _____

c. 土 → _____

d. 日 → _____

e. 心 → _____

6. Circle the wrong character(s) in each sentence and make the correction in the brackets provided.

a. 听说<u>张伯伯</u>穿的衣服都是他自己做的。　　（　　　）

b. 夏天有很多好吃的水果，我最 xǐ 欢吃西爪。　（　　　）

c. <u>钟名然</u>在水果滩旁边儿仔细地桃着水果。　（　　　）（　　　　）

d. <u>谢里</u>在风景好看的<u>雪山城</u>找了个假期公作。　（　　　）

VOCABULARY EXERCISES

1. Combine a character from column A with one from column B, and then write the word in brackets. No character can be used more than one time.

A	B	
马	游	（　　　　）
自	车	（　　　　）
堵	期	（　　　　）
轻	里	（　　　　）
假	害	（　　　　）
公	上	（　　　　）
利	己	（　　　　）
旅	松	（　　　　）

2. Write two different characters next to the Pinyin in each group of homonyms, then form a word or phrase with each character.

a. { jí (　　　) _____
     jí (　　　) _____

b. { jìn (　　　) _____
     jìn (　　　) _____

c. { yuè (　　　) _____
     yuè (　　　) _____

d. { jiǔ (　　　) _____
     jiǔ (　　　) _____

e.
$$\begin{cases} \text{zhì (\quad)} & \underline{\hspace{4cm}} \\ \text{zhì (\quad)} & \underline{\hspace{4cm}} \end{cases}$$

f.
$$\begin{cases} \text{qīng (\quad)} & \underline{\hspace{4cm}} \\ \text{qīng (\quad)} & \underline{\hspace{4cm}} \end{cases}$$

g.
$$\begin{cases} \text{jiào (\quad)} & \underline{\hspace{4cm}} \\ \text{jiào (\quad)} & \underline{\hspace{4cm}} \end{cases}$$

3. **Write two different pronunciations for each of the following characters, then make a word or phrase with each.**

a. 和
$$\begin{cases} (\quad) & \underline{\hspace{4cm}} \\ (\quad) & \underline{\hspace{4cm}} \end{cases}$$

b. 着
$$\begin{cases} (\quad) & \underline{\hspace{4cm}} \\ (\quad) & \underline{\hspace{4cm}} \end{cases}$$

c. 仔
$$\begin{cases} (\quad) & \underline{\hspace{4cm}} \\ (\quad) & \underline{\hspace{4cm}} \end{cases}$$

4. **Find the word that is not in the same category as the other three words and write it in the brackets provided.**

a. 毛衣, 牛仔裤, 外衣, 汗衫　(　　　　)

b. 附近, 对面, 假期, 旁边儿　(　　　　)

c. 车站, 火车, 飞机, 出租车　(　　　　)

d. 着急, jǐn 张, 暖和, 生气　(　　　　)

e. 下雪, 刮风, 下雨, 下班　(　　　　)

5. **Give the antonym for each of the following words.**

a. jǐn 张 → (　　　　)　　c. 凉快 → (　　　　)

b. 远 → (　　　　)　　d. 进 → (　　　　)

6. **Give a synonym for each of the following words.**

a. 钟头 → (　　　　)　　c. 饭馆儿 → (　　　　)

b. 也许 → (　　　　)

STRUCTURE EXERCISES

1. Write the correct classifier character to complete each of the following phrases.

一＿＿＿＿外衣	一＿＿＿＿大河	四＿＿＿＿行李
两＿＿＿＿牛仔裤	那＿＿＿＿路	这＿＿＿＿水果摊
一＿＿＿＿假期工作	三＿＿＿＿西瓜	

2. Complete the following sentences using the pattern 越……越……and the words in brackets.

a. 他的汉字＿＿＿＿＿＿＿＿＿＿＿＿＿＿＿＿＿＿＿＿。(写)

b. 中文 ＿＿＿＿＿＿＿＿＿＿＿＿＿＿＿＿＿＿＿＿。(学)

c. 他说得＿＿＿＿＿＿＿我＿＿＿＿＿＿＿＿＿＿＿。(快)

d. 你＿＿＿＿＿＿＿＿考试成绩＿＿＿＿＿＿＿＿。(用功)

e. 她＿＿＿＿＿＿＿＿＿＿＿＿＿＿＿＿＿＿。(吃)

3. Translate the following sentences into Chinese, using Chinese characters for learned words.

a. My home is very close to the city center, so I often go downtown to do window-shopping.

＿＿＿＿＿＿＿＿＿＿＿＿＿＿＿＿＿＿＿＿＿＿＿＿＿＿＿＿＿

b. It takes at least four hours to go from Shanghai to Beijing by train.

＿＿＿＿＿＿＿＿＿＿＿＿＿＿＿＿＿＿＿＿＿＿＿＿＿＿＿＿＿

c. Over holidays, the more beautiful the scenery of a place is, the greater the number of tourists.

＿＿＿＿＿＿＿＿＿＿＿＿＿＿＿＿＿＿＿＿＿＿＿＿＿＿＿＿＿

d. How hot is it here in summer? Not very hot, it's relatively cool.

＿＿＿＿＿＿＿＿＿＿＿＿＿＿＿＿＿＿＿＿＿＿＿＿＿＿＿＿＿

e. The later you leave, the heavier the traffic jam.

＿＿＿＿＿＿＿＿＿＿＿＿＿＿＿＿＿＿＿＿＿＿＿＿＿＿＿＿＿

WRITING EXERCISE

1. **Write a short paragraph about your traveling experience.**

_____

_____

_____

_____

_____

_____

_____

_____

SUPPLEMENTARY READING

READING 1

知之为知之, 不知为不知

　　你们知道 "知之为知之, 不知为不知" 是什么意思吗? 这也是 2000 多年前写的中文, 意思是 "知道就说知道, 不知道就说不知道, 这样才能学到东西"。

Comprehension questions

1. "知之为知之，不知为不知" 这句话是什么意思？

_____

2. "知之为知之，不知为不知" 是什么时候写的？

_____

READING 2

走马看花

　　以前有一个名叫贵良[1]的男子，他长得很好看，可是 tuǐ 有点儿问题，所以走路很不方便。他想找一个漂亮的女孩子做他的太太，他请他的朋友华汉给他介绍女朋友。

　　华汉家对面住着一个很漂亮的女孩子，她的名字叫叶青[2]。叶青想找一个好看的男朋友，可是因为她的 bízi 长得不好看，所以没找着。华汉想把叶青介绍给贵良认识。

　　在八月八日的那一天，华汉让贵良 qí 着马从叶青家门口经过[3]，又叫叶青手里拿着花站在她家门口。叶青看到 qí 在马上的贵良，没有看出贵良的 tuǐ 有问题，叶青很 xǐ 欢贵良。贵良只看到叶青手上拿的花，没有看到叶青的 bízi，贵良也爱上了叶青。后来叶青做了贵良的太太。他们常常说起 "走马看花" 的那件事。现在这句话成了一句成语，意思是 "只是很快地看了一遍，没仔细地看清楚"。

_____

1. 贵良 Guì Liáng "name of a male"
2. 叶青 Yè Qīng "name of a female"
3. 经过 jīngguò "pass through"

Comprehension questions

1. 为什么华汉要给贵良介绍女朋友?

   _____

2. 华汉为什么把吐青介绍给贵良认识?

   _____

3. "走马看花" 是什么意思?

   _____

CHARACTER PRACTICE

工	工								
马	马								
己	己								
瓜	瓜								
至	至								
利	利								
远	远								
近	近								
附	附								

松	松							
果	果							
急	急							
挑	挑							
旅	旅							
害	害							
假	假							
堵	堵							
景	景							
游	游							
越	越							
暖	暖							
摊	摊							

轻	轻								
较	较								
旁	旁								
旅	旅								
站	站								

TEXT

　　江太太知道江兴成今天下午不用去上班，就叫他上附近的超市替她买点儿东西。她说假期快到了，她想带孩子们去度假，所以要买点儿吃的、喝的、用的什么的。当然，还要买几斤现成的饺子。江太太还要他买东西的时候，不要被偷了钱和信用 kǎ。江兴成刚出门，他太太又叫住他，告诉他买东西回来的时候从高速公路去学校接孩子回家。江兴成不高兴地说："知道了。真讨厌！"

　　两个小时以后，江兴成带着四个孩子回来了。孩子们又吵又闹，江兴成要他们安静些。孩子们不但不听，而且越来越吵了。大女儿一进家就要唱 kǎ拉 OK，二女儿要给同学打电话，小女儿要玩电 nǎo，小儿子要看电 shì 上的足球 sài。一会儿，二女儿跟小儿子打架了，儿子哭了，他的手被姐姐抓 pò 了，流血了，二女儿也生气了。江兴成说家里有四个孩子真是吵死了，孩子们都应

该去学校宿舍住。可是，假期的时候孩子们天天在家怎么办? 自己还是天天
去办公楼上班，不在家最好。

生词 NEW WORDS

江兴成	Jiāng Xīngchéng	(N) a personal name
超市	chāoshì	(PW) supermarket
度假	dù jià	(VO) spend one's holiday
-斤	-jīn	(Cl) unit of weight (0.5 kilograms, slightly more than a pound)
被	bèi	(CV) (a marker for passive-voice sentence)
偷	tōu	(V) steal
信用 kǎ	xìnyòngkǎ	(N) credit card (Cl -张)
高速公路	gāosù gōnglù	(N) highway, freeway
接	jiē	(V) meet, pick (somebody) up
讨厌	tǎoyàn	(SV) be a pain in the neck
闹	nào	(V) make noise, stir up trouble, etc.
不但……而且……	búdàn…érqiě…	(Pat) Not only X, but also Y
唱	chàng	(V) sing
kǎ 拉 OK	kǎlā-ōukēi	(N) karaoke
电 nǎo	diànnǎo	(N) computer (lit. "electric brain")
足球 sài	zúqiúsài	(N) soccer match
一会儿	yìhuǐr	(TD) a while, a short time
打架	dǎ jià	(VO) scuffle
哭	kū	(V) cry, weep
手	shǒu	(N) hand
抓	zhuā	(V) grab, scratch, arrest
流血	liú xiě	(VO) bleed
-死	-sǐ	(RVC) (indicates extremeness of state)
应该	yīnggāi	(Aux) ought to
宿舍	sùshè	(PW) dormitory
怎么办?	Zěnme bàn?	(Ex) What the heck do we do
办公楼	bàngōnglóu	(PW) office building

COMPREHENSION QUESTIONS

1. Read the text of this chapter and for each statement below indicate whether it is true or false.

a. (　　　　) <u>江太太</u>知道<u>江兴成</u>下午要去上班, 所以叫他替她买东西。

b. (　　　　) <u>江太太</u>要<u>江兴成</u>去买东西, 因为她想带孩子们去度假。

c. (　　　　) <u>江太太</u>买东西的时候被偷了钱和信用 kǎ。

d. (　　　　) <u>江兴成</u>从高速公路去学校接孩子回家。

e. (　　　　) 因为<u>江兴成</u>不 xǐ 欢他的太太说得太多, 所以他说: "真讨厌!"

2. In pairs, fill in the boxes with the relevant information from the text.

People	Description
大女儿	
二女儿	
小女儿	
小儿子	

WRITING HELP

INDEPENDENT CHARACTERS

Character	Basic meaning	No. of strokes	Stroke order	Radical	Components	Structure
*斤 jīn	0.5 kilo-grams	4	㇒ ㇀ ㇁ 斤	斤	斤	☐
办 (辦) bàn	to do	4	㇆ 力 办 办	力	办	☐
且 qiě	also	5	㇑ ㄇ 𠕁 月 且	一	且	☐
血 xiě	blood	6	㇒ ㇀ 白 血 血	血	血	☐

COMPOUND CHARACTERS

The following are the new compound characters with learned radicals in this chapter: 讨, 厌, 但, 足, 抓, 应, 拉, 该, 舍, 度, 架, 被, 速, 哭, 流, 偷, 接, 唱, 球, 宿, and 超.

Character	Basic meaning	No. of strokes	Stroke order	Radical	Meaning clue	Phonetic clue	Components	Structure
讨 (討) tǎo	to ask for	5	讠 讨	讠	讠		讠 寸	
*厌 (厭) yàn	disgusting	6	厂 厌 厌	厂			厂 犬	
但 dàn	but	7	亻 但 但	亻		旦 dàn	亻 日 一	
*足 zú	foot	7	口 甲 昂 昆 足	口			口 止	
抓 zhuā	to grab	7	扌 扩 扪 抓	扌	扌	爪 zhuǎ	扌 爪	
应 (應) yīng	should	7	广 庐 应 应	广			广 丷 一	
拉 lā	to pull	8	扌 拉	扌	扌		扌 立	
该 (該) gāi	should	8	讠 讠 诊 该	讠		亥 hài	讠 亥	
*舍 shè	inn	8	人 今 舍	人	人	舌 shé	人 干 口	
*度 dù	size	9	广 广 庐 庐 庐 度	广			广 廿 又	
架 jià	shelf, frame	9	力 加 架	木	木	加 jiā	力 口 木	
被 bèi	quilt*, by... -ed	10	衤 被	衤	衤	皮	衤 皮	

Character	Basic meaning	No. of strokes	Stroke order	Radical	Meaning clue	Phonetic clue	Components	Structure
*速 sù	speed	10	一 曰 申 束 速	辶	辶	束 shù	辶 束	
哭 kū	to cry	10	口 吅 哭 哭	口	口, 犬		口口犬	
流 liú	to flow	10	氵 汁 浐 浐 浐 浐 流	氵	氵		氵 云 丿 川	
偷 tōu	to steal	11	亻 仒 伶 偷 偷	亻	亻		亻俞	
接 jiē	to meet	11	扌 拉 接	扌	扌	妾 qiè	扌 立 女	
唱 chàng	to sing	11	口 呾 唱	口	口	昌 chāng	口 日 曰	
球 qiú	ball	11	王 玒 玒 玒 玒 玒 球 球	王		求 qiú	王 求	
*宿 sù	to stay over-night	11	宀 宀 宿	宀	宀, 亻, 百		宀 亻 百	
超 chāo	to sur-pass	12	走 起 超	走	走	召 zhāo	走 刀 口	

哭: This is better remembered as a person with arms stretched 大, two 口 are like two eyes on the top and one dot is the tear from the eye

宿: This is better remembered like this: There are hundreds 百 of people 人 living under one roof = dormitory.

EXERCISES

CHARACTER EXERCISES

1. **Find the independent characters you have learned hidden in the following characters.**

宿 _____　　　超 _____　　　被 _____　　　哭 _____

偷 _____　　　接 _____　　　闹 _____　　　度 _____

2. **Write in brackets the component that is common to each set of characters below.**

度, 假, 被, 瘦 → (　　　　)　　　　架, 为, 办, 边 → (　　　　　)

偷, 期, 用, 胖 → (　　　　)　　　　流, 能, 去, 公 → (　　　　　)

厌, 哭, 美, 因 → (　　　　)　　　　该, 刻, 孩 → (　　　　)

3. **Form new characters by using different components of the following characters, e.g. 工 (from 功) + 𠂇 (from 有) → 左.**

| 超　抓　经　较　速　杯　吧 |

_____ (from _____) + _____ (from _____) → _____

_____ (from _____) + _____ (from _____) → _____

_____ (from _____) + _____ (from _____) → _____

_____ (from _____) + _____ (from _____) → _____

_____ (from _____) + _____ (from _____) → _____

4. **Form five characters each using each of the following components.**

a. 寸 → _____

b. 扌 → _____

c. 日 → _____

d. 衤 → _____

e. 讠 → _____

f. 立 → _____

g. 亻 → _____

h. 子 → _____

5. Write as many characters as you can remember with the following radicals indicating the meanings in the brackets.

a. 辶 (road/walking movement)

→ _____

b. 讠 (language/speech related)

→ _____

c. 木 (wood/tree related)

→ _____

6. Circle the wrong character(s) in each sentence and make the correction in the brackets provided.

a. <u>江兴成</u>上班的地方在这个办工楼的四楼。 　　　(　　)

b. 他买了几斤现成的饺子, 没时间做饭的时候可以吃饺子。 (　　)

c. <u>江兴成</u> jué 得孩子们因该去学校宿舍住, 因为他们太吵了。 (　　)

d. 小儿子的手被二女儿抓 pò 了,流皿了。 　　　　　(　　)

e. 考完试以后, <u>钟名然</u>想去<u>雪山城</u>度架, 轻松一下。 　(　　)

VOCABULARY EXERCISES

1. Combine a character from column A with one from column B, and then write the word in brackets. No character can be used more than one time.

A	B	
讨	血	(　　　　)
足	舍	(　　　　)
宿	该	(　　　　)
应	架	(　　　　)
安	假	(　　　　)
流	静	(　　　　)
打	厌	(　　　　)
度	球	(　　　　)

2. Write two different characters next to the Pinyin in each group of homonyms, then form a word or phrase with each character.

a. $\begin{cases} \text{kuài (} & \text{)} \underline{\hspace{4cm}} \\ \text{kuài (} & \text{)} \underline{\hspace{4cm}} \end{cases}$

b. $\begin{cases} \text{dù (} & \text{)} \underline{\hspace{4cm}} \\ \text{dù (} & \text{)} \underline{\hspace{4cm}} \end{cases}$

c. $\begin{cases} \text{jià (} & \text{)} \underline{\hspace{4cm}} \\ \text{jià (} & \text{)} \underline{\hspace{4cm}} \end{cases}$

d. $\begin{cases} \text{sù (} & \text{)} \underline{\hspace{4cm}} \\ \text{sù (} & \text{)} \underline{\hspace{4cm}} \end{cases}$

e. $\begin{cases} \text{bèi (} & \text{)} \underline{\hspace{4cm}} \\ \text{bèi (} & \text{)} \underline{\hspace{4cm}} \end{cases}$

f. $\begin{cases} \text{xiě (} & \text{)} \underline{\hspace{4cm}} \\ \text{xiě (} & \text{)} \underline{\hspace{4cm}} \end{cases}$

3. How many words and phrases can you form using the following characters?

a. 家 → \underline{\hspace{9cm}}

b. 子 → \underline{\hspace{9cm}}

c. 高 → \underline{\hspace{9cm}}

4. Write two different pronunciations for each of the following characters, then
   make a word or phrase with each.

a. 行 (   ) \underline{\hspace{5cm}}

   (   ) \underline{\hspace{5cm}}

b. 得 (   ) \underline{\hspace{5cm}}

   (   ) \underline{\hspace{5cm}}

c. 便 (   ) \underline{\hspace{5cm}}

   (   ) \underline{\hspace{5cm}}

5. For each of the objects below find a verb from the text that can go with the object and write the verb in the brackets.

a. (　　　) kǎ 拉 OK   e. (　　　) 超市

b. (　　　) 孩子   f. (　　　) 电话

c. (　　　) 电 nǎo   g. (　　　) 宿舍

d. (　　　) 足球 sài

6. Find the word that is not in the same category as the other three words and write it in the brackets provided.

a. 办公楼, 超市, 利害, 宿舍   (　　　)

b. 听说, 打架, 流血, 堵车   (　　　)

c. 应该, 能, 被, 可以   (　　　)

d. 抓, 挑, 接, 闹   (　　　)

e. 高速公路, 公共汽车, 火车, 飞机 (　　　)

7. Give the antonym for each of the following words.

a. 笑 → (　　　)   c. 吵 → (　　　)

b. xǐ 欢 → (　　　)   d. 上班 → (　　　)

STRUCTURE EXERCISES

1. Write the correct classifier character to complete each of the following phrases.

一＿＿＿＿信用 kǎ   一＿＿＿＿高速公路   几＿＿＿＿饺子

两＿＿＿＿饭   四＿＿＿＿课   三＿＿＿＿皮 xié

2. Rearrange the elements below to form a grammatical sentence.

a. 而且, 卖, 不但, 吃, xǐ 欢, 大女儿, 超市, 小儿子, 饺子, 也, 的, xǐ 欢

→ ＿＿＿＿＿＿＿＿＿＿＿＿＿＿＿＿＿＿＿＿＿＿＿＿＿＿＿

b. 的, 上课, 都, 学校, 假期, 天天, 孩子们, 用, 不, 时候, 在, 去, 家

→ ＿＿＿＿＿＿＿＿＿＿＿＿＿＿＿＿＿＿＿＿＿＿＿＿＿＿＿

c. 在, 被, 了, 不过, 他, 信用 kǎ, 钱, 的, 偷, 还

→ _____

d. 了, 又, 作业, 气, 孩子们, <u>江兴成</u>, 吵, 而且, 做, 不但, 闹, 又, 没, 死, 还

→ _____

3. Translate the following sentences into Chinese, using Chinese characters for learned words.

a. The story he told made me split my sides in laughter.

_____

b. The dishes on the table have all been eaten up by him. The other people are not yet full.

_____

c. He didn't move until the house had been sold.

_____

d. Living in the university dormitory is not only comfortable but also convenient for university students.

_____

e. This supermarket is not only close to his home, but the things there are also comparatively cheap.

_____

SUPPLEMENTARY READING

READING 1

<u>Xiāng 山</u>

　　你知道 <u>Xiāng 山</u>在哪儿吗? <u>Xiāng 山</u>就在<u>北京</u>的西北部。因为 <u>Xiāng 山</u>那儿的风景很美, 所以一年春夏秋冬都有很多人到那儿去玩儿。很多住在<u>北京</u>的人也 xǐ 欢在星期六和星期日带家人去爬山。春天, <u>Xiāng 山</u>的山上开了很多的花, 花被风 chuī 下来的时候, 很好看。夏天不但不热, 而且很凉快。秋天的风景更漂亮, 远远看去, 红 sè、黄 sè、绿 sè 的山, 美极了。冬天虽然冷, 又下雪, 可是<u>Xiāng 山</u>还是很美, 跟春天、夏天和秋天的美不一样。要是你们有机会去<u>北京</u>, 一定要去<u>Xiāng 山</u>玩儿。

Comprehension questions

1. <u>Xiāng</u> 山在哪儿?

_____

2. <u>Xiāng</u> 山一年春夏秋冬的风景都一样吗? 有什么不同?

_____

READING 2

张大千

　　<u>张大千</u> (1899–1984) 是一个很有名的画家。他从小就跟他妈妈学画画儿。他父母一共有十个孩子, 他是第八个。他七岁开始上学, 九岁开始学画画儿, 十二岁就能画山水、花和人。他 1917 年跟他哥哥去<u>日本</u>学画画儿。1919 年从<u>日本</u>回<u>上海</u>后就跟一位很有名的画家学书画[1]。 他去过很多个国家, 也住过很多个国家, 他在<u>美国</u>住了八年。<u>张大千</u>画画儿画了六十多年, 他很用功。在这么长的时间里, 他画了三万多张画儿。

　　<u>张大千</u>不但 xǐ 欢画画儿, 他也 xǐ 欢买画儿。听说有一次他已经跟朋友说好要买他朋友的房子, 可是后来他看到有人要卖一幅很有名的画儿。 他看了那幅画儿以后高兴得睡不着觉。过了几天, 他跟他的朋友说他不买他的房子了, 他把买房子的钱都拿去买画儿了。

---

1. 书画 shūhuà "painting and calligraphy"

Comprehension questions

1. 张大千是谁? 他几岁就开始学画画儿?

   _____

2. 张大千画画儿画了多少年? 他一共画了多少张画儿?

   _____

3. 张大千不但 xǐ 欢画画儿, 而且还喜欢做什么?

   _____

CHARACTER PRACTICE

斤	斤								
办	办								
且	且								
血	血								
市	市								

讨	讨							
厌	厌							
级	级							
但	但							
足	足							
抓	抓							
应	应							
拉	拉							
该	该							
舍	舍							
度	度							
架	架							
被	被							
速	速							

哭	哭								
流	流								
偷	偷								
接	接								
唱	唱								
球	球								
宿	宿								
超	超								

COMPLETE THE DIALOGUE

Complete the following dialogue in Chinese characters. When words are provided in brackets, you should use them.

A: 明天是<u>黄志</u>的生日, 我想送他一个 lǐwù。

B: <u>黄志</u>最 xǐ 欢看书了。

A: 那, _____? (书店)

B: 好, 市中心有一家很大的书店, 我们到那儿去看看。

A: _____?

B: 不远, 走路只要十五分钟。

A: _____。

B: 走吧。

FILL IN THE BLANK

Fill in each blank by choosing the most appropriate word from the alternatives provided in the box. You should not use any word more than ONCE. There are more choices than blanks.

1.

| 从 替 的时候 了 能 当然 当中 中间 连 |
| 现在 不 以前 不过 得 用 来 好 几 |

国汉的父母是中国人, _____ 他们很久以前就到美国来念书和工作了。国汉 _____ 小就住在美国, 他不会说中文, 也不会写汉字。去年国汉上大学 _____, 他学了很多不同的课。在大学所有的课 _____, 他最想学中文, 因为他的父母是中国人。可是, 他太忙了, 没有时间学中文。

今年他有机会到上海学一年的中文。刚到上海 _____, 他 _____ 一个朋友也没有, 谁也不认识, 所以他很想家。几个月以后, 他开始认识了一些朋友, 有中国的、日本的, 也有美国的。_____, 他 xǐ 欢住在上海了。上海很热闹, 也很方便, 那儿的东西很好看, 也很便宜。衣服很时 máo, 小吃很好吃, 坐公交车上学也很方便。以前, 国汉一句中文也听 _____ 懂, 现在他会说 _____ 些中文了, 也会写一些汉字了。现在, 他能 _____ 中文做很多事了, 买东西、坐公交车都没什么大问 tí 了。

2.

| 带 着 不必 地 而是 急 吵 双 可是 穿 在 |
| 安静 热闹 就是 极 很 dài 的 到 fù 得 太 |

今天是十月三十号, 大明的生日。早上他去超市买了很多菜和啤酒, 晚上大明请他的朋友们一块儿来家里做饭。他的好朋友英英, 最会做饺子了, 她做的饺子好吃 _____ 了。他们喝 _____ 中国啤酒吃饺子。因为大明现在在大学学中文, 所以大明的朋友们送给他一本中文词典。除了中文词典以外, 他们还送大明一 _____ 很时 máo 的 mò 镜。大明 _____ 上又时 máo 又好看的 mò 镜, 真是太好看了。大明很 xǐ 欢他的生日 lǐwù。

他们 liáo 天一直 liáo＿＿＿＿＿半夜。他们越 liáo 越高兴, 也越来

越＿＿＿＿＿, 英英要他们安静, 大明轻松＿＿＿＿＿说:"没关系, 我的邻 jū

们不是去旅游, ＿＿＿＿＿不在家, 所以＿＿＿＿＿jǐn 张。"虽然已经很晚

了, 他们还不想回家。＿＿＿＿＿, 明天他们还要上课呢。大明请他的朋友们回

家, 等到星期六再来玩。他的朋友们想开车回家, 大明说:"喝了酒以后不可以开

车。"所以大明 bāng 他们叫了出租车, 他们就坐出租车回家了。

TRANSLATION

Translate each of the following passages into Chinese. For characters you have not yet been taught, you may use *Hànyǔ Pīnyīn* romanization together with the tone marks.

1.

My friend *Xiaoping* really likes to go to China for a holiday. He says that the food at the restaurants there is not only cheap, but it is also very delicious. On April 23 of last year he went on holiday to Beijing again. As he was on his way from Beijing University to the train station by bus, his leather briefcase got stolen. Inside the briefcase were his passport, credit card, and $105. He said, "This is really infuriating!"

＿＿＿＿＿＿＿＿＿＿＿＿＿＿＿＿＿＿＿＿＿＿＿＿＿＿＿＿＿＿

＿＿＿＿＿＿＿＿＿＿＿＿＿＿＿＿＿＿＿＿＿＿＿＿＿＿＿＿＿＿

＿＿＿＿＿＿＿＿＿＿＿＿＿＿＿＿＿＿＿＿＿＿＿＿＿＿＿＿＿＿

＿＿＿＿＿＿＿＿＿＿＿＿＿＿＿＿＿＿＿＿＿＿＿＿＿＿＿＿＿＿

＿＿＿＿＿＿＿＿＿＿＿＿＿＿＿＿＿＿＿＿＿＿＿＿＿＿＿＿＿＿

＿＿＿＿＿＿＿＿＿＿＿＿＿＿＿＿＿＿＿＿＿＿＿＿＿＿＿＿＿＿

2.

Xiao Fang: *Dawen*, are you able to make out those two characters on the blackboard?

Dawen: (They) are *zhǔnbèi*. What about your glasses?

Xiao Fang: I got up late this morning and didn't have time to look (for them).

Dawen: (If you) don't wear glasses, are you able to see things?

Xiao Fang: (I) can make them out, but I can't see them clearly.

Dawen: I hope that your glasses are not lost.

Xiao Fang: (If they are) lost it also doesn't matter. They are old and they aren't a famous brand.

Dawen: How much per pair are your glasses?

Xiao Fang: Two hundred sixty dollars a pair.

Dawen: If mine were lost then I would never be able to afford to buy (another pair) again.

_____

_____

_____

_____

_____

_____

_____

_____

_____

3.

This morning, as soon as I woke up, I felt sick. My throat hurt, as did my head and my back. I felt pain everywhere. I couldn't even eat breakfast ("I could not swallow any breakfast"). Therefore, I had to visit the doctor. I took a bus to the hospital and I didn't need to change buses. It was quite convenient. After seeing the doctor I returned home and had some medicine. I now feel a lot better.

_____

_____

_____

_____

_____

_____

4.

It will be *Zhang Jing*'s birthday tomorrow. Yesterday I went to New World Shoe Shop to buy her a pair of shoes. New World Shoe Shop is not far from my house. It only takes 10 minutes to walk there from my house.

As soon as I finished my breakfast, I went to the shoe shop to have a look at shoes. The shoes in the New World Shoe Shop were beautiful, but they were getting more and more expensive. I knew that there was a newly opened shoe shop not far from New World Shoe Shop. I heard that the shoes in the newly opened shoe shop were comparatively cheaper. I walked out of New World Shoe Shop and went to the new shoe shop to have a look. The shoes in the new shoe shop were slightly more expensive than those in New World Shoe Shop, but they were a lot more beautiful than those in New World Shoe Shop. I bought a pair of dark blue shoes. I know that *Zhang Jing* will certainly like them.

_____

_____

_____

_____

_____

_____

_____

_____

_____

_____

_____

_____

_____

5.

Last Saturday I went to a shop downtown to buy a sweater. The sweaters sold in that shop were quite pretty. There were red ones, blue ones, yellow ones, purple ones, and pink ones. I liked that shop's sweaters very much, but they were too expensive, so I could not afford one. I additionally went to another shop to have a look. I saw that up ahead there was a shop with many people inside. I walked in to have a look. The sweaters that that shop sold were both cheap and good-looking. No wonder there were that many people.

_____

_____

_____

_____

_____

_____

_____

_____

6.

Last night *Xiaoming* went to sleep late, so he didn't get out of bed until 8:30 this morning. Although his home is not far from university, it still takes 20 minutes to walk there. Driving is faster than walking, but the day before yesterday his friend *Xiao Zhang* borrowed his car. This morning he had to be at French class at 9:00, so as soon as he got out of bed he headed off to class. In class, because he forgot to bring his glasses, he couldn't clearly see the words that the teacher wrote on the blackboard. As soon as he got out of class he returned home to look for his glasses, and looked everywhere but he couldn't find them anywhere. The next day *Xiao Zhang* returned the car to him. He found his glasses inside his car. He was extremely happy.

_____

_____

_____

_____

_____

_____

_____

_____

_____

READING COMPREHENSION

Read each of the following passages and answer the questions that follow it.

1.

今天南西 ("Nancy") 的好朋友从英国来看她。因为她太高兴了, 所以昨天她一个晚上都睡不好。今天早上她很早就起床了, 她连早饭都没吃就去机场接她朋友了。从她家坐公共汽车去机场要一个小时, 坐出租车只要半个小时。坐出租车要五十多块钱, 坐公共汽车只要六块钱。她看时间已经不早了, 还是打的去吧!

半小时后, 她到了机场。南西下了出租车就跑进机场, 她想她的朋友一定等了很久了, 可是她在机场找来找去都找不到她的朋友。她看看她的手 biǎo, 再看看机场的钟。她的手 biǎo 的时间是七点半, 可是机场的钟才六点半, 她早到了一个小时。

她在 yǐ 子上坐下, 肚子开始饿了。她站起来走去对面的中国小吃店买了一包小吃, 然后又回到 yǐ 子上坐, 正想吃小吃的时候, 坐在她旁边儿的那位 dài 眼镜的先生说: "小姐, 等人吗?"

"是呀! 还得等一个小时呢。"

"那, 先看报吧! 这是今天的报, 刚买的。"

"谢谢。"

南西吃着小吃看报。过了一会儿, 坐在她旁边儿的那位先生也开始吃起她买的小吃来。她想: "啊! 因为他想吃我的东西, 所以才给我看他的报。"过了两分钟, 那位先生说: "我朋友来了, 这些中国小吃给你吧!"

"这是你的?"

"是呀! 你的在你的行李上呢。"

"对不起, 我 yǐwéi 是我的。"

"没关系。你吃吧!"

南西的 liǎn 红了, 那位先生对她笑了笑就走了。

a. 南西为什么去机场?

_____

b. 南西是怎么去机场的?

_____

c. 南西到了机场, 她的朋友到了吗? 南西为什么早到了一个小时?

_____

d. 南西肚子饿了, 她去哪儿买吃的东西?

_____

e. 南西和那位 dài 眼镜的先生吃的小吃是谁的? 南西的小吃在哪儿?

_____

2.

    高明 liàng 是住在英国的中国人。他以前连一个汉字都不会写，现在他不只会写汉字，还会用毛笔写呢! 他的毛笔字很好看，我想跟他学，他说:"好呀! 我教你写毛笔字，你请我吃饭怎么样?"我说:"没问题。"

    我家对面有一家中国饭馆，这家饭馆的牛肉炒白菜很有名。我知道高明 liàng 最爱吃牛肉，就对他说:"明 liàng，我请你吃牛肉炒白菜怎么样?"高明 liàng 说:"当然好。可是你不是不会用筷子吗?""吃牛肉炒白菜不一定要用筷子。我不会用筷子，我用刀子和叉子。"我说。高明 liàng 说:"不行，吃中国菜一定要吃米饭，吃米饭当然要用筷子。""好吧。我跟你学吧。"我说。

    我跟他一块儿说着话吃饭。我问他为什么要学毛笔字，现在很少人用毛笔写字了。他说他的朋友都笑他，说他是中国人，可是不会用毛笔，不会写汉字。他不好意思就学用毛笔写汉字。他问我:"那，你呢?"我说:"我 xǐ 欢中国画儿，我想学画中国画儿。画中国画儿得学写毛笔字。"

Identify the following statements as being either true or false, based on the information in the passage. Circle the appropriate word.

a. 高明 liàng 请我吃晚饭。   对 or 不对

b. 高明 liàng 以前不会写汉字。   对 or 不对

c. 我和高明 liàng 去中国饭馆吃饭。 对 or 不对

d. 高明 liàng 的朋友都是中国人。   对 or 不对

e. 我会写毛笔字因为我会画中国画儿。 对 or 不对

Answer the following questions based on the information in the passage provided.

a. 高明 liàng 是哪国人?

_____

b. 我为什么要高明 liàng jiāo 我写毛笔字?

_____

c. 高明 liàng 为什么说吃牛肉炒白菜一定要用筷子?

_____

3.

    志中是美国人，今年二月他去了上海学中文。在上海的时候，志中每天早上都会去大学旁边儿的小吃店买早饭。店里的王老板很有意思，他不会说英语，可是他很 xǐ 欢跟志中说话。志中每次去那儿吃早饭，王老板都要志中少给一点儿钱。有的时候，还会请志中喝一杯咖啡，不必给钱。王老板有一个儿子跟志中一样大，他在外国工作，一年只能回来一次。王老板很想他的儿子，他一看到志中，就想到他的儿子，所以他对志中 tè 别好。

有一天, 王老板对志中说: "你下个星期六不用上课, 晚上来我家吃饭吧。" 志中高兴地说: "好啊!" 王老板说: "我的太太会做几个家常菜 ("home cooking"), 我们一块儿吃吧。" 志中听不懂什么是"家常菜", 所以他问王老板那是什么菜。王老板笑着说: "就是在家里常常做的和吃的菜。"

志中常常去找王老板 liáo 天, 因为王老板说话很有意思, 也可以跟他学到很多学校没有教过的生词。当然, 志中也会跟王老板练习学校里学过的中文。

到了星期六, 志中走路去王老板的家, 王老板的家很容 yì 找, 就在他的小吃店的后面。王太太很客气, 她做了很多好吃的中国菜, 有饺子、炒上海白菜、炒牛肉和 yú 汤。王太太做的饺子很地道, 比外面卖的还要好吃, 所以志中吃了很多饺子。王老板拿出他的好酒来, 跟志中一块儿喝。志中不太会喝酒, 所以只喝了一点儿, 就喝不下了。王老板对他说: "没关系, 那我们喝中国茶吧。" 志中很 xǐ 欢喝中国茶, 他们就在客厅里喝茶 liáo 天, 到了十二点, 志中才回宿舍去。

今年十二月, 志中就要回美国去了。他不太想回去, 因为在中国他学了很多以前没学过的东西, 也认识了很多朋友。不过, 他也很高兴, 因为他很快就可以见到他的家人和朋友了。明年他会在美国的大学念书, 他很 jǐn 张, 因为他已经有一年没在美国的大学念书了, 有很多的东西都忘了。志中 xīwàng jiāng 来能再回到中国去学中文, 因为以后他想跟中国人做生意。

a. 说说王老板这个人。
Focus: In what way 王老板 is nice to 志中.

1. _____

2. _____

b. 为什么王老板给志中喝中国茶?

_____

c. 为什么王老板对志中 tè 别好?
Focus: Reasons that 王老板对志中 tè 别好.

_____

d. 为什么志中吃了很多王太太做的饺子?

_____

e. 明年志中回美国以后会做什么?

_____

4.

汤米从小就和王老太太住在一块儿。王老太太 xǐ 欢 liáo 天, 她天天都跟汤米 liáo 天。他们什么都 liáo, 吃饭的时候话儿 tè 别多。

汤米五岁的时候, 他回去跟他父母住。汤米已经 xíguàn 了吃饭的时候 liáo 天。

"Bàba, 因为你小的时候 xǐ 欢爬山, 所以现在你的耳朵很红, 对吗?"

"谁说的?"

"王老太太说的。" 汤米说, "王老太太还说, 你小的时候没有人 xǐ 欢你, 因为你 xǐ 欢打人。你 dài 眼镜, 因为你小的时候不 xǐ 欢开着灯看书。"

汤米的 bàba 不高兴了: "要说话就别吃饭。" 汤米不想饿肚子, 吃饭的时候只好 不说话了。

有一天, 汤米看着 bàba, 想说什么又不说了。等 bàba 吃饱了, 汤米问: "bàba, 好吃吗?"

"好吃。" Bàba 说, "为什么?"

"你刚吃了一条虫 (chóng, "worm")。" 汤米说。

汤米的 bàba 听了汤米的话以后, 肚子就开始疼。晚上, 汤米的妈妈还得带他 bàba 去看医生呢。

a. 王老太太最 xǐ 欢跟汤米做什么?

_____

b. 汤米什么时候回去跟他父母住?

_____

c. 王老太太说汤米的 bàba 小的时候 xǐ 欢做什么? 不 xǐ 欢做什么?

_____

d. 汤米的 bàba 为什么肚子疼?

_____

5.

红红和她的几个朋友一块儿住在大学的宿舍里。大学的宿舍 lí 咖啡店和图书馆都很近, 吃饭、借书、还书、看书都很方便。走路到最近的咖啡店只要三分钟。红红和她的朋友们 xǐ 欢到宿舍对面的那家咖啡店喝着咖啡看书。那家店的咖啡又好喝又便宜, 老板也很客气, 客人喝第二杯咖啡都不必给钱。店里卖的午饭 wèi.dào 也很好。

宿舍的旁边儿是图书馆。红红很 xǐ 欢到图书馆去看书, 因为在图书馆里看书, 不但很安静, 而且借书也很方便。Tè 别是做作业的时候, 要找很多的书。在图书馆里做作业、找书、借书和还书都很方便。

这个月他们最忙了, lí 考试越来越近了, 有些学生已经开始考试了。他们常常要看书看到很晚才睡觉。昨天晚上, 红红在家看书。过了半夜了, 有人在楼上走来走去, 红红想, 这会是谁呢?

她起来, 慢慢地走上楼, 看到厨房的灯开着, 有一个人在那儿吃东西。那不是美美吗? 她说: "美美, 是你啊, 我 yǐwéi 是谁呢!" 美美说: "啊! 对不 qǐ, 是不是我太吵了?" 她问美美, 为什么这么晚了还在吃东西。美美: "因为要考试了, 我在准备明天的考试, 一直看书看到现在, 又饿又累, 所以到厨房里来找东西吃。找来找去找不到好吃的东西, 我就做了个炒饭。我想我太吵了, 对不 qǐ!"

红红说: "没关系! 你炒了什么饭?" 美美说: "我炒了个牛肉炒饭。红红, 你要尝尝 (chángchang, "have a taste") 吗?" 红红说: "我最 xǐ 欢吃牛肉炒饭了, 谢谢。"

她吃了以后很 xǐ 欢, 她对<u>美美</u>说她的炒饭跟饭馆儿卖的一样好吃, <u>美美</u>客气地说:
"哪里哪里, 你真会说话。来, 再多吃一点儿。" 她们吃完了以后, 看看时间已经是
早上五点了。<u>美美</u>说她得去睡觉了, 因为今天下午两点十五分她有中文考试。<u>红
红</u>想<u>美美</u>是应该休息一下了, <u>红红</u>对<u>美美</u>说: "今天你考完试, 我请你到大学对面
的<u>中国</u>饭馆儿去吃饭。" <u>美美</u>高兴地说: "太好了, 谢谢你! 考完试以后, 我到那家
饭馆儿去找你。"

Answer the following questions in Chinese characters; use *Hànyǔ Pīnyīn* with original tone marks only if the character has not been learned. The answer should be
in your own words based on the information in the text. Directly copying from the
text will be penalized.

a. 为什么<u>红红</u>和她的朋友们都 xǐ 欢到那家咖啡店喝咖啡?

_____

_____

b. 为什么<u>红红</u> xǐ 欢到图书馆去做作业?

_____

_____

c. 这么晚了, 厨房的灯为什么还开着?

_____

_____

d. <u>美美</u>做的炒饭 wèi.dào 怎么样?

_____

_____

e. 为什么<u>美美</u>是应该休息一下了?

_____

_____

6.

    <u>谢里</u>已经学了一年半的中文了, 我想他一定会说汉语。刚考完试, 我想到<u>北
京</u>去玩儿, 轻松一下, 可是我汉语说得不好。我想<u>谢里</u>一定也想去, 我给他打电话,
他说: "好啊!"
    七月十八号我们从<u>美国</u>坐飞机去<u>北京</u>。到了<u>北京</u>, 我们就坐出租车去旅馆
(lǚguǎn, "hotel")。我们住的旅馆附近有很多商店, 商店的前面有很多摊子。第二
天晚上我们吃了晚饭就到摊子那儿去买东西。

　　我们下了楼，走出旅馆大门，往右拐，走了五分钟，看见前边有很多人。我们走过去看看，看见有人在唱 gē tiào wǔ，很热闹。看了一会儿，我们就到对面的饺子馆去吃饺子。我们喜欢吃牛肉饺子，可是饺子馆的先生听不懂我们说的汉语。<u>谢里</u>就在纸上写："我们要两碗午内校了。"先生看了半天还是看不懂。他说："我们不卖这个。我给你来两碗白菜饺子吧！"我最讨厌吃白菜了，可是他听不懂我们的汉语，也看不懂我们的汉字，我们只好吃白菜饺子了。

　　吃完了饺子，我正想给钱。怎么我的皮包开着？我的信用 kǎ、hùzhào、钱都不见了。<u>谢里</u>说："别着急！再找找看。"我在皮包里找来找去怎么也找不着。我说："一定是被偷了。我们快给 jǐngchá 打电话吧！"<u>谢里</u>给了钱，我们就回旅馆去打电话。到了旅馆，我们马上跑上楼，进了 wòshì，正想打电话。<u>谢里</u>说："<u>路 yì</u>，你的信用 kǎ、hùzhào、钱不都在床上吗？"我想起来了，刚才我忘了把这些东西放进皮包里了。

Answer the following questions in Chinese based on the information in the passage provided. All answers should be in your own words.

a. <u>路 yì</u> 为什么给<u>谢里</u>打电话？

　　_____

　　_____

b. <u>谢里</u>的汉语说得怎么样？

　　_____

　　_____

c. <u>谢里</u>把什么字写成 "午内校了"？

　　_____

　　_____

d. <u>路 yì</u> 为什么找不到他的信用 kǎ、hùzhào 和钱？

　　_____

　　_____

Vocabulary Index

被	bèi	(CV) (a marker for passive-voice sentence) (20)
-倍	-bèi	(Cl) -fold, number + times (18)
北边儿	běi.biānr	(PS/PW) the north (10)
北京	Běijīng	(PW) capital city of the People's Republic of China (9)
北京 Jiē	Běijīng Jiē	(PW) name of a street (9)
北京街	Běijīng Jiē	(PW) name of a street (13)
-本	-běn	(Cl) volume (for books) (5)
笨	bèn	(SV) be stupid (8)
笔	bǐ	(N) pen, writing instrument (9)
比	bǐ	(CV) compared to (18)
-遍	-biàn	(VCL) times (17)
别	bié	(Conj) don't (imperative) (12)
别的	biéde	(N) other (14)
别人	bié.rén	(N) other people (14)
比较	bǐjiào	(Adv) comparatively (19)
病	bìng	(N) illness, (V) be ill (13)
冰水	bīngshuǐ	(N) ice water (7)
伯伯	bóbo	(N) uncle (father's elder brother) (7)
伯母	bómǔ	(N) aunt (wife of father's elder brother) (7)
不	bù-, bú-, -bu-	(Adv) not (4)
不过	búguò	(Conj) still, however (12)
不必	búbì	(Aux) need not, not have to (7)
不错	búcuò	(SV) be pretty good (12)
不但……而且……	búdàn…érqiě…	(Pat) Not only X, but also Y (20)
不是……(而)是	búshì…(ér)shì	(Pat) it's not…but rather (14)
不是……就是	búshì…jiùshì	(Pat) if not…then it's (15)
不同	bùtóng	(SV) be different (18)
不行	bùxíng	(Ex) Can't be done. (6)
不用	búyòng	(Aux) need not, not have to (13)

C

才	cái	(Conj) then (later than expected) (13)
菜	cài	(N) food, dishes (10)
厕所	cèsuǒ	(PW) toilet (15)

出租(汽)车	chūzū (qì)chē	(N) taxi (19)
-次	-cì	(VCL) times (16)
词 diǎn	cídiǎn	(N) dictionary (Cl -本) (5)
词典	cídiǎn	(N) dictionary (Cl -本) (6)
从	cóng	(CV) from (11)
从……dào……	cóng…dào…	(Pat) from…to…(11)
cōng 明	cōngming	(SV) be intelligent, be smart (8)

D

大	dà	(SV) be big, be large (4)
打的	dǎ dī	(VO) take a taxi (slang) (11)
打电话	dǎ diànhuà	(VO) make a phone call (10)
打架	dǎ jià	(VO) scuffle (20)
大 shēng	dà shēng	(Adv) loud (16)
带	dài	(V) take or bring along, lead around (16)
大家	dàjiā	(N) everyone (15)
大门	dàmén	(N) main entrance (9)
当然	dāngrán	(Adv) of course (12)
dāng 中	dāngzhōng	(PS/PW) the middle (more abstract) (10)
当中	dāngzhōng	(PS/PW) the middle (more abstract) (16)
到	dào	(CV) to (12)
到	dào	(V) arrive (12)
-到	-dào	(VC) (reach a point) (17)
刀子	dāozi	(N) knife (Cl -把) (10)
大人	dàrén	(N) adult (10)
大学	dàxué	(N) university (11)
大学生	dàxuésheng	(N) university student (10)
的	de	(P) indicates possession, used to join a modifying clause with the noun it modifies (9)
得	de	(P) (marks the manner or extent of an action) (14)
-地	-de	(P) (marks the manner in which a single instance of an action is carried out) (13)

……的时候	…de shíhou	(Part) at the time of…(13)
得	děi	(Aux) must (6)
灯	dēng	(N) lamp, lights (11)
等	děng	(V) wait (13)
第-	dì-	(Pre) (indicates numerical order) (13)
-点	-diǎn	(Cl) (number) o'clock (12)
电脑	diànnǎo	(N) computer (lit. "electric brain") (20)
电视	diànshì	(N) television (6)
电梯	diàntī	(N) elevator (15)
电影	diànyǐng	(N) movie (12)
地道	dìdao	(SV) be authentic (8)
弟弟	dìdi	(N) younger brother (6)
地方	dìfang	(PW) place, location (9)
地图	dìtú	(N) map (Cl -张), atlas (Cl -本) (8)
懂	dǒng	(V) understand (14)
-懂	-dǒng	(VC) understand (17)
东边儿	dōng.biānr	(PS/PW) the east (9)
冬天	dōngtiān	(TW) winter (15)
东西	dōngxi	(N) thing (physical) (7)
都	dōu	(Adv) in all cases (8)
堵车	dǔ chē	(VO) jam up (of traffic) (19)
度假	dù jià	(VO) spend one's holiday (20)
对	duì	(SV) be correct (8)
对	duì	(CV) to, toward (10)
对了	duì le	(Ex) by the way, it occurred to me that (8)
对面	duìmiàn	(PW) side directly opposite (12)
-顿	-dùn	(Cl) used with 饭 to mean "meal" (14)
多	duō	(SV) many, be abundant (11)
多久?	duō jiǔ?	(QW) how long? (19)
多少?	duōshao?	(Q) How many? How much? (12)
肚子	dùzi	(N) stomach (13)

E

饿	è	(SV) be hungry (7)
二	èr	(Nu) two (4)

告诉	gàosu	(V) tell, inform (6)
高速公路	gāosù gōnglù	(N) highway, freeway (20)
高兴	gāoxìng	(SV) be happy (12)
-个	-ge	(Cl) (general classifier) (5)
哥哥	gēge	(N) older brother (6)
给	gěi	(CV) for, to (10)
给	gěi	(V) give, give to (16)
跟	gēn	(Conj) and (usually joins nouns) (16)
跟	gēn	(CV) (together) with (16)
更	gèng	(Adv) even more (18)
公共汽车	gōnggòng qìchē	(N) public bus (11)
公 jiāo 车/公车	gōngjiāochē/gōngchē	(N) same as 公共汽车 (11)
功课	gōngkè	(N) schoolwork, homework (11)
公里	gōnglǐ	(Cl) kilometers (19)
公寓	gōngyù	(PW) apartment (15)
公寓楼	gōngyù lóu	(PW) apartment building (15)
工作	gōngzuò	(N) job (19)
够	gòu	(V) be enough, sufficient, adequate (18)
刮风	guā fēng	(VO) have wind gusts (15)
拐	guǎi	(V) turn (11)
guàng 街	guàng jiē	(VO) go window-shopping, stroll around the streets (14)
贵	guì	(V) be expensive (18)
-过	-guo	(P) (Used after a verb to indicate an experience) (10)
过	guò	(V) surpassing, more than, pass by (14)
故事	gùshi	(N) story, narrative account (10)

H

还	hái	(Adv) also, additionally (7)
还……呢	hái…ne	(Pat) (continuation of an action) (12)
海明	Hǎimíng	(N) a personal name (12)
还是	háishi	(Conj) or (9)
还是	háishi	(Adv) still (best to…) (14)
孩子	háizi	(N) child, youngster (10)
韩国	Hánguó	(PW) Korea (14)
汗衫	hànshān	(N) T-shirt (Cl -件) (9)

J

挤	jǐ	(SV) be crowded (13)
几-	jǐ-	(Q) a few, several (classifier required) (5)
几?	jǐ?	(Q) How many? (classifier required) (5)
记	jì	(V) remember (17)
家	jiā	(N) family, home (6)
-家	-jiā	(Cl) (for businesses) (7)
家具	jiājù	(N) furniture (Cl -件) (15)
-件	-jiàn	(Cl) (for clothing covering the upper half of the body, e.g. "shirt" and "jacket") (9)
-见	-jiàn	(VC) perceive (16)
讲	jiǎng	(V) speak, say (16)
江兴成	Jiāng Xīngchéng	(N) a personal name (20)
jiāng 来	jiānglái	(TW) in the future, future (14)
教	jiāo	(V) teach (10)
叫	jiào	(V) be called, call (8)
饺子	jiǎozi	(N) "Chinese ravioli", "Chinese dumpling" (17)
假期	jiàqī	(TW) vacation, holiday period (19)
家人	jiārén	(N) family members (9)
街	jiē	(N) street (Cl -条) (11)
接	jiē	(V) meet, pick (somebody) up (20)
借	jiè	(V) borrow, lend (17)
姐姐	jiějie	(N) older sister (6)
介绍	jièshào	(V) introduce (10)
几乎	jīhū	(Adv) almost, nearly (18)
机会	jīhuì	(N) opportunity (10)
......极了	...jíle	(Adv) extremely (17)
-斤	-jīn	(Cl) unit of weight (0.5 kilograms, slightly more than a pound) (20)
进	jìn	(V) enter (15)
近	jìn	(SV) be near (19)
今年	jīnnián	(TW) this year (15)
今天	jīntiān	(TW) today (13)
jǐn 张	jǐnzhāng	(SV) be nervous, be tense (17)
九	jiǔ	(Nu) nine (4)

酒	jiǔ	(N) liquor (Cl -杯, -瓶) (7)
久	jiǔ	(SV) take/be a long time (13)
旧	jiù	(SV) be old (of objects, *not* living things) (8)
就	jiù	(Adv) only, just (9)
就	jiù	(Conj) then (11)
就	jiù	(Conj) then (earlier than expected) (13)
jué 得	juéde	(V) think, feel (13)

K

咖啡	kāfēi	(N) coffee (7)
咖啡馆儿	kāfēiguǎnr	(PW) café (14)
开	kāi	(V) open, operate, drive (a car), turn on (11)
开始	kāishǐ	(V) begin (13)
kǎ 拉 OK	kǎlā-ōukēi	(N) karaoke (20)
看	kàn	(V) look, read, watch (9)
看	kàn	(V) consider, be of the opinion (14)
看病	kàn bìng	(VO) to see a doctor (13)
看医生	kàn yīshēng	(VO) (same as 看病) (13)
考试	kǎoshì	(VO) take a test or examination (10)
考试	kǎoshì	(N) test or examination (10)
课	kè	(N) lesson, class, course (10)
-刻(钟)	-kè (zhōng)	(Cl) quarter hour, 15 minutes (12)
可不是吗?	Kě búshi ma?	(Ex) Isn't that so? (19)
客人	kè.rén	(N) guest, shop/restaurant customer (7)
可口可乐	Kěkǒu Kělè	(N) Coca-Cola (Cl -罐, -瓶) (7)
可乐	kělè	(N) cola, Coke (Cl -罐, -瓶) (7)
可能	kěnéng	(Adv) possibly (19)
客气	kèqi	(SV) be polite (7)
可是	kěshì	(Conj) but, however (8)
可 shì	kěshì	(Conj) but, however (5)
客厅	kètīng	(PW) living room (15)
可以	kěyǐ	(Aux) allowed to, can (5)
-口	-kǒu	(Cl) (classifier for persons) (6)
哭	kū	(V) cry, weep (20)
快	kuài	(SV) be fast, be quick (14)

-块	-kuài	(Cl) dollars (8)
-块	-kuài	(Cl) a piece of (also used for "watch") (9)
快(要)……了	kuài (yào)…le	(Pat) about to…(7)
筷子	kuàizi	(N) chopsticks (Cl -双) (10)
裤子	kùzi	(N) pants, trousers (Cl -条) (18)

L

来	lái	(V) come (11)
-来	-lái	(VC) come (16)
蓝	lán	(SV) be blue (14)
兰兰	Lánlan	(N) a personal name (7)
老	lǎo	(SV) be old (usually of person or living things for a long time) (16)
老	lǎo	(Adv) always, invariably (17)
老板	lǎobǎn	(N) boss, owner (9)
老 shī	lǎoshī	(N) teacher (10)
老师	lǎoshī	(N) teacher (12)
了	le	(P) (indicates a new situation) (7)
了	le	(P) (indicates completed action) (12)
累	lèi	(SV) be physically drained, be tired (14)
冷	lěng	(SV) be cold (15)
里	lǐ	(PS/PW) inside (14)
里边儿	lǐ.biānr	(PS/ PW) inside (12)
连……都/ 也……	lián…dōu/yě…	(Pat) even…(18)
两	liǎng	(Q) two (classifier required) (5)
凉快	liángkuài	(SV) be (comfortably) cool (said of air temperature) (17)
练习	liànxí	(V/N) practice (13)
-了	-liǎo	(VC) able to (17)
liáo 天	liáotiān	(VO) chat (11)
利害*	lìhai	(SV) be formidable, be fierce (19)
邻 jū	línjū	(N) neighbor (16)
六	liù	(Nu) six (9)
流血	liú xiě	(VO) bleed (20)
-楼	-lóu	(Cl) floor (15)

lóu 上	lóushàng	(PW) upstairs (9)
楼上	lóushàng	(PS/PW) upstairs (17)
楼梯	lóutī	(N) stairs (15)
lóu 下	lóuxià	(PW) downstairs (9)
楼下	lóuxià	(PS/PW) downstairs (17)
路	lù	(N) road (Cl -条) (18)
绿	lǜ	(SV) be green (14)
旅游	lǚyóu	(V) tour (19)

M

吗	ma	(P) (indicates a question) (5)
买	mǎi	(V) buy (6)
卖	mài	(V) sell (7)
妈妈	māma	(N) mother (6)
慢	màn	(SV) be slow (14)
忙	máng	(SV) be busy (7)
màn 画(书)	mànhuà(shū)	(N) comic book, manga (Cl -本) (6)
-毛	-máo	(Cl) dimes (6)
毛乐生	Máo Lèshēng	(N) a personal name (8)
毛 bǐ	máobǐ	(N) writing brush (Cl -支) (5)
毛笔	máobǐ	(N) writing brush (see Chapter 5) (8)
毛衣	máoyī	(N) sweater (Cl -件) (9)
马上	mǎshàng	(Adv) right away (19)
没关 xi	méi guānxi	(Ex) Never mind. It doesn't matter. (7)
没关系	méi guānxi	(Ex) Never mind. It doesn't matter. (16)
没问 tí	méi wèntí	(Ex) Not a problem. (8)
没(.yǒu)	méi(.yǒu)	(V) not have, has not (7)
没(有)	méi(.yǒu)	(V) not have, has not (8)
没有	méi.yǒu	(V) there isn't, there aren't (9)
美国	Měiguó	(PW) America (10)
妹妹	mèimei	(N) younger sister (6)
美思大学	Měisī Dàxué	(PW) name of a university (11)
门	mén	(N) door (16)
-门	-mén	(Cl) (for a course taken at school) (10)
米饭	mǐfàn	(N) cooked rice (10)
明白	míngbai	(V) understand (8)
明年	míngnián	(TW) next year (12)

名 pái 儿	míngpáir	(N) famous brand, nameplate (16)
明天	míngtiān	(TW) tomorrow (13)
名字	míngzi	(N) name (8)

N

拿	ná	(V) take, bring, pick up (11)
那	nà	(Pr) that (8)
那	nà	(Conj) in that case (14)
难	nán	(SV) be difficult (14)
南	nán	(PS) the south (15)
男-	nán-	(Pre) male (human) (14)
南京	Nánjīng	(PW) a city in China (11)
南京路	Nánjīng Lù	(PW) name of a street (18)
闹	nào	(V) make noise, stir up trouble, etc. (20)
哪儿	nǎr	(PW) where? (9)
那儿	nàr	(PW) there, that place (9)
呢	ne	(P) (forms a reverse question) (5)
呢	ne	(P) (used at the end of sentences for emphasis) (8)
内衣	nèiyī	(N) underwear (Cl -件) (9)
那么	nème (nàme)	(Adv) in that way, that (11)
能	néng	(Aux) can (16)
你	nǐ	(Pr) you (singular) (5)
年	-nián	(TD) year(s) (12)
念书	niàn shū	(VO) study (academically) (10)
你们	nǐmen	(Pr) you (plural) (5)
牛奶	niúnǎi	(N) milk (8)
牛肉	niúròu	(N) beef (10)
牛仔 kù	niúzǎikù	(N) denim jeans (Cl -条) (9)
牛仔裤	niúzǎikù	(N) denim jeans (Cl -条) (18)
女-	nǚ-	(Pre) (female) (human) (16)
女儿	nǚ'ér	(N) daughter (5)
暖和	nuǎnhuo	(SV) be (comfortably) warm (said of weather) (19)
女 de	nǚde	(N) woman, female (6)
女的	nǚde	(N) woman, female (10)

P

爬山	pá shān	(VO) climb a mountain (15)
胖	pàng	(SV) be fat (of humans) (18)
旁边儿	páng.biānr	(PS/PW) the side (19)
跑	pǎo	(V) run (16)
朋友	péngyou	(N) friend (8)
便宜	piányi	(SV) be cheap (6)
啤酒	píjiǔ	(N) beer (16)
平常	píngcháng	(Adv) usually (14)
皮 xié	píxié	(N) leather shoes (Cl -双) (8)

Q

七	qī	(Nu) seven (4)
-起	-qǐ	(VC) afford to (16)
起床	qǐ chuáng	(VO) get out of bed, get up (14)
千	qiān	(Nu) thousand (5)
前	qián	(PS/PW) in front (11)
钱	qián	(N) money (13)
浅	qiǎn	(SV) be shallow, be light (14)
钱希平	Qián Xīpíng	(N) a personal name (15)
铅笔	qiānbǐ	(N) pencil (17)
前边儿	qián.biānr	(PS/PW) in front (9)
前天	qiántiān	(TW) the day before yesterday (14)
汽车	qìchē	(N) automobile (15)
起来	qǐlai	(V) rise (up), get up (15)
请	qǐng	(V) please, treat, hire, invite (8)
请客	qǐng kè	(VO) to treat someone to food or entertainment (7)
清楚	qīngchu	(SV) be clear (16)
轻松	qīngsōng	(SV) be relaxed (19)
秋天	qiūtiān	(TW) autumn, fall (12)
去	qù	(V) go to (a place) (8)
去年	qùnián	(TW) last year (12)
裙子	qúnzi	(N) dress, skirt (Cl -条) (14)

R

然后	ránhòu	(Conj) and then…(13)
热	rè	(SV) be hot (15)
人	rén	(N) person, human being (4)
热闹	rènao	(SV) be bustling (18)
认识	rènshi	(V) be acquainted with (9)
日本	Rìběn	(PW) Japan (4)
日文	Rìwén	(N) Japanese (language) (4)
日语	Rìyǔ	(N) Japanese (language) (5)
容 yì	róngyì	(SV) be easy (8)

S

三	sān	(Nu) three (4)
山	shān	(N) hill, mountain (15)
上	shàng	(V) go or come up (15)
-上	-shàng	(VC) come/go up (16)
上班	shàng bān	(VO) go to work (15)
上课	shàng kè	(VO) have class, attend class (10)
商先生	Shāng xiānsheng	(N) Mr. Shang (17)
上学	shàng xué	(VO) go to school (15)
上(个)月	shàng(ge)yuè	(TW) last month (12)
上边儿	shàng.biānr	(PS) above (9)
商场	shāngchǎng	(PW) market, bazaar (14)
商 diàn	shāngdiàn	(PW) shop, store (Cl -家) (9)
商店	shāngdiàn	(PW) shop, store (Cl -家) (14)
上海	Shànghǎi	(PW) a city in Eastern China (10)
上午	shàngwǔ	(TW) in the morning (12)
少	shǎo	(SV) lack, be deficient, lose, be missing (16)
谁	shéi/shuí	(Pr) who (12)
深	shēn	(SV) be deep, be dark, be profound (14)
生词	shēngcí	(N) new words, new vocabulary (17)
生气	shēngqì	(SV) be angry (17)
生日	shēngrì	(N) birthday (12)
生意	shēngyi	(N) (commercial) business (7)
什么	shénme	(QW) what (5)

| 所有的 | suǒyǒude | (N) every-, all of something (17) |
| 宿舍 | sùshè | (PW) dormitory (20) |

T

他	tā	(Pr) he, him (5)
她	tā	(Pr) she, her (7)
太	tài	(SV) overly, too (7)
太太	tàitai	(N) Mrs., wife (5)
她们	tāmen	(Pr) they, them (all females) (6)
他们	tāmen	(Pr) they, them (5)
汤	tāng	(N) soup (8)
讨厌	tǎoyàn	(SV) be a pain in the neck (20)
特别	tèbié	(SV) be special (14)
疼	téng	(V) feel pain (13)
替	tì	(CV) in place of (10)
-天	-tiān	(TD) day(s) (13)
天天	tiāntiān	(Pat) (Cl-Cl) every…(19)
挑	tiāo	(V) choose, select (19)
-条	-tiáo	(Cl) (for things that are seen as long, narrow, and flexible) (11)
听	tīng	(V) listen (16)
听说	tīngshuō	(V) hear it said that…(19)
同心街	Tóngxīn Jiē	(PW) a street name (11)
同学	tóngxué	(N) fellow student, classmate (11)
偷	tōu	(V) steal (20)
头	tóu	(N) head (13)
图书馆	túshūguǎn	(PW) library (11)

V

| V 来 V 去 | V+lái+V+qù | (Pat) indicates a thorough repetition (16) |
| (VO)V 得…… | (VO)V de… | (Pat) (indicates customary manner or the extent of an action) (14) |

W

| 外边儿 | wài.biānr | (PS/PW) outside (11) |
| wài 衣 | wàiyī | (N) jacket (Cl -件) (9) |

外衣	wàiyī	(N) jacket (Cl -件) (19)
-完	-wán	(VC) finish, complete (16)
晚	wǎn	(SV) be late (13)
万	wàn	(N) a Chinese surname (Q) ten thousand (6)
万文生	Wàn Wénshēng	(N) a personal name (6)
玩(儿)	wán(r)	(V) have fun, have a good time, enjoy oneself (15)
晚饭	wǎnfàn	(N) supper (8)
王	Wáng	(N) a Chinese surname (4)
往	wǎng	(CV) toward (11)
忘	wàng	(V) forget (9)
王欢兰	Wáng Huānlán	(N) a personal name (10)
王太太	Wáng tàitai	(N) Mrs. Wang (5)
王先生	Wáng xiānsheng	(N) Mr. Wang (5)
王中书	Wáng Zhōngshū	(N) a personal name (4)
完全	wánquán	(Adv) completely (18)
晚上	wǎnshang	(TW) in the evening (11)
袜子	wàzi	(N) socks (Cl -双 "pair", -zhī 只 "single") (9)
-位	wèi	(Cl) (polite, for persons) (10)
为什么?	wèishénme?	(Adv) why? (9)
问	wèn	(V) ask (a question) (5)
问 lù	wèn lù	(VO) ask the way (11)
问 tí	wèntí	(N) question (10)
文文	Wénwen	(N) a personal name (5)
我	wǒ	(Pr) I, me (4)
我们	wǒmen	(Pr) we, us (6)
五	wǔ	(Nu) five (4)
午饭	wǔfàn	(N) lunch (7)

X

下	xià	(V) get off, disembark (13)
下	xià	(V) go or come down (15)
-下	-xià	(VC) come/go down (16)
下班	xià bān	(VO) finish work (15)
下车	xià chē	(VO) get off a bus or train (13)
下课	xià kè	(VO) finish class (12)

兴趣	xìngqù	(N) interest (in something) (18)
薪水	xīnshuǐ	(N) salary (18)
Xīn 西 lán	Xīnxīlán	(PW) New Zealand (4)
新西兰	Xīnxīlán	(PW) New Zealand (19)
信用 kǎ	xìnyòngkǎ	(N) credit card (Cl. -张) (20)
兄弟姐妹	xiōngdì-jiěmèi	(N) brothers and sisters, siblings (6)
休息	xiūxi	(V) rest (13)
学	xué	(V) study, learn (10)
雪山城	Xuěshānchéng	(PW) Snowy Mountain Town (19)
学生	xuésheng	(N) student (11)
学校	xuéxiào	(PW) school (15)

Y

Y 分之 X	Y fēn zhī X	(Pat) (indicates X/Y fractions) (18)
呀	ya	(P) (tells listener s/he really should have known that) (9)
眼睛	yǎnjing	(N) eye (16)
眼 jìng	yǎnjìng	(N) eyeglasses (Cl -副) (9)
眼镜	yǎnjìng	(N) eyeglasses (Cl -副) (16)
颜 sè	yánsè	(N) color (14)
药	yào	(N) medicine (13)
要	yào	(V) want, want to (6)
要	yào	(Aux) going to, will, must, should (7)
要……了	yào…le	(Pat) about to…(15)
要是(的 话)……就	yàoshi (de huà)…jiù	(Pat) if…then (14)
也	yě	(Adv) also (4)
-页	-yè	(Cl) page (14)
也许	yěxǔ	(Adv) perhaps (15)
一	yī, yì, yí	(Nu) one (4)
一……就	yī…jiù…	(Pat) as soon as (16)
一半	yíbàn	(Q) half (6)
一 diǎn 儿	yìdiǎnr	(Q) a bit, a little (7)
一点儿	yìdiǎnr	(Q) a bit, a little (13)
一 dìng	yídìng	(Adv) definitely (10)
一定	yídìng	(Adv) definitely (12)
衣 fu	yīfu	(N) clothing (Cl -件) (9)

Z

再	zài	(Adv) again, additionally (7)
在	zài	(CV) at, in (9)
在	zài	(V) be located at, be present (9)
再	zài	(Adv) and then (13)
在	zài	(Adv) be...ing (14)
再见	Zàijiàn!	(Ex) Goodbye, au revoir! (5)
咱们	zánmen	(Pr) we, us (inclusive of listener) (14)
早	zǎo	(SV) be early (15)
早饭	zǎofàn	(N) breakfast (8)
早上	zǎoshang	(TW) in the morning (13)
杂志	zázhì	(N) magazine (Cl -本 or -份) (9)
怎么	zěnme	(Adv) how? why? (11)
怎么办?	Zěnme bàn?	(Ex) What the heck do we do? (20)
怎么了?	Zěnme le?	(Ex) What's going on? What's the matter? (13)
-张	-zhāng	(Cl) for flat objects like tables, paper, paintings) (17)
张伯伯	Zhāng bóbo	(N) Uncle Zhang (18)
-着	-zháo	(VC) successfully complete (16)
找	zhǎo	(V) to give change, to look for (something) (9)
着急	zháojí	(SV) be anxious (19)
-着	-zhe	(P) (attached to verbs to indicate action in progress) (10)
这	zhè	(Pr) this (8)
这么	zhème	(Adv) in this way, this (11)
真	zhēn	(Adv) really, truly (5)
真气死人!	Zhēn qìsǐ rén!	(Ex) How infuriating! (17)
......着(呢)	...-zhe (ne)	(Pat) description of a state (11)
正(在)......(着)(呢)	zhèng(zài)...(zhe)(ne)	(Pat) right in the middle of...(11)
这儿，这里	zhèr, zhèlǐ	(PW) here, this place (12)
-支	-zhī	(Cl) (for pens, pencils) (5)
只	zhǐ	(Adv) only, just (5)
纸	zhǐ	(N) paper (Cl -张) (17)
知道	zhī.dào	(V) know, know of, know that (7)

至少	zhìshǎo	(Adv) at the very least (19)
只要	zhǐyào	(Conj) All you need to do is…(17)
钟	zhōng	(N) clock (time as measured in hours/minutes) (12)
钟名然	Zhōng Míngrán	(N) a personal name (19)
中本 一也	Zhōngběn Yīyě	(N) a Japanese personal name (4)
中 guó	Zhōngguó	(PW) China (4)
中国	Zhōngguó	(PW) China (8)
中 jiān	zhōngjiān	(PS/PW) the middle (more concrete) (10)
中间	zhōngjiān	(PS) the middle (19)
钟头	zhōngtóu	(N) hour (14)
中文	Zhōngwén	(N) Chinese (language) (4)
中午	zhōngwǔ	(TW) noon (14)
中学	zhōngxué	(PW) high school (11)
中 xué 生	zhōngxuéshēng	(N) secondary school students (5)
住	zhù	(V) reside (9)
-住	-zhù	(VC) make secure or firm (16)
抓	zhuā	(V) grab, scratch, arrest (20)
准备	zhǔnbèi	(V) prepare (14)
桌子	zhuōzi	(N) table (16)
字	zì	(N) (Chinese) character(s) (Cl -个) (6)
自己	zìjǐ	(Pr) self (19)
仔 xì	zǐxì	(SV) be careful, be detailed (13)
仔细	zǐxì	(SV) be careful, be detailed (17)
自行车	zìxíngchē	(N) bicycle (Cl -辆) (6)
走	zǒu	(V) walk, go, move along, leave (11)
最	zuì	(Adv) most (12)
做	zuò	(V) do, take the role of (7)
坐	zuò	(V) sit, ride, take (a means of transportation) (11)
做生意	zuò shēngyi	(VO) engage in commerce (18)
左边儿	zuǒ.biānr	(PS/PW) the left (11)
昨天	zuótiān	(TW) yesterday (13)
作业	zuòyè	(N) schoolwork, homework (12)
左右	zuǒyòu	(Adv) about, more or less (14)
足球 sài	zúqiúsài	(N) soccer match (20)

Alphabetized Character Index

Note: An asterisk (*) next to one of a character's multiple English meanings indicates that *for that particular English meaning* the character cannot stand alone in modern Chinese as an independent word.

Pinyin	Character	Chapter	Radical	Traditional character
A				
ā	阿	17	阝	阿
á	啊	16	口	啊
āi	哎	6	口	哎
ài	爱	15	爪	愛
ān	安	12	宀	安
B				
ba	吧	8	口	吧
bā	八	4	八	八
bǎ	把	17	扌	把
bái	白	8	白	白
bǎi	百	5	一	百
bān	搬	15	扌	搬
bān	班	15	王	班
bǎn	板	9	木	板
bàn	半	6	八	半

Pinyin	*Character*	*Chapter*	*Radical*	*Traditional character*
bàn	办	20	力	辦
bāo	包	17	勹	包
bǎo	饱	8	饣	飽
bào	报	9	扌	報
bēi*	杯	13	木	杯
běi	北	9	丨	北
bèi	备	14	田	備
bèi*	倍	18	亻	倍
bèi	被	20	衤	被
běn*	本	4	木	本
bèn	笨	8	**竹**	笨
bǐ	笔	8	**竹**	筆
bǐ	比	18	比	比
bì*	必	7	心	必
biān	边	9	辶	邊
biàn/pián*	便	11	亻	便
biàn*	遍	17	辶	遍
bié	别	12	刂	別
bīng	冰	7	冫	冰
bìng	病	13	疒	病
bó*	伯	7	亻	伯
bù-, bú-, -bu-	不	4	一	不

C

cái	才	13	一	才
cài	菜	10	艹	菜
cè*	厕	15	厂	廁

Pinyin	Character	Chapter	Radical	Traditional character
chā*	叉	10	又	叉
chá	茶	10	艹	茶
chà	差	12	羊	差
cháng	常	13	巾	常
cháng	长	18	丿	長
chǎng	场	14	土	場
chàng	唱	20	口	唱
chāo	超	20	走	超
chǎo	炒	11	火	炒
chǎo	吵	16	口	吵
chē	车	6	车	車
chèn*	衬	9	衤	襯
chéng	城	9	土	城
chéng	成	17	戈	成
chī	吃	7	口	吃
chū	出	15	山	出
chú	除	10	阝	除
chú*	厨	15	厂	廚
chǔ*	楚	16	木	楚
chuān	穿	18	穴	穿
chuáng	床	14	广	床
chūn*	春	12	日	春
cí	词	5	讠	詞
cì*	次	16	冫	次
cóng	从	11	人	從
cuò	错	12	钅	錯

Pinyin	Character	Chapter	Radical	Traditional character
D				
dǎ	打	10	扌	打
dà	大	4	大	大
dài	带	16	巾	带
dàn	但	20	亻	但
dāng	当	12	小	当
dāo	刀	10	刀	刀
dào	道	7	辶	道
dào	到	12	刂	到
de	的	9	白	的
de/děi	得	13	彳	得
de/dì	地	13	土	地
děi/de	得	6	彳	得
dēng	灯	11	火	燈
děng	等	13	竹	等
dì*	弟	6	八	弟
dì/de	地	8	土	地
dì	第	13	竹	第
diǎn*	典	6	八	典
diǎn	点	12	灬	點
diàn	电	6	曰	電
diàn	店	14	广	店
dìng	定	12	宀	定
dōng	东	7	一	東
dōng	冬	14	夂	冬
dǒng	懂	14	忄	懂

Pinyin	Character	Chapter	Radical	Traditional character
dōu	都	8	阝	都
dǔ	堵	19	土	堵
dù*	肚	13	月	肚
dù*	度	20	广	度
duì	对	8	又	對
dùn*	顿	14	页	頓
duō	多	11	夕	多
duǒ*	朵	16	木	朵
E				
è	饿	7	饣	餓
ér*	儿	5	儿	兒
ér	而	14	一	而
ěr*	耳	16	耳	耳
èr	二	4	一	二
F				
fā	发	13	又	發
fǎ*	法	8	氵	法
fàn	饭	7	饣	飯
fāng	方	9	方	方
fáng	房	15	户	房
fàng	放	17	攵	放
fēi*	啡	7	口	啡
fēi	飞	17	乙	飛
fēn	分	6	八	分
fěn	粉	14	米	粉

Pinyin	*Character*	*Chapter*	*Radical*	*Traditional character*
fèn*	份	6	亻	份
fēng	风	15	风	風
fú (noun*)	服	11	月	服
fù*	父	6	父	父
fù	附	19	阝	附
G				
gāi	该	20	讠	該
gāng	刚	16	刂	剛
gāo	高	9	亠	高
gào	告	6	口	告
gē	哥	6	口	哥
gè*	个	5	人	個
gěi	给	10	纟	給
gēn	跟	16	足	跟
gèng	更	18	一	更
gōng*	公	11	八	公
gōng	功	11	工	功
gōng*	工	19	工	工
gòng*	共	6	八	共
gòu	够	18	夕	够
gù*	故	10	攵	故
guā	刮	15	刂	刮
guā	瓜	19	瓜	瓜
guǎi	拐	11	扌	拐
guān	关	7	八	關
guǎn*	馆	7	饣	館

Pinyin	*Character*	*Chapter*	*Radical*	*Traditional character*
guì	贵	18	贝	貴
guó	国	8	口	國
guǒ*	果	19	木	果
guò	过	10	辶	過
H				
hái/huán	还	7	辶	還
hái*	孩	10	子	孩
hǎi	海	10	氵	海
hài	害	19	宀	害
hán	韩	14	十	韓
hàn*	汉	7	氵	漢
hàn	汗	9	氵	汗
háng*/xíng	行	12	彳	行
hǎo	好	6	女	好
hào	号	12	口	號
hē	喝	7	口	喝
hé/huó	和	11	禾	和
hé	河	18	氵	河
hěn	很	6	彳	很
hóng	红	14	纟	紅
hòu*	后	10	口	後
hòu (time*)	候	13	亻	候
hū	乎	18	丿	乎
huā	花	13	艹	花
huá*	华	17	十	華
huà	话	5	讠	話

Pinyin	Character	Chapter	Radical	Traditional character
huà	画	6	凵	畫
huài	坏	13	土	壞
huān*	欢	8	又	歡
huán/hái	还	17	辶	還
huáng	黄	14	艹	黄
huī	灰	14	火	灰
huí	回	12	口	回
huì	会	5	人	會
huó/hé	和	19	禾	和
huǒ	火	11	火	火
J				
jī*	机	10	木	機
jí	极	17	木	极
jí	急	19	心	急
jǐ*	几	5	几	幾
jǐ	挤	13	扌	擠
jǐ*	己	19	己	己
jì	记	17	讠	記
jì*	绩	18	纟	績
jiā	家	6	宀	家
jià	假	19	亻	假
jià (quarrel*)	架	20	木	架
jiān	间	17	门	間
jiàn	见	5	见	見
jiàn*	件	9	亻	件
jiāng	江	18	氵	江

Pinyin	Character	Chapter	Radical	Traditional character
jiǎng	讲	16	讠	講
jiāo	教	10	攵	教
jiǎo	饺	17	饣	餃
jiào	叫	8	口	叫
jiào*	觉	16	见	覺
jiào	较	19	车	較
jiē	街	11	彳	街
jiē	接	20	扌	接
jiě	姐	6	女	姐
jiè*	介	10	人	介
jiè	借	17	亻	借
jīn	今	13	人	今
jīn*	斤	20	斤	斤
jìn	进	15	辶	進
jìn	近	19	辶	近
jīng*	京	9	亠	京
jīng	经	12	纟	經
jīng*	睛	16	目	睛
jǐng*	景	19	日	景
jìng*	镜	16	钅	鏡
jìng	静	18	青	靜
jiǔ	酒	7	氵	酒
jiǔ	久	13	丿	久
jiù	九	4	丿	九
jiù	旧	8	日	舊
jiù	就	9	亠	就
jù*	具	15	八	具

Pinyin	Character	Chapter	Radical	Traditional character
K				
kā*	咖	7	口	咖
kāi	开	11	一	開
kàn*	看	9	目	看
kǎo	考	10	十	考
kě	可	5	口	可
kè	客	7	宀	客
kè	课	10	讠	課
kè	刻	12	刂	刻
kòng	空	18	穴	空
kǒu	口	6	口	口
kū	哭	20	口	哭
kù*	裤	18	衤	褲
kuài	快	7	忄	快
kuài*	块	8	土	塊
kuài*	筷	10	竹	筷
L				
lā	拉	20	扌	拉
lái	来	11	一	來
lán	蘭	6	八	蘭
lán	蓝	14	艹	藍
lǎo	老	9	耂	老
le/liǎo	了	7	乙	了
lè	乐	7	丿	樂
lèi	累	14	田	累

Pinyin	Character	Chapter	Radical	Traditional character
lěng	冷	15	冫	冷
lǐ*	里	12	里	裏
lǐ	李	17	木	李
lì	利	19	刂	利
lián	连	18	辶	連
liàn	练	13	纟	練
liáng	凉	17	冫	凉
liǎng*	两	5	一	兩
liǎo/le	了	17	乙	了
lín*	邻	16	阝	鄰
liú	流	20	氵	流
liù	六	9	亠	六
lóu	楼	15	木	樓
lù	路	18	足	路
lǚ*	旅	19	方	旅
lǜ	绿	14	纟	綠

M

ma	吗	5	口	嗎
mā	妈	6	女	媽
mǎ	马	19	马	馬
mǎi	买	6	乙	買
mài	卖	7	十	賣
màn	慢	14	忄	慢
máng	忙	7	忄	忙
máo	毛	5	毛	毛
me*	么	5	丿	麼

Pinyin	Character	Chapter	Radical	Traditional character
méi	没	7	氵	没
měi	美	10	羊	美
mèi*	妹	6	女	妹
men*	们	5	亻	們
mén	门	9	门	門
mǐ	米	10	米	米
miàn	面	12	一	面
míng*	名	8	口	名
míng*	明	8	日	明
mǔ*	母	6	母	母
N				
ná	拿	11	人	拿
nǎ	哪	9	口	哪
nà	那	8	阝	那
nǎi	奶	8	女	奶
nán	南	11	十	南
nán	难	14	又	難
nán*	男	14	田	男
nào	闹	18	门	鬧
ne	呢	5	口	呢
nèi	内	9	冂	内
néng	能	16	月	能
nǐ	你	5	亻	你
nián	年	12	丿	年
niàn	念	10	心	念
niú	牛	8	牛	牛

Pinyin	Character	Chapter	Radical	Traditional character
nǚ*	女	5	女	女
nuǎn	暖	19	日	暖
P				
pá	爬	15	爪	爬
páng*	旁	19	方	旁
pàng	胖	18	月	胖
pǎo	跑	16	足	跑
péng*	朋	8	月	朋
pí	皮	8	皮	皮
pí*	啤	16	口	啤
pián*/biàn	便	6	亻	便
piào	票	15	西	票
píng	平	14	一	平
Q				
qī	七	4	一	七
qī*	期	12	月	期
qǐ	起	14	走	起
qì	气	7	气	氣
qì	汽	11	氵	汽
qiān	千	5	十	千
qiān	铅	17	钅	鉛
qián*	前	7	八	前
qián	钱	13	钅	錢
qiǎn	浅	14	氵	淺
qiě	且	20	一	且

Pinyin	Character	Chapter	Radical	Traditional character
qīng	清	16	氵	清
qīng	轻	19	车	輕
qǐng	请	7	讠	請
qiū*	秋	12	禾	秋
qiú	球	20	王	球
qù	去	8	土	去
qù*	趣	18	走	趣
quán	全	18	人	全
qún*	裙	14	衤	裙
R				
rán*	然	12	灬	然
rè	热	15	灬	熱
rén	人	4	人	人
rèn	认	9	讠	認
rì*	日	4	日	日
róng*	容	8	宀	容
ròu	肉	10	冂	肉
S				
sān	三	4	一	三
shān*	衫	9	衤	衫
shān	山	15	山	山
shāng*	商	9	亠	商
shàng	上	9	一	上
shāo	烧	13	火	燒
shǎo	少	12	小	少

Pinyin	Character	Chapter	Radical	Traditional character
shào*	绍	10	纟	紹
shè*	舍	20	人	舍
shéi/shuí	谁	12	讠	誰
shēn	深	14	氵	深
shén*	什	5	亻	甚
shēng	生	5	生	生
shī*	师	12	巾	師
shí	十	4	十	十
shí	时	13	日	時
shǐ*	始	13	女	始
shì	是	8	日	是
shì	识	9	讠	識
shì	事	10	一	事
shì (noun*)	试	10	讠	試
shì*	市	14	亠	市
shǒu	手	9	手	手
shòu	瘦	18	疒	瘦
shū	书	4	乙	書
shū	叔	8	又	叔
shū*	舒	11	人	舒
shuāng*	双	8	又	雙
shuí/shéi	谁	12	讠	誰
shuǐ	水	7	水	水
shuì	睡	16	目	睡
shuō	说	5	讠	說
sī*	思	8	心	思
sǐ	死	17	歹	死

Pinyin	Character	Chapter	Radical	Traditional character
sì	四	8	口	四
sōng	松	19	木	松
sòng	送	7	辶	送
sù*	诉	6	讠	訴
sù*	宿	20	宀	宿
sù*	速	20	辶	速
suī	虽	18	口	雖
suì*	岁	15	山	歲
suǒ*	所	15	户	所
T				
tā	他	5	亻	他
tā	她	6	女	她
tài	太	5	大	太
tān (noun*)	摊	19	扌	攤
tāng	汤	8	氵	湯
tǎo	讨	20	讠	討
téng	疼	13	疒	疼
tī*	梯	15	木	梯
tì	替	10	日	替
tiān	天	11	大	天
tiāo	挑	19	扌	挑
tiáo*	条	11	木	條
tīng	听	13	口	聽
tīng*	厅	15	厂	廳
tóng*	同	11	冂	同
tōu	偷	20	亻	偷

Pinyin	Character	Chapter	Radical	Traditional character
tóu	头	13	大	頭
tú	图	8	口	圖
W				
wà*	袜	9	衤	襪
wài*	外	11	夕	外
wán	玩	15	王	玩
wán	完	16	宀	完
wǎn	晚	8	日	晚
wàn	万	6	一	萬
wáng	王	4	王	王
wàng	忘	9	心	忘
wàng	往	11	彳	往
wèi	为	9	丶	為
wèi*	位	10	亻	位
wén*	文	4	文	文
wèn	问	5	口	問
wǒ	我	4	戈	我
wǔ	五	4	一	五
wǔ*	午	7	丿	午
X				
xī	西	4	西	西
xī*	息	13	心	息
xī*	希	15	巾	希
xí*	习	13	乙	習
xì (relate to*)	系	16	丿	系

Pinyin	Character	Chapter	Radical	Traditional character
xì	细	17	纟	細
xià	下	9	一	下
xià	夏	15	夂	夏
xiān	先	5	儿	先
xiàn*	现	12	王	現
xiāng*	箱	17	竹	箱
xiǎng	想	7	心	想
xiǎo	小	4	小	小
xiào	笑	10	竹	笑
xiào*	校	15	木	校
xiě	写	17	冖	寫
xiě/xuě	血	20	血	血
xiè	谢	10	讠	謝
xīn	心	11	心	心
xīn	新	15	斤	新
xīn*	薪	18	艹	薪
xìn	信	10	亻	信
xīng	星	12	日	星
xíng/háng	行	6	彳	行
xǐng	醒	16	酉	醒
xìng	姓	6	女	姓
xìng*	兴	12	八	興
xiōng*	兄	6	口	兄
xiū*	休	13	亻	休
xǔ	许	15	讠	許
xué	学	10	子	學

Pinyin	Character	Chapter	Radical	Traditional character
xuě	雪	15	雨	雪
xuě/xiě	血	20	血	血
Y				
ya	呀	6	口	呀
yán*	颜	14	页	顏
yǎn	眼	9	目	眼
yàn*	厌	20	厂	厭
yàng*	样	18	木	樣
yào	要	6	女	要
yào	药	13	艹	藥
yě	也	4	乙	也
yè*	业	12	业	業
yè*	页	14	页	頁
yè	夜	16	亠	夜
yī*	衣	9	衣	衣
yī*	医	13	匚	醫
yī, yì, yí	一	4	一	一
yí*	宜	6	宀	宜
yí	姨	17	女	姨
yǐ	以	5	人	以
yǐ*	己	12	己	己
yì*	意	7	心	意
yīn	因	9	口	因
yín	银	12	钅	銀
yīng*	英	10	艹	英

Pinyin	Character	Chapter	Radical	Traditional character
yīng	应	20	广	應
yòng	用	10	门	用
yóu	游	19	氵	遊
yǒu*	友	8	又	友
yǒu	有	8	月	有
yòu*	右	9	口	右
yòu	又	16	又	又
yǔ*	语	5	讠	語
yǔ	雨	15	雨	雨
yù*	寓	15	宀	寓
yuǎn	远	19	辶	遠
yuàn	院	13	阝	院
yuè	月	12	月	月
yuè (verb*)	越	19	走	越

Z

zá	杂	9	木	雜
zǎi*/zǐ*	仔	9	亻	仔
zài	再	5	一	再
zài	在	8	土	在
zán	咱	14	口	咱
zǎo	早	8	日	早
zěn*	怎	11	心	怎
zhàn	站	19	立	站
zhāng (classifier*)	张	17	弓	張
zhǎo	找	9	扌	找

Pinyin	Character	Chapter	Radical	Traditional character
zhe*	着	10	羊	著
zhě*	者	15	日	者
zhè	这	8	辶	這
zhēn	真	5	十	真
zhèng	正	11	一	正
zhī*	支	5	十	支
zhī	知	7	口	知
zhī*	之	18	丶	之
zhí	直	11	十	直
zhǐ	只	5	口	只
zhǐ	纸	17	纟	紙
zhì*	志	9	心	志
zhì	至	19	土	至
zhōng	中	4	丨	中
zhōng	钟	12	钅	鐘
zhù	住	9	亻	住
zhuā	抓	20	扌	抓
zhǔn	准	14	冫	准
zhuō*	桌	15	木	桌
zǐ*/zǎi*	仔	13	亻	仔
zǐ*	子	5	子	子
zì	字	6	宀	字
zì	自	6	自	自
zǒu	走	11	走	走
zū	租	11	禾	租
zú*	足	20	口	足

Pinyin	Character	Chapter	Radical	Traditional character
zuì	最	12	日	最
zuó*	昨	13	日	昨
zuǒ	左	11	工	左
zuò	做	7	亻	做
zuò	坐	11	土	坐
zuò	作	12	亻	作

Character Index by
Radical Stroke Count

Radical	Character	Pinyin	Number of strokes	Chapter first introduced	Traditional character
丶	之	zhī	3	18	之
丶	为	wèi	4	9	為
一	一	yī, yì, yí	1	4	一
一	二	èr	2	4	二
一	七	qī	2	4	七
一	三	sān	3	4	三
一	万	wàn	3	6	萬
一	上	shàng	3	9	上
一	下	xià	3	9	下
一	才	cái	3	13	才
一	不	bù-, bú-, -bu-	4	4	不
一	五	wǔ	4	4	五
一	开	kāi	4	11	開
一	东	dōng	5	7	東
一	正	zhèng	5	11	正
一	平	píng	5	14	平
一	且	qiě	5	20	且
一	百	bǎi	6	5	百
一	再	zài	6	5	再

Radical	Character	Pinyin	Number of strokes	Chapter first introduced	Traditional character
一	而	ér	6	14	而
一	两	liǎng	7	5	兩
一	来	lái	7	11	來
一	更	gèng	7	18	更
一	事	shì	8	10	事
一	面	miàn	9	12	面
丨	中	zhōng	4	4	中
丨	北	běi	5	9	北
丿	九	jiǔ	2	4	九
丿	么	me	3	5	麼
丿	久	jiǔ	3	13	久
丿	午	wǔ	4	7	午
丿	乐	lè	5	7	樂
丿	长	cháng	5	18	長
丿	乎	hū	5	18	乎
丿	年	nián	6	12	年
丿	系	xì	7	16	系
乙	了	le/liǎo	2	7	了
乙	也	yě	3	4	也
乙	习	xí	3	13	習
乙	飞	fēi	3	17	飛
乙	书	shū	4	4	書
乙	买	mǎi	6	6	買
亠	六	liù	4	9	六
亠	市	shì	5	14	市
亠	京	jīng	8	9	京
亠	夜	yè	8	16	夜

Radical	Character	Pinyin	Number of strokes	Chapter first introduced	Traditional character
亠	高	gāo	10	9	高
亠	商	shāng	11	9	商
亠	就	jiù	12	9	就
冫	冰	bīng	6	7	冰
冫	次	cì	6	16	次
冫	冷	lěng	7	15	冷
冫	准	zhǔn	10	14	准
冫	凉	liáng	10	17	涼
冖	写	xiě	5	17	寫
讠	认	rèn	4	9	認
讠	记	jì	5	17	記
讠	讨	tǎo	5	20	討
讠	许	xǔ	6	15	許
讠	讲	jiǎng	6	16	講
讠	词	cí	7	5	詞
讠	诉	sù	7	6	訴
讠	识	shì	7	9	識
讠	话	huà	8	5	話
讠	试	shì	8	10	試
讠	该	gāi	8	20	該
讠	说	shuō	9	5	說
讠	语	yǔ	9	5	語
讠	请	qǐng	10	7	請
讠	课	kè	10	10	課
讠	谁	shéi/shuí	11	12	誰
讠	谢	xiè	12	10	謝
十	十	shí	2	4	十

Radical	Character	Pinyin	Number of strokes	Chapter first introduced	Traditional character
十	千	qiān	3	5	千
十	支	zhī	4	5	支
十	考	kǎo	6	10	考
十	华	huá	6	17	華
十	卖	mài	8	7	賣
十	直	zhí	8	11	直
十	南	nán	9	11	南
十	真	zhēn	10	5	真
十	韩	hán	12	14	韓
厂	厅	tīng	4	15	廳
厂	厌	yàn	6	20	厭
厂	厕	cè	8	15	廁
厂	厨	chú	12	15	廚
匸	医	yī	7	13	醫
刂	刚	gāng	6	16	剛
刂	别	bié	7	12	別
刂	利	lì	7	19	利
刂	到	dào	8	12	到
刂	刻	kè	8	12	刻
刂	刮	guā	8	15	刮
冂	内	nèi	4	9	内
冂	用	yòng	5	10	用
冂	肉	ròu	6	10	肉
冂	同	tóng	6	11	同
八	八	bā	2	4	八
八	分	fēn	4	6	分
八	公	gōng	4	11	公

Radical	Character	Pinyin	Number of strokes	Chapter first introduced	Traditional character
八	兰	lán	5	6	蘭
八	半	bàn	5	6	半
八	共	gòng	6	6	共
八	关	guān	6	7	關
八	兴	xìng	6	12	興
八	弟	dì	7	6	弟
八	典	diǎn	7	6	典
八	具	jù	8	15	具
八	前	qián	9	7	前
勹	包	bāo	5	17	包
人	人	rén	2	4	人
人	个	gè	3	5	個
人	以	yǐ	4	5	以
人	介	jiè	4	10	介
人	从	cóng	4	11	從
人	今	jīn	4	13	今
人	会	huì	6	5	會
人	全	quán	6	18	全
人	舍	shè	8	20	舍
人	拿	ná	10	11	拿
人	舒	shū	12	11	舒
亻	们	men	4	5	們
亻	什	shén	4	5	甚
亻	他	tā	5	5	他
亻	仔	zǎi/zǐ	5	9	仔
亻	份	fèn	6	6	份
亻	件	jiàn	6	9	件

Radical	Character	Pinyin	Number of strokes	Chapter first introduced	Traditional character
亻	休	xiū	6	13	休
亻	你	nǐ	7	5	你
亻	伯	bó	7	7	伯
亻	住	zhù	7	9	住
亻	位	wèi	7	10	位
亻	作	zuò	7	12	作
亻	但	dàn	7	20	但
亻	便	pián/biàn	9	6	便
亻	信	xìn	9	10	信
亻	候	hòu	10	13	候
亻	借	jiè	10	17	借
亻	倍	bèi	10	18	倍
亻	做	zuò	11	7	做
亻	假	jià	11	19	假
亻	偷	tōu	11	20	偷
几	几	jǐ	2	5	幾
儿	儿	ér	2	5	兒
儿	先	xiān	6	5	先
又	又	yòu	2	16	又
又	叉	chā	3	10	叉
又	双	shuāng	4	8	雙
又	友	yǒu	4	8	友
又	对	duì	5	8	對
又	发	fā	5	13	發
又	欢	huān	6	8	歡
又	叔	shū	8	8	叔
又	难	nán	10	14	難

Radical	Character	Pinyin	Number of strokes	Chapter first introduced	Traditional character
阝	那	nà	6	8	那
阝	邻	lín	7	16	鄰
阝	阿	ā	7	17	阿
阝	附	fù	7	19	附
阝	除	chú	9	10	除
阝	院	yuàn	9	13	院
阝	都	dōu	10	8	都
凵	画	huà	8	6	畫
刀	刀	dāo	2	10	刀
力	办	bàn	4	20	辦
氵	汉	hàn	5	7	漢
氵	汤	tāng	6	8	湯
氵	汗	hàn	6	9	汗
氵	江	jiāng	6	18	江
氵	没	méi	7	7	沒
氵	汽	qì	7	11	汽
氵	法	fǎ	8	8	法
氵	浅	qiǎn	8	14	淺
氵	河	hé	8	18	河
氵	酒	jiǔ	10	7	酒
氵	海	hǎi	10	10	海
氵	流	liú	10	20	流
氵	深	shēn	11	14	深
氵	清	qīng	11	16	清
氵	游	yóu	12	19	遊
忄	忙	máng	6	7	忙
忄	快	kuài	7	7	快

Radical	Character	Pinyin	Number of strokes	Chapter first introduced	Traditional character
忄	慢	màn	14	14	慢
忄	懂	dǒng	15	14	懂
宀	字	zì	6	6	字
宀	安	ān	6	12	安
宀	完	wán	7	16	完
宀	宜	yí	8	6	宜
宀	定	dìng	8	12	定
宀	客	kè	9	7	客
宀	家	jiā	10	6	家
宀	容	róng	10	8	容
宀	害	hài	10	19	害
宀	宿	sù	11	20	宿
宀	寓	yù	12	15	寓
广	床	chuáng	7	14	床
广	应	yīng	7	20	應
广	店	diàn	8	14	店
广	度	dù	9	20	度
门	门	mén	3	9	門
门	间	jiān	7	17	間
门	闹	nào	8	18	鬧
辶	边	biān	5	9	邊
辶	过	guò	6	10	過
辶	还	hái/huán	7	7	還
辶	这	zhè	7	8	這
辶	进	jìn	7	15	進
辶	连	lián	7	18	連
辶	近	jìn	7	19	近

Radical	Character	Pinyin	Number of strokes	Chapter first introduced	Traditional character
辶	远	yuǎn	7	19	遠
辶	送	sòng	9	7	送
辶	速	sù	10	20	速
辶	道	dào	12	7	道
辶	遍	biàn	12	17	遍
扌	打	dǎ	5	10	打
扌	报	bào	7	9	報
扌	找	zhǎo	7	9	找
扌	把	bǎ	7	17	把
扌	抓	zhuā	7	20	抓
扌	拐	guǎi	8	11	拐
扌	拉	lā	8	20	拉
扌	挤	jǐ	9	13	擠
扌	挑	tiāo	9	19	挑
扌	接	jiē	11	20	接
扌	搬	bān	13	15	搬
扌	摊	tān	13	19	攤
工	工	gōng	3	19	工
工	功	gōng	5	11	功
工	左	zuǒ	5	11	左
土	去	qù	5	8	去
土	地	de/dì	6	8	地
土	在	zài	6	8	在
土	场	chǎng	6	14	場
土	至	zhì	6	19	至
土	块	kuài	7	8	塊
土	坐	zuò	7	11	坐

Radical	Character	Pinyin	Number of strokes	Chapter first introduced	Traditional character
土	坏	huài	7	13	壞
土	城	chéng	9	9	城
土	堵	dǔ	11	19	堵
艹	花	huā	7	13	花
艹	英	yīng	8	10	英
艹	茶	chá	9	10	茶
艹	药	yào	9	13	藥
艹	菜	cài	11	10	菜
艹	黄	huáng	11	14	黄
艹	蓝	lán	13	14	藍
艹	薪	xīn	16	18	薪
大	大	dà	3	4	大
大	太	tài	4	5	太
大	天	tiān	4	11	天
大	头	tóu	5	13	頭
小	小	xiǎo	3	4	小
小	少	shǎo	4	12	少
小	当	dāng	6	12	當
口	口	kǒu	3	6	口
口	只	zhǐ	5	5	只
口	可	kě	5	5	可
口	兄	xiōng	5	6	兄
口	叫	jiào	5	8	叫
口	右	yòu	5	9	右
口	号	hào	5	12	號
口	吗	ma	6	5	嗎
口	问	wèn	6	5	問

Radical	Character	Pinyin	Number of strokes	Chapter first introduced	Traditional character
口	告	gào	6	6	告
口	吃	chī	6	7	吃
口	名	míng	6	8	名
口	后	hòu	6	10	後
口	回	huí	6	12	回
口	呀	ya	7	6	呀
口	吧	ba	7	8	吧
口	听	tīng	7	13	聽
口	吵	chǎo	7	16	吵
口	足	zú	7	20	足
口	呢	ne	8	5	呢
口	哎	āi	8	6	哎
口	咖	kā	8	7	咖
口	知	zhī	8	7	知
口	哪	nǎ	9	9	哪
口	咱	zán	9	14	咱
口	虽	suī	9	18	雖
口	哥	gē	10	6	哥
口	啊	á	10	16	啊
口	哭	kū	10	20	哭
口	啡	fēi	11	7	啡
口	啤	pí	11	16	啤
口	唱	chàng	11	20	唱
口	喝	hē	12	7	喝
口	四	sì	5	8	四
口	因	yīn	6	9	因
口	国	guó	8	8	國

Radical	Character	Pinyin	Number of strokes	Chapter first introduced	Traditional character
口	图	tú	8	8	圖
巾	师	shī	6	12	師
巾	希	xī	7	15	希
巾	带	dài	9	16	帶
巾	常	cháng	11	13	常
山	山	shān	3	15	山
山	出	chū	5	15	出
山	岁	suì	6	15	歲
彳	行	xíng/háng	6	6	行
彳	往	wàng	8	11	往
彳	很	hěn	9	6	很
彳	得	de/děi	11	6	得
彳	街	jiē	12	11	街
夕	外	wài	5	11	外
夕	多	duō	6	11	多
夕	够	gòu	11	18	够
饣	饭	fàn	7	7	飯
饣	饱	bǎo	8	8	飽
饣	饺	jiǎo	9	17	餃
饣	饿	è	10	7	餓
饣	馆	guǎn	11	7	館
己	已	yǐ	3	12	已
己	己	jǐ	3	19	己
弓	张	zhāng	8	17	張
子	子	zǐ	3	5	子
子	学	xué	8	10	學
子	孩	hái	9	10	孩

Radical	Character	Pinyin	Number of strokes	Chapter first introduced	Traditional character
女	女	nǚ	3	5	女
女	奶	nǎi	5	8	奶
女	好	hǎo	6	6	好
女	妈	mā	6	6	媽
女	她	tā	6	6	她
女	姐	jiě	8	6	姐
女	妹	mèi	8	6	妹
女	姓	xìng	8	6	姓
女	始	shǐ	8	13	始
女	要	yào	9	6	要
女	姨	yí	9	17	姨
夂	冬	dōng	5	14	冬
夂	夏	xià	10	15	夏
纟	红	hóng	6	14	紅
纟	纸	zhǐ	7	17	紙
纟	绍	shào	8	10	紹
纟	经	jīng	8	12	經
纟	练	liàn	8	13	練
纟	细	xì	8	17	細
纟	给	gěi	9	10	給
纟	绿	lǜ	11	14	綠
纟	绩	jì	11	18	績
马	马	mǎ	3	19	馬
灬	点	diǎn	9	12	點
灬	热	rè	10	15	熱
灬	然	rán	12	12	然
文	文	wén	4	4	文

Radical	Character	Pinyin	Number of strokes	Chapter first introduced	Traditional character
户	房	fáng	8	15	房
户	所	suǒ	8	15	所
方	方	fāng	4	9	方
方	旅	lǚ	10	19	旅
方	旁	páng	10	19	旁
火	火	huǒ	4	11	火
火	灯	dēng	6	11	燈
火	灰	huī	6	14	灰
火	炒	chǎo	8	11	炒
火	烧	shāo	10	13	燒
心	心	xīn	4	11	心
心	必	bì	5	7	必
心	忘	wàng	7	9	忘
心	志	zhì	7	9	志
心	念	niàn	8	10	念
心	思	sī	9	8	思
心	怎	zěn	9	11	怎
心	急	jí	9	19	急
心	息	xī	10	13	息
心	想	xiǎng	13	7	想
心	意	yì	13	7	意
王	王	wáng	4	4	王
王	现	xiàn	8	12	現
王	玩	wán	8	15	玩
王	班	bān	10	15	班
王	球	qiú	11	20	球
木	本	běn	5	4	本

Radical	*Character*	*Pinyin*	*Number of strokes*	*Chapter first introduced*	*Traditional character*
木	机	jī	5	10	機
木	杂	zá	6	9	雜
木	朵	duǒ	6	16	朵
木	条	tiáo	7	11	條
木	极	jí	7	17	極
木	李	lǐ	7	17	李
木	板	bǎn	8	9	板
木	杯	bēi	8	13	杯
木	果	guǒ	8	19	果
木	松	sōng	8	19	松
木	架	jià	9	20	架
木	校	xiào	10	15	校
木	桌	zhuō	10	15	桌
木	样	yàng	10	18	樣
木	梯	tī	11	15	梯
木	楼	lóu	13	15	樓
木	楚	chǔ	13	16	楚
歹	死	sǐ	6	17	死
车	车	chē	4	6	車
车	轻	qīng	9	19	輕
车	较	jiào	10	19	較
戈	成	chéng	6	17	成
戈	我	wǒ	7	4	我
比	比	bǐ	4	18	比
日	日	rì	4	4	日
日	旧	jiù	5	8	舊
日	早	zǎo	6	8	早

Radical	Character	Pinyin	Number of strokes	Chapter first introduced	Traditional character
日	时	shí	7	13	時
日	明	míng	8	8	明
日	者	zhě	8	15	者
日	是	shì	9	8	是
日	春	chūn	9	12	春
日	星	xīng	9	12	星
日	昨	zuó	9	13	昨
日	晚	wǎn	12	8	晚
日	替	tì	12	10	替
日	最	zuì	12	12	最
日	景	jǐng	12	19	景
日	暖	nuǎn	13	19	暖
曰	电	diàn	5	6	電
水	水	shuǐ	4	7	水
贝	贵	guì	9	18	貴
见	见	jiàn	4	5	見
见	觉	jiào	9	16	覺
父	父	fù	4	6	父
牛	牛	niú	4	8	牛
手	手	shǒu	4	9	手
毛	毛	máo	4	5	毛
气	气	qì	4	7	氣
攵	放	fàng	8	17	放
攵	故	gù	9	10	故
攵	教	jiāo	11	10	教
斤	斤	jīn	4	20	斤
斤	新	xīn	13	15	新

Radical	Character	Pinyin	Number of strokes	Chapter first introduced	Traditional character
爪	爬	pá	8	15	爬
爪	爱	ài	10	15	愛
月	月	yuè	4	12	月
月	有	yǒu	6	8	有
月	肚	dù	7	13	肚
月	朋	péng	8	8	朋
月	服	fú	8	11	服
月	胖	pàng	9	18	胖
月	能	néng	10	16	能
月	期	qī	12	12	期
风	风	fēng	4	15	風
耂	老	lǎo	6	9	老
母	母	mǔ	5	6	母
穴	空	kòng	8	18	空
穴	穿	chuān	9	18	穿
生	生	shēng	5	5	生
立	站	zhàn	10	19	站
疒	病	bìng	10	13	病
疒	疼	téng	10	13	疼
疒	瘦	shòu	14	18	瘦
衤	衬	chèn	8	9	襯
衤	衫	shān	8	9	衫
衤	袜	wà	10	9	襪
衤	被	bèi	10	20	被
衤	裙	qún	12	14	裙
衤	裤	kù	12	18	褲
业	业	yè	5	12	業

Radical	Character	Pinyin	Number of strokes	Chapter first introduced	Traditional character
目	看	kàn*	9	9	看
目	眼	yǎn	11	9	眼
目	睛	jīng	13	16	睛
目	睡	shuì	13	16	睡
田	男	nán	7	14	男
田	备	bèi	8	14	備
田	累	lèi	11	14	累
钅	钟	zhōng	9	12	鐘
钅	钱	qián	10	13	錢
钅	铅	qiān	10	17	鉛
钅	银	yín	11	12	銀
钅	错	cuò	13	12	錯
钅	镜	jìng	16	16	鏡
禾	和	hé/huó	8	11	和
禾	秋	qiū	9	12	秋
禾	租	zū	10	11	租
白	白	bái	5	8	白
白	的	de	8	9	的
瓜	瓜	guā	5	19	瓜
皮	皮	pí	5	8	皮
衣	衣	yī	6	9	衣
羊	美	měi	9	10	美
羊	差	chà	9	12	差
羊	着	zhe	11	10	著
米	米	mǐ	6	10	米
米	粉	fěn	10	14	粉
耳	耳	ěr	6	16	耳

Radical	Character	Pinyin	Number of strokes	Chapter first introduced	Traditional character
西	西	xī	6	4	西
西	票	piào	11	15	票
页	页	yè	6	14	頁
页	顿	dùn	10	14	頓
页	颜	yán	15	14	顏
竹	笔	bǐ	10	8	筆
竹	笑	xiào	10	10	笑
竹	笨	bèn	11	8	笨
竹	第	dì	11	13	第
竹	等	děng	12	13	等
竹	筷	kuài	13	10	筷
竹	箱	xiāng	15	17	箱
自	自	zì	6	6	自
血	血	xiě/xuě	6	20	血
走	走	zǒu	7	11	走
走	起	qǐ	10	14	起
走	越	yuè	12	19	越
走	超	chāo	12	20	超
走	趣	qù	15	18	趣
酉	醒	xǐng	16	16	醒
里	里	lǐ	7	12	裏
足	跑	pǎo	12	16	跑
足	跟	gēn	13	16	跟
足	路	lù	13	18	路
青	静	jìng	14	18	靜
雨	雨	yǔ	8	15	雨
雨	雪	xuě	11	15	雪

Radical Index
(Introduced Radicals Only)

Radical	Number of strokes	General meaning	Independent character?	Chapter first introduced
一	1	one	Y	4
丨	1	(a vertical line)	N	9
乙	1	/	Y	13
人	2	human	Y	5
亻	2	human	N	5
儿	2	son	Y	5
十	2	ten	Y	5
讠	2	speech	N	5
八 or 丷	2	eight	Y	6
冫	2	cold, ice	N	7
又	2	again, hand	Y	8
阝	2	ear	N	8
冖	2	coverage	N	9
冂	2	border	N	10
刂	2	knife	N	12
厂	2	factory, cover	Y	15
宀	2	cover	N	17
勹	2	/	N	17
口	3	mouth	Y	5

Radical	Number of strokes	General meaning	Independent character?	Chapter first introduced
女	3	female	Y	6
宀	3	roof	N	6
彳	3	double human	N	6
忄	3	heart, mind	N	7
氵	3	water	N	7
辶	3	road, walking	N	7
饣	3	food	N	7
忄	3	heart, mind	N	7
囗	3	enclosure	Y	8
土	3	soil	Y	8
扌	3	hand	N	9
子	3	child	Y	10
纟	3	silk	N	10
艹	3	grass, plant	N	10
夕	3	evening	Y	11
工	3	work	Y	11
小	3	little	Y	12
巾	3	towel	Y	12
匚	3	three-fourths enclosure	N	13
大	3	big, large	Y	13
广	3	extensive	Y	14
夂	3	retreat	N	14
山	3	mountain	Y	15
弓	3	bow	Y	17
门	3	door	Y	17
心	4	heart, mind	Y	7
心	4	heart, mind	Y	7

Radical	Number of strokes	General meaning	Independent character?	Chapter first introduced
日	4	sun	Y	8
月	4	moon, flesh	Y	8
木	4	wood, tree	Y	9
攵	4	culture, language	N	10
火	4	fire	Y	11
灬	4	fire	N	12
王	4	king, jade	Y	12
户	4	door or family	Y	15
斤	4	0.5 kilograms, axe	Y	15
爪	4	paw	Y	15
见	4	see	Y	16
比	4	compare	Y	18
贝	4	shell, money	Y	18
方	4	square, direction	Y	19
车	4	vehicle	Y	19
白	5	white, light	Y	9
目	5	eye	Y	9
衤	5	clothing	N	9
禾	5	grain	Y	11
钅	5	metal, money	N	12
疒	5	illness, disease	N	13
田	5	field	Y	14
穴	5	cave, hole	Y	18
立	5	stand	Y	19
竹	6	bamboo	Y	8
羊	6	goat	Y	10
米	6	rice	Y	14

Radical	Number of strokes	General meaning	Independent character?	Chapter first introduced
页	6	page	Y	14
西	6	west	Y	15
走	7	walk	Y	14
足	7	foot	Y	16
酉	7	wine	Y	16
雨	8	rain	Y	15
青	8	glassy green	Y	18

English Translations of the Reading Passages

CHAPTER 4

TEXT 1

I read books and I also buy books. I have Chinese books. I also have Japanese books—one, two, three, four, five, six, seven, eight, nine, ten. My books are not large, nor are they small. Do you have Chinese books or Japanese books?

TEXT 2

He is Chinese and is called *Wang Zhongshu*. He speaks Chinese and can also speak English. I am Japanese. My family name is *Nakamoto* and my personal name is *Kazuya*. My friend is a New Zealander. He speaks English. We both study Chinese and *Wang Zhongshu* teaches us Chinese.

SUPPLEMENTARY READING

Wang Xiaowen:	Good morning!
Nakamoto Kazuya:	Good morning!
Wang Xiaowen:	Are you Chinese or Japanese?
Nakamoto Kazuya:	I am Japanese. Are you Chinese?
Wang Xiaowen:	I am Chinese. My name is *Wang Xiaowen*. What is your name?
Nakamoto Kazuya:	My name is *Nakamoto Kazuya*.

CHAPTER 5

TEXT 1

Mr. Wang has 1,254 books. He has Chinese books, English books, and even Japanese books. He asked *Wenwen* what books she has and how many she has. *Wenwen* only has a few English works of fiction. Mr. Wang said that *Wenwen* can read his Chinese books. However, *Wenwen* doesn't understand Chinese. *Wenwen* can't speak Chinese and can't read it either. *Wenwen* can only say "Hello! Goodbye." *Wenwen* wants to learn Chinese. Mr. Wang said that he could teach *Wenwen* Chinese. He even gave *Wenwen* a Chinese-English dictionary.

TEXT 2

I am a New Zealander. I can speak English and Japanese. I can also write a few Chinese characters. Mrs. Wang's son and daughter are middle school students. I teach them to speak Japanese. Mrs. Wang gave me three brush pens. I asked her, "Can you teach me to write with a brush pen?" She said, "Sure." She's really good! And what about you? Do you want to learn how to write with a brush pen? I can give you two.

SUPPLEMENTARY READING

Nakamoto Kazuya:	Hello! May I ask, can you speak Japanese?
Wang Wen:	I can only say "one", "two", "three", "four", "five", "six", "seven", "eight", "nine", and "ten". Are you Japanese?
Nakamoto Kazuya:	Yes, I am. However, my wife is Chinese.
Wang Wen:	You can speak Chinese. Can your wife speak Japanese?
Nakamoto Kazuya:	Yes, she can.
Wang Wen:	Is he your son?
Nakamoto Kazuya:	Yes.
Wang Wen:	Can your son speak Chinese or Japanese?
Nakamoto Kazuya:	He can speak Chinese and he can also speak Japanese.

CHAPTER 6

TEXT 1

I have a good friend whose family name is *Wan* and whose full name is *Wan Wensheng*. There are altogether eight people in his family: his father, mother, an older sister, two younger sisters, an older brother, a younger brother, and *Wensheng*. Half of the siblings are male and half are female. His older sister has four Japanese dictionaries, two Chinese magazines, and three New Zealand works of fiction. Both of his younger sisters are elementary school students and they don't like to read fiction. They want to read comic books. They say that comic books are nice to read and don't have many words either. Neither *Wensheng* nor his younger brother likes to read books. They want to watch TV. They say that TV is very nice to watch.

TEXT 2

Neither my older sister nor I have a bicycle. I must buy one. Bicycles are $740.95 each, neither expensive nor cheap. My older sister also wants to buy one. How much altogether are two? Tell me, OK? Oh my! Altogether its $1,481.90. No way. We only have $1,000 and can only buy one. My parents have a lot of money. They have tens of thousands of dollars. They said they could give us two bicycles. My parents are really good!

SUPPLEMENTARY READING 1

Daxi: *Wensheng*, who is in your family?
Wensheng: My dad, mom, an older sister, two younger sisters, an older brother, and me.
Daxi: Can everyone in your family speak Chinese?
Wensheng: They can all speak Chinese. How many brothers and sisters do you have?
Daxi: I only have one younger brother.
Wensheng: Can your younger brother speak Chinese?
Daxi: He can only speak English.

SUPPLEMENTARY READING 2

That Japanese car that *Nakayama Kazuya* bought wasn't cheap, but he says it wasn't expensive. He said a good Japanese car will cost thirty or forty thousand dollars. His was only ten thousand dollars. The car he bought really wasn't expensive.

CHAPTER 7

TEXT

It is about the time for lunch. I'm really hungry, but don't want to cook. I'd like to go to a Chinese restaurant for some simple dishes, and then have a bit to drink.

Simple Chinese dishes are quite delicious, but are not easy to make. *Lanlan* also hasn't eaten lunch. She also wants to go to eat lunch. I know what she wants to eat. She wants to eat Japanese food and drink ice water and Coca-Cola. *Lanlan*'s uncle and aunt are the proprietors of a Japanese restaurant. Their business is very brisk and their customers are also numerous. The dishes of their restaurant are very delicious. However, their coffee isn't good-tasting. They also used to sell liquor before but now they don't. *Lanlan* even says that her uncle won't take our money, as he really likes to treat people to a meal. We needn't be over-polite or give him anything. It doesn't matter. (After all,) he is *Lanlan*'s uncle. However, her uncle likes to speak Chinese. When we go to his restaurant to eat we'll have to speak Chinese. That's great! I can speak a little Chinese and I also like to speak Chinese. I can even write a few Chinese characters.

SUPPLEMENTARY READING 1

Wenhan: *Xiaolan*, are these simple Chinese dishes cooked by you?
Xiaolan: Yes.
Wenhan: They are really delicious.
Xiaolan: (If you feel that they) are delicious then have a bit more.
Wenhan: Really? In that case I won't be polite.
Xiaolan: No problem, eat as much as you can. Don't be polite.

SUPPLEMENTARY READING 2

I really like to drink ice water, but Chinese people say that drinking ice water is not good. Chinese restaurants neither sell ice water nor give it to customers. Chinese people say that drinking Chinese tea is better. My American friend says that drinking cola is better. What do you say?

CHAPTER 8

TEXT

This is my good friend. His name is *Mao Lesheng*. *Xiao Mao* is French. He is really interesting, as he likes buying authentic French things. That pair of French leather shoes he wears is very expensive, more than $400 a pair. I only buy cheap leather shoes. All of my old leather shoes are only $80 a pair. Some people say that *Xiao Mao* is quite clever, but I say that he is really stupid. Look, he wears expensive French leather shoes, but has no money left to buy something to eat. He no longer eats breakfast, and just drinks milk. And he no longer eats lunch, either, and just drinks a bit of soup. It's really not easy not to eat. I asked him if he was hungry or not and he said it's not a problem. I really don't get it. He cannot not eat, right? I'd like to treat him to dinner. He really likes authentic French things, but he doesn't like to eat French food. That's right, he likes eating Chinese food. I'll invite *Xiao Mao* to go to my uncle's Chinese restaurant for dinner. *Xiao Mao* hasn't eaten breakfast or lunch, so (he must be) too hungry. He says that the dishes made by that restaurant are outstandingly delicious. He is no longer hungry and is full now. My uncle even gave *Xiao Mao* a Chinese writing brush and a Chinese atlas.

SUPPLEMENTARY READING 1

Owner:	Are you buying a bicycle?
Wan Wensheng:	How much is this bicycle?
Owner:	Eight hundred dollars.
Wan Wensheng:	Six hundred, okay?
Owner:	No. Seven hundred!
Wan Wensheng:	That's too expensive. How about one thousand two hundred for two?
Owner:	One thousand three hundred!
Wan Wensheng:	That's too expensive. I'm no longer interested.
Owner:	Okay, I'll sell them to you for just one thousand two hundred.
Wan Wensheng:	Okay, here's one thousand five hundred.
Owner:	And here's your three hundred in change.

SUPPLEMENTARY READING 2

I wanted to buy apples. I asked the owner how much one catty of apples cost. He said, "One dollar fifty." He asked me how many catties I wanted and I said that they were too expensive. I asked him if he would sell them to me for fifty cents a catty and he said that I needed to buy five catties (to get that price). I said, "Okay!" I gave him $7.50. Do you think that this was the right amount or not?

CHAPTER 9

TEXT

There is a famous store downtown. That store sells many things. Upstairs they sell clothing and (leather) shoes. There are shirts, T-shirts, jackets, underwear, sweaters, dresses, and denim jeans. The things are all very cheap. Look, is this sweater

I am wearing good-looking? It was only $40. That's not expensive, eh. The socks and shoes sold there are also very good-looking. Downstairs to the east of the main entrance they sell watches and eyeglasses. The watches there are not cheap—more than $1,000 each; the eyeglasses are also quite expensive—more than $600 a pair. That store does not have cheap watches or eyeglasses, so you don't want to buy watches there and you don't want to buy eyeglasses there either. To the west of the main entrance they sell food, books, newspapers, magazines, writing implements, and maps. In front of the main entrance they sell things to eat and drink. Do you want to go there to shop? Do you want to drink cold milk or a cola? Oh my! I forgot to inform you where the store is located. It is on Beijing Street. It's not difficult to find. The proprietor of the shop is surnamed *Fang*. He is called *Fang Yisi*. He is quite tall. I know him. He lives to the right of our place. His house is quite large. There are four rooms upstairs and two rooms downstairs. Fang Laoban and the (other) people in his family are all very busy, and so are very infrequently at home. I like going to shop at his store very much. Why? Because the things he sells are very good. Do you know where I want to go now? I want to go to *Fang Laoban*'s store. Do you want to go with me?

SUPPLEMENTARY READING 1

Owner: Good morning! What are looking for?

Gao Yilan: I'm just looking. How much for this sweater?

Owner: Four hundred and eighty dollars.

Gao Yilan: That's too expensive.

Owner: It's not expensive.

Gao Yilan: How about three hundred and eighty?

Owner: Impossible. Four hundred and fifty!

Gao Yilan: Four hundred and twenty!

Owner: Okay, okay, four hundred and twenty! Do you want anything else?

Gao Yilan: Just this. Thank you.

SUPPLEMENTARY READING 2

You all know what the meaning of "door" is. Your home has a front door and a back door. However, do you know what "There is no door" means? (For instance), if all of you want to go see a movie but you want me to stay home and watch the door. You would say, "We're going to watch a movie. You stay home alone and watch the door." I would say, "You want me to stay home alone and watch the door. There is no door." What does "watch the door" mean here? What about "There is no door"? Does it mean that the house doesn't have a door or "No way, impossible"?

CHAPTER 10

TEXT

Gao Xiaomei is an American who lives in China. She lives on Shanghai Road, between a bookstore and a coffee shop. Before, her children were small and she had to be at home to look after the kids, so she didn't have an opportunity to study Chinese and could only speak English. Now her four kids are all older so she can now go study. Mrs. Gao couldn't write any Chinese characters before. Now she is a university student. She studies Chinese and French. Chinese is not easy, (as) the teacher always uses Chinese to teach, and the Chinese books are all written in Chinese. It is almost exam time, and Mrs. Gao is too busy. With the exception of class she doesn't go anywhere. She doesn't watch television and she also doesn't cook. The adults and kids all go to the restaurant behind their house to eat dinner. In addition to Chinese she also has a French exam. She says that she has to read more than ten books. Some are Chinese books and some are French books.

Mrs. Gao has a friend named *Wang Huanlan*. She is female. Among Mrs. Gao's friends, only *Wang Hanlan* is Chinese. Miss Wang lives to the north of Mrs. Gao. Mrs. Gao can use Chinese to phone *Wang Huanglan* and can speak with her in Chinese. *Wang Huanlan* also uses Chinese to speak with Mrs. Gao and tells her Chinese stories. *Wang Huanlan* can use a brush pen to write Chinese characters. She writes Chinese letters to the Chinese teacher with a brush pen for Mrs. Gao. Mrs. Gao is also very good to Huanlan, inviting her to go to a Chinese restaurant for a meal. *Wang Huanlan* has taught Mrs. Gao how to use chopsticks to eat rice. Mrs. Gao has never drunk Chinese tea before, so *Wang Huanlan* has introduced her to Chinese tea. Mrs. Gao makes English tea for *Wang Huanlan*, and teaches her how to use a knife and fork to eat beef. They like to laugh together as they eat and drink tea. Mrs. Gao thinks it is really great to have a Chinese friend. She'll definitely not have any trouble with the exam. She really must thank *Wang Huanlan*.

SUPPLEMENTARY READING 1

Zhigao: *Xiaohuan*, let me introduce the two of you. This is my friend *Fang Han*.

Xiaohuan: Hello, *Fang Han*. My name is *Xiaohuan*.

Fang Han: Hello, *Xiaohuan*.

Zhigao: *Xiaohuan* is my neighbor. She is a student at Peking University. *Fang Han* is also a student.

Fang Han: I am a university student but I am only taking two courses. What about you?

Xiaohuan: I am taking five courses. Which two courses are you taking?

Fang Han: Chinese and French.

Xiaohuan: You're studying Chinese! Can you write Chinese characters with a brush pen?

Fang Han: I can't, *Zhigao* can, but I would very much like to learn.

Xiaohuan: In that case, *Zhigao*, you teach us, okay?

Zhigao: No problem.

SUPPLEMENTARY READING 2

Chinese people like to say "No problem." (So, for example,) you say to the store owner, "This clothing is too large. Give me smaller size, okay?" The owner will say, "No problem." Eating at a restaurant, I said to the restaurant owner, "I can't use chopsticks, would it be possible to give me a knife and fork?" The owner said, "No problem." Before eating I said to my Chinese friend *Xiao Wang*, "*Xiao Wang*, sorry but I am no longer going to eat." Xiao Wang asked, "Why (not)?" I said, "I don't have any money." *Xiao Wang* said, "No money? No problem, I have money here." After eating, *Xiao Wang* said to me, "Oh no! There's a problem." I asked, "What problem?" He said, "I don't have any money either." You also don't have any money. I think this really is a problem.

CHAPTER 11

TEXT

Bai Jingyi is my middle school classmate and is now a student at Peking University. He is very bright and his homework is quite good. But he doesn't know how to drive a car and goes everywhere by bicycle. He says riding a bus is very cheap, but too many people ride the bus, so it's too uncomfortable. Taking a taxi is very convenient and comfortable, but it is too expensive. Therefore, he goes everywhere by bicycle.

    Bai Jingyi one night gave me a call and asked what I was doing. I said that I was right then reading. He asked me if I had free time. I said that I'm free. Come on over to my place for a chat and some drinks. He said great, but he didn't know how to get to my place. I told him that my home is on Tongxin Street and there was a train station on the left-hand side. Turn left at the train station and keep on going straight from the train station you will get to my house. To the right of my home is a primary school and to the left is a library. There's a light outside of the library, so it's not hard to find. *Bai Jingyi* rode from this street to that street asking directions, but no one knew where Tongxin Street was, so *Bai Jingyi* stopped riding his bicycle and took a taxi to come to my home. I asked him why he didn't buy a map. Looking for the street while holding the map would be (so much) easier. He's really stupid, not the least bit bright.

That night *Bai Jingyi* and I drank Chinese liquor and chatted, eating the small Shanghai snacks, Nanjing stir fried dishes that my wife made for us. *Bai Jingyi* said that because there are such delicious dishes and such tasty spirits, he likes coming to my house to drink and shoot the breeze with me very much.

SUPPLEMENTARY READING 1

Gao Zhiming: Hello, excuse me, where is the train station?
Pedestrian: Up ahead.
Gao Zhiming: How do I get there (asking for directions)?
Pedestrian: Keep going straight ahead. When you get to the intersection turn left and you'll be there.
Gao Zhiming: Thank you!
Pedestrian: Don't mention it.

SUPPLEMENTARY READING 2

Chinese has very many four character idioms. Some idioms have stories behind them, (while) others don't. "One day, three autumns (days creep by like years)", "Nine ox, a single strand of hair (a drop in the bucket)", and "old man under the moon (act as the go-between in a marriage)" are all idioms and they all have stories behind them.

CHAPTER 12

TEXT

Last spring, *Fang Meichun* and her classmates came to Beijing to learn Chinese. They had already been studying Chinese in England for a year. None of them have been to China before. They will be in Beijing for a year and a half and will return home next autumn. Except for Saturdays and Sundays, they have classes every day. In the morning they have class from 8:10 to 11:30. In the afternoon they are in class from 1:35 to 4:00, and in the evening they have to do a lot of homework. They love most of all to go to the library to do their homework, because it's very quiet and the students work very hard.

On Saturdays and Sundays, *Fang Meichun* and her classmates are very happy, because they can chat at home, cook, and they can go watch a movie, go to a store to shop. *Fang Meichun* had never cooked before, but now she can cook delicious Chinese fried rice. She likes to invite her classmates and teachers to come have dinner with her. All of her friends love to eat the Chinese fried rice that she makes.

On the 20th of last month, a Sunday, it was *Fang Meichun*'s birthday. Her boyfriend *Haiming* said that because it was *Meichun*'s birthday, (he told her) don't cook at home (and that instead) he wanted to invite *Meichun* and her friends to a good restaurant for dinner. He said that the new British restaurant opposite the bank is very good and he wanted to go there. *Meichun* said of course. However, there must be no fried rice in a British restaurant. (Therefore) *Meichun* took a lot of fried rice to the restaurant. Almost all of *Meichun*'s classmates and friends came. Do you know how many people came altogether? More than twenty! They even invited the British boss to eat with them. "It's good that I haven't had Chinese fried rice in a British restaurant," *Haiming* said. "This is great. I have never eaten Chinese fried rice at a British restaurant." The British boss even said that when he has free time he wants to learn from *Meichun* how to cook Chinese fried rice.

SUPPLEMENTARY READING 1

Gao Xiaochun: *Wenhai*, where are you going?
Wang Wenhai: I'm going to class.
Gao Xiaochun: When do you start?
Wang Wenhai: Two o'clock.
Gao Xiaochun: What time is it now?
Wang Wenhai: Ten minutes before two.
Gao Xiaochun: In that case, you'd better hurry up!
Wang Wenhai: Bye.
Gao Xiaochun: Bye.

SUPPLEMENTARY READING 2

Chinese people often say *"Méi shìr."* (For instance,) you said to your friend that you would wait for him at the cinema at seven o'clock, but you only arrived at 7:30. You say to him, "Sorry, I'm late." He says, *"Méi shìr."* (Or), a friend invites you to go to a restaurant to eat and you forget to go. The next day you phone your friend and say, "Sorry, last night I forgot the fact that you invited me to eat." Your friend says, *"Méi shìr."* Do you know what the two *"méi shìr"* here mean? Here, *"méi shìr"* means "It doesn't matter, it's nothing."

CHAPTER 13

TEXT

I most dislike going to see a doctor. Seeing a doctor you have to spend a lot of money, and (even) if you take medicine you won't necessarily get better. But this morning I went to the hospital to see a doctor.

Yesterday *Bai Jingyi* came looking for me to practice Chinese and to shoot the breeze. In the evening we drank a lot of alcohol and ate a lot of delicious things. In the evening after *Bai Jingyi* left I (started to) feel uncomfortable. My head hurt, my stomach hurt, and I was uncomfortable everywhere.

My wife said, "This isn't good. You're sick!" She first gave me a bit of water to drink and then she gave me some medicine to take. However, I was still uncomfortable everywhere. I thought, "In the past I have drunk liquor but was never once uncomfortable. What's going on today?" My wife said that I drank too much yesterday and ate too many things. I ate to the point of getting sick. Therefore you're not feeling well. She said, "It's too late today. Drink a glass of water and rest. Tomorrow you must go see Dr. Gao, who I know."

This morning I still had a headache. I ate breakfast and immediately went to see the doctor.

I took a bus to the hospital from the bus stop in front of my home. It was very crowded on the bus. There was no place to sit. I got off at Beijing Road. The hospital was to the left of the Bank of China. Dr. Gao is a famous doctor at this hospital. There were many people at the hospital who had come to see a doctor. I waited a very long time before I could (finally) be seen. After observing me very carefully Dr. Gao said that I didn't have a fever, so my sickness wasn't a big problem, that I didn't need to take any medicine, that I should (simply) go home and rest and I should be fine. He told me that for these few days I shouldn't eat meat and that I shouldn't drink alcohol and that I should drink a lot of water. In the future before drinking alcohol I should have a bit to eat, that I shouldn't drink on an empty stomach.

I rested at home for a day and the day after that I was much better. I don't know whether *Lao Bai* also got sick. I still haven't phoned him. He is not at home now. I have to ring his mobile.

SUPPLEMENTARY READING 1

Taxi Driver:	Hello, where to?
Passenger:	Beijing Hospital
Taxi Driver:	Okay, get in.
Passenger:	Thank you.
Taxi Driver:	We're there. That'll be $12.
Passenger:	Here's $20.
Taxi Driver:	Have you got $2? I'll give you $10.
Passenger:	Sorry, I don't have $2.
Taxi Driver:	No problem, here's $8 in change.
Passenger:	Thank you.

SUPPLEMENTARY READING 2

Some people like to drink liquor and are very good at it. They drink beer and they also drink *baijiu*. Five or six people are able to drink 40–50 bottles. Many people say that if you want to conduct business with someone who can drink a lot you first need to learn how to drink. When conducting business with them and they invite you to drink, then you will have to drink. If you don't, then they will think that you are not sincere about wanting to do business with them.

CHAPTER 14

TEXT

The day before yesterday was a Saturday, and at around 9:00 in the morning, even before *Fang Meichun* had even gotten out of bed, her boyfriend *Haiming* phoned her. He said that he wanted to invite her to go downtown to see a movie. He said that he'd wait for her at the main entrance to the large market downtown at 10:00. From where *Fang Meichun* lives to where the market is located takes about an hour. If there are many people on the street or there's lots of traffic, then it takes more than an hour. Right after *Fang Meichun* got up she went out the door without even eating breakfast.

   She first rode the bus downtown and then walked to the market. When she got off the bus it was already five minutes to 10:00. She thought, "Oh no, I'm late. *Haiming* is certainly already waiting for me at the entrance to the market. I'll have to walk a bit quicker (than normal)." It normally takes *Meichun* fifteen minutes to walk from the bus stop to the market, but that day she walked quickly, and got to the market at just 10:05. *Haiming* was already there and had been waiting for quite a while, having arrived at just 9:45.

   Haiming asked *Meichun* where she wanted to go. She said, "Before we watch the movie let's first go walk around. It's almost winter. I'd like to buy a skirt to wear in winter." *Haiming* said, "Okay." The market had a lot of good-looking clothing, including very many skirts of all colors—red ones, pink ones, gray ones, yellow ones, light blue ones, white ones, and dark green ones. *Haiming* asked *Meichun* which color dress she liked best. She said, "With this many colors I don't know which one I like best." *Haiming* said, "In that case why don't you simply try them on one at a time and see which one looks the best on you." *Meichun* tried on quite a few, taking more than an hour, but she didn't like even one of them." Some weren't good-looking, some were too expensive. She said, "I'm hungry. I didn't eat breakfast and it's almost noon. Why don't we go to that famous Korean restaurant and have some lunch. After lunch we can go to some other markets to have a look." *Haiming* said, "You go by yourself. I'll be reading in the café in front. After you have bought your skirt, come look for me."

Meichun went to three markets and none of them had a skirt she liked, so she went to the café to look for *Haiming*. He was just drinking coffee while reading. He reads very quickly, so he had already read several dozen pages. He really didn't understand how buying a skirt could be this difficult. *Meichun* does everything else so quickly. It is only shopping where she is particularly slow.

Meichun said, "I'm exhausted. Let's go home. (We can) come again tomorrow." *Haiming* unhappily said, "I won't be coming tomorrow. I have to prepare for next week's test. We didn't come today to go shopping and we didn't come today to read. Rather, we came to watch a movie. If you didn't shop for a skirt then we could have seen a movie. In the future, if you want to go shopping don't come looking for me. Look for someone else to go with you."

SUPPLEMENTARY READING 1

Owner:	What do you think? Is this shirt okay?
Wan Xiaodong:	It's a bit big. Do you have something a bit smaller size?
Owner:	This one is a medium. Is it okay?
Wan Xiaodong:	I don't like yellow. Do you have one in a different color?
Owner:	I also have one in light blue.
Wan Xiaodong:	Let me have a look.
Owner:	Here, it's very nice.
Wan Xiaodong:	How much?
Owner:	Six hundred and fifty dollars.
Wan Xiaodong:	It's that expensive! How about making it a bit cheaper, okay? Five hundred dollars.
Owner:	I can't do it. The cheapest I can go is $600.
Wan Xiaodong:	Okay, okay, here's six hundred dollars.

SUPPLEMENTARY READING 2

This is an email message written by *Xuewen* to *Meichun*.

Meichun:

Saturday of next week is my birthday. I would like to go to the Beijing Restaurant for dinner. The Beijing Restaurant is downtown, so you can take a train downtown and then walk to the restaurant. The train station is across from the library. From the library keep on going straight. When you get to the bank turn left and go for two blocks. The Beijing Restaurant is between a shoe store and a denim jeans shop. You can also take a taxi to the Beijing Restaurant. Taking a taxi is very comfortable and it is also very convenient. However, it is very expensive.

I have also invited *Wang Xiaolan*. *Xiaolan* has just come back from Britain. I think that you would certainly want to chat with her. Besides *Xiaolan*, I have also invited *Bai Jingyi* and *Zhiming*. *Bai Jingyi* prefers to ride a bicycle. He says that it only takes half an hour to ride from his house to the Beijing Restaurant. That's right, *Zhiming* is your neighbor. You can come together with him.

> *Xuewen*
> August 21

After reading the message *Meichun* phoned *Zhiming*. She asked *Zhiming* if he was going or not. *Zhiming* said, "Of course. However, I hate riding the bus. Let's take a taxi there!" She said, "Okay!"

CHAPTER 15

TEXT

Qian Xiping has been living on the east side of the city for seven years. The day after tomorrow he is moving because starting this year he will be teaching at a new school, and this school is located on the south side of the city. Taking a bus from the east side of the city to the south side takes an hour and a half. Where they are (now) is very hot in summer and very cold in winter. It even often snows. In the spring, if the wind isn't blowing then it is raining. It is really inconvenient to go outside. Every day the round-trip bus ticket is seven or eight dollars, not cheap at all. *Qian Xiping*'s wife said that they certainly needed to move to the south side of the city.

Qian Xiping's new home is located in an apartment building on the third floor. Their new house is very large: four bedrooms, a study, a living room, a dining room, and beyond that, a very large kitchen and two bathrooms. Inside the building is an elevator, but their family ordinarily won't be using it, as they are only on the third floor and don't have to use it. It is just fine to go up and down using the stairs. The houses on the south side of the city are truly expensive. Buying this home cost *Qian Xiping* $560,000.

They're about to move and *Qian Xiping* still needs to buy a lot of furniture. His parents, older brother, and older sister all think that because he has bought a house, perhaps he has run out of money. Therefore everyone wants to buy some furniture to give to him. Next month is *Qian Xiping*'s fortieth birthday. The new (pieces of) furniture are the birthday gifts that they are giving him. The furniture is all very beautiful, and the piece that *Qian Xiping* likes the best is the dining table given to him by his older sister. It is especially beautiful and made in Japan.

After he moves into his new home *Qian Xiping* will no longer need to travel to and from work by bus. It is also very convenient for his children to go to school and for his wife to go out and shop. Behind (their building) is the city's highest mountain, South Mountain. On Saturdays and Sundays they can take the children to climb the mountain. The children all like mountain climbing, as the children all love to climb mountains. In the morning he doesn't need to get up early and in the afternoon after finishing work he can walk home in fifteen minutes. While his wife cooks dinner he can either play with the children or have a rest. The entire family is very happy that he can return home this early.

SUPPLEMENTARY READING 1

Xiaoping: *Xuewen*, I've heard that you moved.

Xuewen: That's right. I bought an apartment downtown.

Xiaoping: On which floor?

Xuewen: The tenth floor.

Xiaoping: You're living that high up!

Xuewen: There is an elevator, so going up and down is very convenient.

Xiaoping: The apartment building that I lived in in China did not have an elevator.

Xuewen: Which floor did you live on?

Xiaoping: The sixth floor.

Xuewen: The sixth floor! You had to use the stairs every day. That certainly must have been very inconvenient.

Xiaoping: It sure was.

SUPPLEMENTARY READING 2

The three works of fiction, *Family*, *Spring*, and *Autumn*, were written by a very famous Chinese author. This author attended middle school in Shanghai and Nanjing and attended college in France. From 1929 to 1937 he wrote many famous works of fiction, and *Family* was written during that time. From 1938 to 1940 he wrote the two works of fiction, *Spring* and *Autumn*. The three works of fiction, *Family*, *Spring*, and *Autumn* are stories written about the Gao family. Many people all like to read works of fiction written by this author.

Note: This author's name is *Ba Jin* (1904–2005).

CHAPTER 16

TEXT

After *Qian Xiping* moved into his new home he invited some twenty-odd friends to go to his home for a meal. His wife busied herself with this for three days, and made more than ten different dishes. *Qian Xiping* additionally bought quite a large number of bottles of alcohol. There was white wine, red wine, rice wine, and of course there was famous brand beer. Both children ran back and forth moving things. *Qian Xiping* has one son and one daughter. His son is thirteen years old now, and just started middle school last year. His daughter is just eight years old this year and is a primary school student. By around five o'clock in the afternoon all of the guests had arrived. Upon entering the door, *Qian Xiping*'s old classmate *Huang Jiashen* loudly said, "Ah, *Xiping*, Look at you! You're able to live in this good a house. I don't know when I'll ever have this much money to afford to buy this nice a house. What about the kids? Come, come, come. These are for you." Every time *Jiashen* comes to their house he always brings things for the kids that they like and plays with them. This time he once again gave them a novel each. The kids also like *Jiashen* a lot. Because *Jiashen* wears glasses the kids call him Uncle Glasses.

Qian Xiping invited the guests to eat the food prepared by his wife. Mrs. Qian's dishes are very authentic, as quite a number (of the dishes) can't be eaten in restaurants. Everyone also drank quite a bit of alcohol; *Jiashen* likes to drink too much. That day, of all the guests, he drank the most and couldn't firmly hold chopsticks. His wife said to him, "You've had quite a bit to drink. You can't drink anymore." However, he said, "It doesn't matter. I can still drink quite a number more glasses of booze. Look, my eyes can still see very clearly. I can see the food on top of the dining table. My ears can still hear very clearly what you are saying. Come, come. Let's drink! Let's drink! Oh the lovely drink." *Qian Xiping* said, "Yes, yes, yes. Everybody, take your time eating, just eat a bit more, drink a bit more. Don't stand on ceremony. Our neighbors are out. Do not worry about making a bit of noise."

Twenty-plus friends ate and ate, drank and drank, and after finishing the meal they chatted. And it wasn't until midnight that everybody finally returned home to sleep. However, the next morning nobody could get up. When *Jiashen* woke up it was already 2:00 in the afternoon.

SUPPLEMENTARY READING 1

I like to go to that Chinese restaurant opposite my home to eat beef fried rice and drink Chinese tea. After learning of this, Dr. Wang said to me that when eating beef it is best not to drink tea. Today I once again went to that restaurant to eat beef fried rice. I said to the owner, "I don't want to drink tea. Please give me hot water." He heard this and was silent for a long time, not knowing what I wanted. I again spoke, "Look, that is tea and it is hot. I want water, water that is hot." The owner then understood. He said, "Oh, you want plain boiled water." I then understood. In Chinese restaurants hot water is not called hot water. It is called plain boiled water.

SUPPLEMENTARY READING 2

There used to be a girl named *Meihuan* who often went to see a doctor. Every time she went to see a doctor, she told the doctor that she had a headache. One day, she went to see a doctor again. The doctor thought for a moment and said to her, "You are too busy. Do what you can do at home, and don't do what you can't do."

A few days later, *Meihuan*'s mother came. She said to the doctor, "My head really hurts." After the doctor saw her, the doctor said to her, "You are too tired. Do what you can do at home, and don't do what you can't do."

After a few weeks, the doctor saw *Meihuan* and her mother in a restaurant. The doctor said to them, "Do you still have a headache?" *Meihuan* said, "My mother and I no longer have a headache. But now my father has a headache."

CHAPTER 17

TEXT

Mr. Shang is an ethnic Chinese New Zealander. He only began to study Chinese when he was sixty. He is very hardworking, but he can never learn it well, as he can never memorize the new vocabulary. He says that having to remember more than fifty new vocabulary items each week is too much, that it is too difficult. Teenagers and twenty-year-olds can't remember this many new words, how is he supposed to remember them!

In the morning he gets up and then both memorizes new vocabulary and writes Chinese characters. He carefully writes down the characters he has already studied on (sheets of) paper, and when he has free time he takes them out to look at. He even puts the characters on the desk next to his bed. Before going to sleep at night he looks at them a few times and after waking up (the next morning) he has another look at them. He says all he has to do is study every day and he can certainly learn Chinese well and can memorize the new words.

Mr. Shang wants to go to China next year to visit his mother's ninety-something sister. It has already been more than fifty years since he last saw her.

In Mr. Shang's house there are Chinese characters here and Chinese characters there. His wife said to his friends that she couldn't read Chinese characters and that as soon as she sees one she gets angry. At home the rooms upstairs and downstairs are completely filled with characters. It really gets her angry. Last year, she also began studying Chinese. Mr. and Mrs. Shang went to the library together to borrow books and to return books. In less than half a year they were already able to speak quite a bit of Chinese and were able to write a large number of Chinese characters. They even learned how to make Chinese dumplings. They thought about it over and over again. "Why do we need to wait (all the way) until next year before we go to China? Let's go now! It is autumn now and Beijing is very cool. Once in China we can practice Chinese very thoroughly and eat ready-made Chinese dumplings."

Last month Mr. and Mrs. Shang brought with them a large suitcase containing all of their Chinese books and other luggage, and went to China.

After they got off the airplane, Mr. Shang used Chinese to speak with a young woman at the airport. He was extremely tense. The young woman couldn't understand his Chinese. Mr. Shang then used a pencil to write down on a piece of paper "Search think sell Chinese self alcohol, you here have buy?" That young woman looked at what he had written for a very long time but she still could not understand what he meant. Do you know why? Mr. Shang had written the character "I" as "search", "white" as "self", and additionally had written the character "buy" as "sell" and "sell" as "buy". Do you think that the young woman could understand what Mr. Shang had written?

SUPPLEMENTARY READING 1

When people say courtyard home/quadrangle home one thinks of Beijing. What, then, is a courtyard home/quadrangle home? A courtyard home/quadrangle home is a type of house that already existed in Beijing one thousand years ago. The center of the home is the courtyard, with rooms sitting on all four of its sides. For this reason it is called a courtyard home/quadrangle home. The family members who live in the northern room(s) are the elders, with the eldest son living in the eastern room, the second eldest son living in the west room, and the daughter(s) living in the rear of the courtyard. A courtyard home/quadrangle home is very special. When you go to Beijing you should have a look.

SUPPLEMENTARY READING 2

San Mao (1943–1991) was a famous female author and enjoyed reading from a very early age. The first book she ever read was a picture story book written and illustrated by *Zhang Leping*. At that time she was only three years old. *San Mao's* English name was *Echo*. Her (real) name was not *San Mao*, as *San Mao* was her pen name. It was because she very much liked the story *San Mao* illustrated by *Zhang Leping* that after she started writing she used *San Mao* as her pen name. *San Mao* visited many countries and understood very many different languages.

CHAPTER 18

TEXT

I live on Nanjing Street. Nanjing Street is very quiet. It is not the least bit noisy, and it is not bustling either. Right across from our house is a very small store selling clothing. Of the two owners of that store, one is surnamed Chang and the other is surnamed Zhang. I call them Uncle Chang and Uncle Zhang. When I have free time I often go there for fun.

   Uncle Chang is very tall and is also very thin. He originally lived north of the Yellow River. Uncle Zhang is not as tall as Uncle Chang, and he is neither fat nor thin. In the past Uncle Zhang lived south of the Yangtze River. He said that the Yangtze River is longer than the Yellow River, while Uncle Chang said that the Yangtze and Yellow Rivers are equally long. I said, "I know (the answer). Our teacher said that the Yangtze River is longer than the Yellow River." Uncle Zhang heard this and was very happy.

Both Uncle Chang and Uncle Zhang are in their fifties. Neither of them is particularly interested in doing business, but they are very interested in making clothing and all of the clothing in their store is made by them. The clothing sold in their shop is both comfortable and inexpensive, the only thing being that it is not fashionable enough. They say that although the clothing sold in other stores is fashionable, it is almost three times as expensive as theirs, so only rich people can afford it.

Both of my parents are teachers. Their salaries are not very high. However, my score on last month's test was especially high. (Therefore) they bought a couple of pair of famous-maker jeans for me. This pair of jeans that I am wearing now is 33% more expensive than the most expensive pair of pants selling in Uncle Chang's store. Uncle Zhang asked me why I didn't buy my pants in their store. I said that this pair of pants I am wearing is completely different from the pants that they sell in their store. My pants are both fashionable and come from a famous maker. This pair I am wearing now still isn't my most expensive pair. I still have another pair that is even more expensive than this pair.

SUPPLEMENTARY READING 1

Do you know who *Mark Rowswell* is? His Chinese name is *Dashan* and he is Canadian. In 1988 he went to China and studied at Peking University. When he was in Beijing he often performed comedy on television, so everyone knows his name. *Dashan* speaks Chinese extremely well. If you only listen to him speak and not see his face, you would certainly think that he was Chinese. *Dashan*'s father's father also lived at one time in China. He was a doctor who worked in a hospital there in 1922. Because the place name has changed, it took *Dashan* ten years to finally find that hospital. Although he is a foreigner, Chinese newspapers say that *Dashan* is not an outsider.

SUPPLEMENTARY READING 2

The Chinese language of more than two thousand years ago is very different from the Chinese language today. The saying "小人之过也，必文" was written two thousand years ago. Do you know what it means? It means "When a vile person commits a bad deed, he must hide it (from others)." Here 过 means "bad deed", 之 means 的, and 文 means "not reveal to others". Although 小人书 is "a book read by young children", 小人 here does not mean "young child". Here it means "a base or vile person", and a base or vile person often does bad things.

CHAPTER 19

TEXT

Zhong Mingran came from Beijing to New Zealand in February of this year to study English. After coming to New Zealand he has been living at my house. *Zhong Mingran* is very hardworking, and over these (past) several months he has come to speak English extremely well. Because he is so worried about his study he hasn't been anywhere to have fun.

After his exams are over he will be relatively free and wants to relax a bit. He has heard that the scenery around Snowy Mountain Town is very beautiful and so he really wants to go travel there, so he gave his classmate *Xie Li* a phone call. *Xie Li* is French and found a job over the vacation in Snowy Mountain Town. He said that he could take *Zhong Mingran* to Snowy Mountain Town for some fun. *Zhong Mingran* heard this and was very happy.

In July it is winter in New Zealand, so Snowy Mountain Town is very cold. Therefore they had to bring more clothing with them (than usual). No denying that. On television they said that it snowed a lot in Snowy Mountain Town, and that all the roads are white and that perhaps you still won't feel warm enough even wearing two sweaters, and a jacket. The more *Zhong Mingran* watched (the report) the colder he felt, so he immediately went to the store and bought another overcoat.

Snowy Mountain Town is very far from my home, altogether more than 700 kilometers, and between (the two places) there's even a big river. Do you know how long it takes to get to Snowy Mountain Town by train? At the very least it takes six hours. It is really not close at all. It is (also) much colder there than here. Although there is no wind, it does snow. The scenery of Snowy Mountain Town is particularly beautiful, so large numbers of foreigners like to go to Snowy Mountain Town.

After *Zhong Mingran* and *Xie Li* arrived at Snowy Mountain Town they came out of the train station and immediately took a taxi to their hotel. The hotel is not far away, but there were lots of cars on the road, and lots of students come here over their break to have fun, so the traffic jams were horrific. They didn't arrive at their hotel until very late. The next day *Zhong Mingran* got up very early. However, the previous night *Xie Li* had gone drinking with his friends, so he went to sleep fairly late. *Zhong Mingran* thought that maybe *Xie Li* couldn't get up in the morning, so he went out by himself to have some fun. After *Xie Li* woke up he couldn't find *Zhong Mingran* and became very worried. He put on his coat and immediately went to search for *Zhong Mingran*. He knew that *Zhong Mingran* loves to eat watermelon the most, so he went to a produce stall near the hotel to look for him. Look! *Zhong Mingran* is right there carefully choosing a watermelon by the side of the stall!

SUPPLEMENTARY READING 1

Do you know the meaning of "知之为知之，不知为不知"? This is Chinese that was written more than two thousand years ago. It means "If you know it, say you do, and if you don't know it, say that you don't. It is only in this way that you can acquire knowledge."

SUPPLEMENTARY READING 2

In the past there was a man named *Gui Liang*. He was very handsome, but there was a bit of a problem with his leg, so it was not easy for him to walk. He wanted to find a pretty girl to be his wife and asked his friend *Hua Han* to introduce a girlfriend to him.

Across from *Hua Han*'s home lived a pretty girl named *Ye Qing*. *Ye Qing* wanted to find a good-looking boyfriend, but she was unable to find one because her nose was unattractive. *Hua Han* wanted to introduce *Ye Qing* to *Gui Liang* for her to get to know him.

On the day of August 8 *Hua Han* had *Gui Liang* ride a horse past the entrance to *Ye Qing*'s home. When *Ye Qing* saw *Gui Liang* riding atop the horse she didn't see that there was a problem with *Gui Liang*'s leg and she really liked him. *Gui Liang* only saw the flowers that *Ye Qing* was holding in her hand and didn't see her nose. He also fell in love with her. Later *Ye Qing* became *Gui Liang*'s wife. They often talked about that time when he "rode quickly past on a horse watching the flowers." Now this expression has become an idiom meaning "to look once very quickly and not carefully see things clearly".

CHAPTER 20

TEXT

Mrs. Jiang knew that *Jiang Xingcheng* didn't need to go to work this afternoon, so she told him to go to the nearby supermarket to buy a few things for her. She said that it is almost vacation time and she'd like to take the kids on a vacation. Therefore she wants (him) to buy some things to eat, to drink, and for them to use, etc. Of course he needs to buy several catties of ready-made Chinese dumplings. While out shopping (for her), Mrs. Jiang also wanted him not to have the money and credit cards stolen. *Jiang Xingcheng* had barely gone out the door when his wife called out to him to stop, telling him that on the way home from shopping he should get off the expressway and go to school to pick up the kids to bring home. *Jiang Xingcheng* unhappily said, "I got it. What a pain!"

Two hours later *Jiang Xingcheng* returned home with four kids. The kids were both noisy and loud, and *Jiang Xingcheng* wanted them to quiet down a bit. Not only did they not listen to him, but they (actually) became noisier and noisier. His elder daughter walked in the door and immediately wanted to sing karaoke. His second daughter wanted to phone classmates, his youngest daughter wanted to play on the computer, and his youngest, a boy, wanted to watch the soccer game on TV. In just a little while his second daughter was fighting with her younger brother, and he started to cry. His hand had been scratched open by his older sister and had started bleeding. *Jiang Xingcheng* said having four kids in a family makes a real racket and that all of them should go live in a school dorm. However, what was he going to do after the start of vacation with the kids at home every day? He should simply go to work every day. Not being at home is the best solution.

SUPPLEMENTARY READING 1

Do you know where Fragrant Mountain is? Fragrant Mountain is in the northwest of Beijing. Because the scenery around Fragrant Mountain is very beautiful, many people go there in all four seasons to enjoy themselves. Many people who live in Beijing like to bring their families there on Saturdays and Sundays to climb it. In the spring, many flowers bloom on its slopes, and when the petals are blown around by the wind it looks very beautiful. In the summer, not only is it not hot (there), it is actually quite cool. The autumn scenery is even more beautiful. Looking from a distance at the red, yellow, and green mountain is absolutely gorgeous. In winter, it is cold, and it additionally snows, but Fragrant Mountain is still very pretty, different from the beauty of spring, summer, or fall. If you have a chance to go to Beijing you definitely must go to Fragrant Mountain and enjoy yourself.

SUPPLEMENTARY READING 2

Zhang Daqian/Chang Ta-ch'ien (1899–1984) was a very famous painter. He studied painting from a young age with his mother. His parents had ten children altogether. He was number eight. He started school at age seven, started learning painting at age nine and by age eleven he was able to paint landscapes, flowers, and people. In 1917 he went to Japan with an older brother to study painting. In 1919 he returned to Shanghai from Japan and studied painting and calligraphy with a very famous painter. He visited many different countries and resided in many different countries, too, (including) the US, where he lived for eight years. *Zhang Daqian* painted for more than sixty years and was very hardworking. In this long period of time he painted more than 30,000 paintings.

　　Zhang Daqian not only liked to paint paintings. He also liked to buy paintings. It is said that one time he had already agreed with a friend to buy that friend's house, but then saw a very famous painting that (the owner) wanted to sell. After viewing that painting he became so excited that he couldn't sleep. After a few days he said to his friend that he was no longer interested in buying his house. (Instead) he used the money originally intended to buy the house to purchase the painting.